Mood Management

Understanding the whole body, brain and mind.

Bernard Allen

www.steaming-training.co.uk

First published in the U.K. in 2017 by Steaming Publishing.

Steaming Publishing
Byways
Lodge Lane
Salfords
Surrey
RH1 5DJ
info@steaming-training.co.uk

"I have striven not to laugh at human actions, not to weep at them, nor to hate them, but to understand them."

Baruch Spinoza - Philosopher - 1632-1677

"I have striven not to weep or hate but you have to laugh…"

Bernard Allen - Nobody - 1954

Table of Contents

Acknowledgements

On the 12th of October 2014, in the early hours of the morning, I found myself at the bar of a hotel in Bournemouth debating with myself whether I should go to bed or stay for another drink. That is an odd concept - debating with yourself. I was also trying to remember my room number.

Then Billy Cliffen came over and said, "So Bern, is there such a thing as free will?".

I realised then that I had reached the limits of my mental capacity. At that moment I was both literally and metaphorically incoherent, because parts of my body and brain were willing me to stay up and others parts were willing me to go to bed. They couldn't all have their own way, which meant that some of them were about to be disappointed. Some of them were about to be deprived of choice in the matter. In fact some of them were about to be deprived of their liberty, by being forced to go somewhere they didn't want to go, or forced to stay somewhere they didn't want to stay. That started me thinking.

Thanks to all who helped, by reading early drafts and correcting huge numbers of my mistakes. That is James Hazelgrove, Gail and James Allen, Brendan Heneghan, Sharon Gray and John Urwin in the UK, along with Nick Burnett and Drew Allison in Australia. The mistakes I have left in are to ensure brand consistency, as all my books seem to contain errors.

Introduction

Words like "consciousness", "awareness", "experience" and "thinking" are used to describe completely different things by different writers and I get confused. Sometimes it is easier to create a new word than keep explaining what you mean by using an existing one to describe different concepts. There is a glossary at the back.

The concepts that the new words describe might not be correct in every detail, but they help me by providing a cognitive framework upon which to hang my current stage of understanding.

I have also failed to follow the traditional academic format. As a reader I find having to flick back and forth frustrating, so I have placed notes and references as footnotes which are easily accessible. We no longer need to plod to the university library and navigate the Dewey index system for information these days. It is easy enough to google a question like "can crows recognise human faces?" and uncover several interesting reference trails.

Every day humans wake up and start doing things, based on some sort of theory about how their own bodies, brains and minds work. Most do not spend much time examining those theories or asking other people to articulate their own. They just go about their business. But when you do ask people to explain themselves it becomes apparent that they have different ideas. They cannot all be right.

Humans may be the most complex creatures on the planet but they are also a bit simple. They do things because they feel like it. If you ask them why they did something they will come up with a plausible explanation, but most of the time they are making it up afterwards. They just felt like it. Feelings drive behaviour.

So what creates those feelings that make humans do whatever they choose to do? And do they really have a choice about whether they have those feelings?

When humans are happy, satisfied and unperturbed they are not motivated to move or do anything much. Happy, satisfied, and unperturbed humans would never have achieved as much as disgruntled ones have. When most living creatures are happy, satisfied and unperturbed, they just sleep most of the time. Every living creature that was ever moved to do anything was stirred into action by an emotion, even if they were not aware of it at the time. Most living creatures are never aware of anything.

Emotions that last for any length of time are called moods. All human behaviour is an attempt at mood management. People do things because they want to feel better. The trouble is that sometimes they end up feeling worse. That is what we need to change.

Human minds are easily distorted by wishful thinking and our inability to tell the truth about ourselves prevents us from seeing the solutions to our problems. Humans are very similar. They are not identical - life would be very weird and complicated if they were. In the wild, mothers needed to be able to recognise and identify their own young and vice versa. In family groups they needed to identify family members, monkeys in troops needed to identify members of their own troop, birds their own flock, fish their own shoal etc.

There are differences between individual humans, but since the human genome was sequenced in 2003 it has become clear that the concept of racial identity has no scientific basis. There are wider differences between individuals within any racial identity group than between the averages of the groups, which means we are all part of the same race.

Our ancestors traditionally lived in family groups and tribes, whose members looked after each other but regarded outsiders as a threat. Unfortunately this tendency to want to identify with groups and treat outsiders as enemies is deeply ingrained.

Individuals choose to exclude others on the basis of a variety of arbitrary characteristics. The most obvious is the colour of their skin, but some people choose to identify with groups according to gender, sexual preference, religion, social class, political affiliation, their favourite sports team or even something as trivial as the newspaper they read. For example, members of the middle class tribe split themselves into "Guardian readers" and "Daily Mail" readers.

The labels for these groups are all terms of abuse because identity group enthusiasts are all obsessed with outsiders. Those who like to categorise individuals into groups of their own choosing then start to chant labels as a term of abuse. They are all running the same mental programme irrespective of what they are chanting. Labels such as "Facist", "Nazi", "Liberal", "Communist", "Racist", "Sexist", "Feminist", "Macho", "Gay", "Farang", and "Kaffir" have all been used as terms of abuse by members of different identity groups. Identity groupies (there, you see I have started doing it now) are happy to point out the stereotyping tendencies of the members of other groups, but are blind to their own behaviour. As they obsess about those they identify as outsiders they become excited, which can lead to aggression and violence. It is ironic that even peace protests can turn violent when humans become excited.

Aggression and violence within the human species is clearly an issue we need to address. When people refer to behaviour problems, what they often mean is violence of one kind or another. In humans, violence seems to be disproportionately exhibited by males, which is the case in many species. Of course there are exceptions. Women fight too. The female praying mantis has a reputation for being a bit rough (although even that reputation is not entirely justified) and some aggressive female hyenas dominate their social groups. But overall, the facts speak for themselves. In many species it tends to be the males that do most of the fighting.

Humans like to think that they have some sort of privileged access to their own thought processes. If you ask them why they did something, or why some idea occurred to them, they will usually come up with a plausible explanation. They also like to think that "they" are in control of their own body and brain. As we will see that is not always true. Sometimes their bodybrain controls them.

Some people like to think of themselves as souls or spirits. I normally think of myself as a combination of a body, brain and mind, but for the purposes of this book I need to be more precise. So I am reserving the term "self" for the conscious part of me which is my mind. I do think that the mind, or self, is generated by the brain but it is not conscious of all the activity in the brain and body. When the mind is in operation, it is only aware of the activity in some of the neural circuits which I am calling the heart & mindbrain. The rest I am calling the bodybrain.

If you believe that you are capable of free will, willpower, morality, ethics, spirituality and stuff like that, then you are probably a heart & mindbrain. That is the system that creates the conscious mind.

There are all sorts of non-conscious, automatic systems and processes going on at the same time which do not seem to involve the conscious mind at all. I am a conscious mind but I am certainly not always in control of my entire bodybrain. That would be exhausting. I like to think that I am in overall charge, but I manage the team with a light touch. The truth is that I just let my bodybrain get on with it most of the time. I am completely switched off for almost a third of the day and even when I am switched on I am not really paying attention to what my bodybrain is doing. My mind has a tendency to wander.

So I will refer to the whole body and brain as the bodybrain, and reserve the term heart & mindbrain for those parts that become conscious now and then.

Chapter 1 - Theories

Maladjusted

I spent most of my career working with children and young people who struggled with their moods. They were first described by professionals as "Maladjusted" (Malad), then as having "Emotional and Behavioural Difficulties" (EBD), then "Social Emotional and Behavioural Difficulties" (SEBD). Then the government changed the order to "Behavioural, Emotional and Social Difficulties" (BESD) to signal a no-nonsense approach towards behaviour in schools. Now they are described as having Social, Emotional and Mental Health difficulties

(SEMH). The experts do not want to talk about "Behaviour" any more.

These changes in emphasis were a deliberate attempt to encourage people to adopt a wider view and pay more attention to the underlying causes of undesirable behaviour, instead of simply trying to control it. However, in my view, simply ignoring behaviour is a mistake. It is a conceptual error based on the false premise that all behaviour which causes problems for society must be a symptom of an individual's social, emotional or mental health difficulties.

Behaviour evolved over millions of years. Human behaviour is generated by a combination of conscious and sub-conscious decision making. The sub-conscious mental programmes that generate automatic behaviour are a mixture of innate and learned habitual programmes. As humans go about their business they get in each other's way. They do things which annoy other people. Some people are just inconsiderate. Others may not realise that their behaviour upsets other people. They find other people annoying and they react instinctively in ways that make things worse. They find themselves repeating patterns of behaviour which bring them unhappiness without understanding what they are doing. Innate and learned behaviours can be the cause of social, emotional and mental health difficulties. I am not sure that medicalising behaviour problems is the right approach.

To begin with, I am not distinguishing between good or bad behaviour, normal and abnormal behaviour, or even between human behaviour and the behaviour of other life forms. I want to make sense of all behaviour, teasing out similarities and differences in the natural world first. Then I want to look at conscious and unconscious behaviour. Finally I want to tread carefully towards the boundary between the majority of sub-conscious information processing and the minority which becomes conscious and appears by magic in my conscious mind. Perhaps it is more correct to speak of the small minority of neural circuits which become my conscious mind now and then. I want to understand the relationship between my "self" and my bodybrain and how I can use them both to extract the most pleasure, fun and satisfaction out of life.

The behaviour of living things seems to be partly innate, partly learned, and partly controlled by the environment. The proportions of those different influences vary in different species. Human bodies, brains and minds still exhibit evidence of our evolutionary past. They slowly adjusted to gradual changes in the environment, which took place over a vast period of time. Yet there have been dramatic changes in the way we live, that have taken place over an extremely short period of time in evolutionary terms. There is no way natural selection could keep up which means that our innate mental programmes no longer equip us to cope as well as they did our ancestors. What is sometimes called natural behaviour is not well adjusted to the modern world and maladjusted behaviour is already getting us into trouble. We will increasingly have to depend on newly learned behaviours in future. So long as we put some effort into understanding what we are really like and take that into account as we attempt to engineer society then hopefully we can meet the challenges of the future.

I have to say that previous grand social engineering projects have not been conspicuously successful.[1] I would not like to live in North Korea or China at present. Karl Popper put forward his own preference for "piecemeal social engineering". That involves making careful, small and reversible changes to society and testing them as we go. To succeed, such an approach needs to be based on a good humoured but blunt and honest assessment of human nature. We need to face up to what we are really like before we can shape a world that we will feel at home in. Unrealistic expectations will always disappoint.

An article in a now defunct American computer magazine, published in 1962, defined a kludge in the following way.

"It is an ill-assorted collection of poorly-matching parts, forming a distressing whole".

Jackson W. Granholm

---

[1] "The Poverty of Historicism" - Karl Popper, 1957

That is us. We are an ill-assorted collection of poorly-matching parts - obsolete technology that evolved for a world that no longer exists. We are maladjusted. But by facing up to our limitations we might at least be able to design some temporary fixes, so that the whole is slightly less distressing. That is a modest aim. I have every confidence that we can, because we are nothing if not creative. Creative thinking is the ability to imagine alternative realities and it is one of the things we are quite good at.

Some writers have described the conscious mind as a railway, with trains of thought. Some think of memory as being like a hologram, or a spiders web. It could be like a river with branching tributaries, or a tree, or the roots of a plant, or like a Google map where you can add detail when you home in on an idea. The body, brain and mind could be like fertile soil which nurtures creative ideas, or a landscape of thoughts, or a company with an executive board and a minute taker. It could be like an orchestra, with the conscious mind being like a conductor in charge, or it could be more like a jazz quartet, with various neural circuits jamming together. It could be like a factory with a production line, or a toolbox of mental programmes. It could be like a garden of ideas, pollinated by the heart & mindbrain bee, or a distillery that purifies and clarifies ideas. It could be a bit like all of them or nothing like any of them, but the ease with which those metaphors flowed out through my fingers does provide a strong hint about how the brain works.

The part of my brain that is writing this book seems to generate metaphors with consummate ease, because that is what it evolved to do. Original ideas are never made up of completely novel components. They are the result of rearrangements of familiar abstractions which are placed into unfamiliar contexts to create something new.

We may need to apply that sort of thinking to the piecemeal social engineering we are going to have to engage in to ensure a better fit between the world we are creating and human nature. And to do that we need to be honest with ourselves. Strangely that appears to be something we struggle to achieve.

Paradoxically, I suspect that intelligence and deception are close relatives. We are so good at deception that we even fool ourselves, or at least other parts of ourselves. This is where it gets confusing. Wishful thinking, self delusion, and a number of other mental distortions are part of our mental make up. We are going to have to be alert to them.

As a general rule, the more emotional humans become the worse they become at thinking. So they become confused about the things they care most passionately about. Perhaps we should encourage people to apply their intellect in areas in which they have no emotional involvement. The idea that victims automatically become experts is a curious one. Often when public policy is discussed victims of various sorts are invited to comment. So mothers of children who died of drug overdoses are invited to advise on drug policy. Road accident victims become experts on road safety. Abuse victims become experts on abuse. They are experts on what it is like to suffer their own experiences but that should not be confused with being experts on the causes of those experiences. Some victims are motivated to becoming experts and some of them have become highly knowledgeable, which is a different thing.

Arguments which are driven by emotions tend to be poor arguments. I have spent the past three years writing about this, so I must care about it, which means it will be probably be littered with errors of reasoning. If you find any, please let me know.

When I started writing this I already knew the title, it was going to be called "Mood Management", but I had no idea what it would turn into. To begin with I was not going to cover behaviour at all in this book and I certainly had no intention of attempting to address what proper psychologists call "the hard problem" - consciousness.

Yet as I began to make progress I realised that it was going to be impossible to understand mood management without considering behaviour. They are indistinguishable. At the same time as Sigmund Freud was becoming famous for inventing controversial ideas that turned out to be wrong, William James, the brother of the novelist Henry James, was at Harvard University developing controversial ideas that turned out to be right.

James trained as a doctor and was appointed to Harvard as a physiologist. James invented psychology as an academic subject. Writing in 1902, he said that the first lecture in psychology he had ever attended was the one he delivered in 1875 in the first academic psychology course ever taught. He had written it during his previous three years at the university and what is astonishing about his work is how much of it has stood the test of time. After inventing psychology, he became bored with it and went on to become a great philosopher.

Amongst the many insights that have been confirmed by subsequent research, James suggested that the experience of emotions was largely caused by feedback from physiological changes in the body.

"The mental aspect of emotion, the feeling, is a slave to its physiology, not vice versa: we do not tremble because we are afraid or cry because we feel sad; we are afraid because we tremble and are sad because we cry."

What is Emotion? - William James 1884

The idea that the bodybrain reacts first, with conscious experience in the heart & mindbrain following later, was controversial at the time because it is so counter-intuitive. But it turned out to be right. According to William James:

"Common sense says, we lose our fortune, are sorry and weep; we meet a bear, are frightened and run; we are insulted by a rival, are angry and strike. The hypothesis here to be defended says that this order of sequence is incorrect … we feel sorry because we cry, angry because we strike, afraid because we tremble."

What is Emotion? - William James, 1884

Nobel Laureate, Daniel Kahneman, describes humans as having two selves. If one of them wants one thing and the other wants something different, which is precisely what Kahneman says is happening for most of the time, which one should we support? Kahneman believes that both selves are conscious, and he talks about the tyranny of the remembering self, which makes decisions that reduce the amount of pleasure available to the remembering self.

The experiencing self only exists in the moment, which according to Kahneman lasts about three seconds, as it has no memories. It cannot think about the past nor can it think about the future. That is not a form of consciousness that I can relate to.

So far as I am concerned, the experiencing self is not me. I am what Kahneman describes as a remembering self. What I experience are simulations, some of which are very recent creations, but I experience them in the context of my memories which are stored simulations.

The philosopher Daniel Dennett has suggested that consciousness might be an illusion.[2] He is certainly correct about thinking that our conscious experience does not accurately correspond to the physical world. But I think he is overly impressed with perceptual illusions, which only demonstrate that the content of our personal experiences can be illusory. We over-estimate the extent of our awareness of the outside world, in the same way that we over-estimate the capacity of our perceptual systems, but the experiences themselves are real even if the content is illusory.

This is a difficult area to discuss because we do not really have enough words. The same term "consciousness" is used to describe the physiological state of a body and brain that is awake and responsive, as opposed to being unconscious or asleep. But it is also used to describe something else entirely. This is a special state of the brain and mind that involves another dimension of altered awareness. To illustrate the difference, it is possible to be unconscious in one sense of the word and conscious in the other, both at the same time. When we are asleep we are unconscious, unaware, and unresponsive to the outside world. But during a phase of light sleep, called rapid eye movement sleep (REM), we start dreaming and experiencing things. The heart & mindbrain becomes conscious while the rest of the bodybrain remains unconscious.

---

2 "Consciousness Explained" by Daniel Dennett 1991

The words "react", "aware" and "respond" are used to describe different things too. When somebody walks up my drive at night the outside lights on the wall of the house come on automatically. You could say the house "reacts" to the people approaching, becomes "aware" of their presence, and "responds" by turning the lights on for them. But it is not really aware of anything. It is not conscious.

My computer is described as going to sleep and waking up too, but even though it does process quite a lot of information more quickly than my body and brain can, it is no more conscious than the dishwasher or any other household appliance. Most tests of consciousness are really sophisticated tests of reaction and responsiveness in the biology and neurology of the body and brain, which brings us back to where we started.

The subjective experience of consciousness is something in addition to the physical processes that cause it. We should take care not to conflate consciousness, attention, self-awareness, wakefulness, and responsiveness to stimuli. They are not the same thing.

Philosophers and psychologists like to pose thought experiments in an effort to clear the mental fog as they consider the complexity of subjective experiences. So we may as well follow suit. Imagine if I was not conscious at all, in the sense of having subjective experiences, but my body and brain reacted and responded just the same as everybody else's. What would be missing?

So long as I never told anyone, how could they ever know that my experience was any different to their own?

How could I know for that matter, never having experienced consciousness? What if your experience of consciousness is not real consciousness, but a very weak imitation of what the rest of us are experiencing. What if we are enjoying a much richer and more wonderful subjective experience than you are. What would that mean? Would you feel cheated?

I knew a psychology professor who was blind in one eye, yet he believed he could see in 3D just as well as anybody else by moving his head from side to side. He had no concept of how different the full experience of binocular 3D is. The brain calculates the relative distance of objects in different ways, for example by measuring relative movement in the visual field when we move our head, but that is nothing like the experience we get from having two eyes processing the world at the same time. I suspect that not all humans with two functioning eyes have the same intensity of 3D experience. Some people were entranced by 3D films but many were not impressed by the effect at all. Perhaps they were not experiencing the same thing. Perhaps there are humans amongst us who are experiencing a much more vivid form of consciousness than we are and others are experiencing a much weaker form.

Meditation and drugs can cause people to experience more vivid forms of consciousness. Alcohol and sedatives can turn down, and eventually turn off, consciousness. The consciousness I am talking about here is a special, subjective experience that I am fairly confident that neither my computer nor my doorbell are capable of experiencing.

Neuroscientists believe that a number of other animals and birds also have some rudimentary form of consciousness, which seems likely, but I doubt they spend much time thinking about this kind of stuff yet.

I agree with Daniel Dennett, that consciousness might be an illusion so far as Kahneman's experiencing self is concerned, but so far as I am concerned, I am definitely experiencing something and I think what I experience is simulations of the real world which produce feelings. Consciousness is important. It is the only part of my mental world that I am really interested in and I do not believe it can be entirely explained away.

"If you're happy and you know it and you really want to show it, if you're happy and you know it clap your hands"

The Scouts Song

How could anyone be happy if they did not know it? If I have a headache that I cannot experience, then I do not really have a headache. I might have some abnormal brain activity, but that is not the same thing. A headache is a conscious experience, not mere neural activity.

As far as I am concerned, the ultimate purpose of life is to create happiness, not headaches, but I need to know that I am happy in order to be happy. I have to notice how I am feeling. I have to be conscious. In order to be conscious of my mood my heart & mindbrain needs to be switched on and paying attention to my feelings. For much of the time, even when I am conscious, it is paying attention to other things. I have been in pleasant environments, engaged in potentially enjoyable activities, which I barely noticed. That is not good mood management. On the other hand I have been in unpleasant environments, engaged in less enjoyable activities, which I barely noticed too. That is good mood management. It is even possible to control pain by directing attention away from it.

When I worked as an aircraft cleaner, I preferred busy shifts because the time seemed to pass more quickly. It was the slow shifts that I hated, when there was nothing to do and time dragged. I could not wait for those shifts to end. I was wishing my life away.

Daniel Kahneman's experiments on the two selves, the experiencing self and the remembering self, involved asking people to report how they felt at regular intervals, as they experienced pain or discomfort. That forced them to direct their attention towards how they were feeling at that moment and compare their current experience with memories of other experiences. I suspect that was really the remembering self answering all the questions. In the real world, most of the time people are not paying attention to how they are feeling.

It is not easy to isolate the two selves. This is my attempt to stay in the moment and record my experiencing self.

"I am typing this sitting up in bed. The time is 07:17 in the morning of Wednesday, 12 October 2016. After my bodybrain wrote that last sentence, my heart & mindbrain paused to consider what it was that I was conscious of at that very moment.

It is now 07:19, so that moment has gone. In fact, as soon as I began to consider what I was conscious of, the moment had already passed and I was looking back at it. It is quite difficult to pin down the experiencing self. Although it feels like we are living in the present, in reality we cannot be, because it takes time for information to travel through our neuronal circuits and be processed. By the time we experience anything, the moment that we are experiencing has already passed and information about another moment is already on its way towards us.

It is a bit like looking at the stars. Some are much further away than others, which means we are not just looking at different places as we look at the stars, we are looking at different times.

Some of the light arriving on our retina from distant galaxies set off on its journey millions of light years before the light arriving from nearer galaxies. Some of those stars will have died before the light gets to us. I know it feels as if we are "in the moment" but that too must be an illusion.

If you touch the end of your nose with a finger, you experience two sensations. One will be at the tip of your finger and the other at the tip of your nose. If you keep your eyes open as you do it, there will be three sensations. You will experience seeing and feeling the two contacts all at the same time. That must be an illusion, because it takes longer for the signals to travel up the long axons of the nerves running from your finger tip, up your arm, into your spine, and up to the brain than it does for the message to pass from the nerves at the tip of the nose to the brain. Somehow the heart & mindbrain must buffer the information from the eyes and nose and wait until the sensation from the finger tip arrives. Then it fabricates a coherent experience."

It is now 08:00 and the alarm has just gone off."

As you can see, that was a dismal failure. My mind wandered and I forgot that I was attempting to stay in the moment. Consciousness is tricky, but I will try to address it more thoroughly towards the end of the book, because it is an integral part of mood management. Only my conscious self is capable of being happy and knowing it; and that is the only self I am really interested in.

Theories About Behaviour

Theories are just plausible stories waiting to be supplanted by better ones. Everyone understands the world according to theories of one sort or another, even if they cannot fully articulate them. Those who believe themselves to be practical, common sense types of people are often basing their ideas on outdated stories they absorbed years ago, then forgot about.

"Madmen in authority, who hear voices in the air, are distilling their frenzy from some academic scribbler of a few years back."

The General Theory of Employment, Interest and Money - John Maynard Keynes, 1936

In the middle ages in Europe the experts believed that people with mental health problems were possessed by demons which needed to be exorcised. In some parts of the world they still believe that. Some believed that children were naturally bad and needed the badness beaten out of them. Others that children were naturally good and if adults simply left them alone they would all grow up to be kind and peaceful citizens. A century ago the idea that women were prone to a special form of mental illness called hysteria, to which rich men with beards were immune, was popular. Another fashionable story was that autism was caused by "refrigerator mothers" who failed to show sufficient affection towards their children. Although fashionable and popular at the time, all of those theories turned out to be wrong.

Experts

"Physician, heal thyself"

Luke 4:23, King James Bible

Experts in the theory of psychology should at least be no worse in the practice of it than the rest of us. For example, it would seem reasonable to expect a psychotherapist to be at least as happy and well adjusted as the average person. Behaviour experts should be able to behave themselves and social psychologists should be socially competent. Most sensible people would not hire a plumber who kept flooding his own house.

Sigmund Freud was nothing if not confident about his own abilities. He has been described as an inventor of psychology and inventor is probably the right word. In reality Freud was a bit of a fraud.[3] He fell out with almost everyone he knew, engaging in bitter feuds throughout most of his adult life; a tradition continued by his daughter, Anna, who was equally disturbed and formed her own cult. Many of the ideas traditionally ascribed to Freud were not really his in the first place and those that were, turned out to be wrong. His cures did not work, so he falsified and fabricated some of the case studies that made him famous. His cure for opium addicts simply turned them into cocaine addicts, which is hardly difficult as cocaine is much more addictive than opium. But Freud was a good writer and he did inspire others to develop better models. Many of his ideas are emotionally appealing, which may explain why they have become so entrenched in our culture. But many of them are also wrong, based on outdated ideas about how the body, brain and mind work.

_____

[3] "Why Freud Was Wrong: Sin, Science and Psychoanalysis " Richard Webster, 2005

Behaviourism was a reaction against the speculative introspections of Victorian psychoanalysts. John B Watson was the founder of the approach which was later popularised by B. F. Skinner. Behaviourists were interested in shaping behaviour through reward and punishment, rather than postulating internal processes. Watson too was confident in his own abilities. He said:

"Give me a dozen healthy infants, well formed and my own specified world to bring them up in and I'll guarantee to take anyone at random and train him to become any type of specialist I might select: doctor, lawyer, artist, merchant-chief and yes, even beggar-man thief, regardless of his talents, pensions, tendencies, abilities, vocations and the race of his ancestors."

Page 82, "Behaviorism" - John B Watson, 1924

Like Freud, Watson was not quite so good at managing his own behaviour. His academic career was short lived, because he was caught conducting clandestine, practical research into the sexual responses of his young research students. He was dismissed. He never worked in academia again, but became a successful advertising executive. I am not sure there is a moral in this story. However he too became estranged from his family and died a recluse.

Konrad Lorenz was more interested in genetics. Rather than speculating about human minds, or training animals to press levers in laboratories, he promoted the ethological approach.

This involved observing animals in their natural environments and trying to work out why they behaved the way they did.

Lorenz was able to show that many behavioural programmes in animals were innate and automatic. He called them fixed action patterns. For example, newly hatched chicks are programmed to imprint on the first large moving object they see and follow it around. As the first large object most chicks see is their mother, following her around is a good way of keeping safe and fed. Lorenz showed that if they hatched next to a moving bucket, being towed by a piece of string, they would imprint on that.

Psychology students are familiar with photographs of this avuncular bearded Austrian, dressed in shorts, being followed around by a line of goslings that had imprinted on him. He looks like a nice man in the photos but Lorenz had some nasty ideas.

In his autobiography Konrad Lorenz claimed to have been captured as a prisoner of war in 1942. The truth is that he was a professor of psychology, at the University of Königsberg, in 1940 and was drafted into the Wehrmacht in 1941. For three years he was engaged in "racial studies" to discover the biological characteristics of "German-Polish half-breeds". He decided who should be allowed to reproduce. Those who failed his test were sent to the death camps. Konrad Lorenz wrote:

"The selection for toughness, heroism, social utility ... must be accompanied by some human institution if mankind ... is not to be ruined

by domestication-induced degeneracy. The racial idea as the basis of our state has already accomplished much in this respect."

Quoted on page 235 of "Sociobiology and the Human Dimension" by Joseph Breuer, 1983.

In ancient times, priests had drilled holes into the skulls of people who were behaving abnormally, supposedly to let out evil spirits. They must have thought they knew what they were doing too. In the 1930s, António Egas Moniz came up with the idea of cutting sections off the front of the brain to cure patients of mental illness. This became popularly known as lobotomy. He was confident that he knew what he was doing too and was awarded a Nobel prize in 1948. He claimed:

"We obtain cures and improvements but no failures."

António Egas Moniz

He was another one who exaggerated his achievements. In 1949 Moniz was shot by a patient and the approach was abandoned in the early 1960s.

The psychology wars of the second half of the last century were fought between cognitive psychologists and behaviourists. In 1959 Noam Chomsky had published a critical review of B.F. Skinner's book "Verbal Behavior" which demolished the idea that language could be explained as simply learned behaviour. Cognitive psychologists wanted to study the logical processes going on inside the brain. For them it seemed unreasonable to maintain, as the behaviourists did, that it was improper to speculate about intentions and internal logical states of the human mind. Software engineers were beginning to write computer programmes that involved intentions and internal logical states for machines. People were beginning to realise that the human brain could be described as a biological computer and it must run on some sort of computer programme too.

In the 21st century, biology and neuroscience have taken centre stage as scientists sequenced the human genome, and those of many plants and animals, to show how closely all life forms are related. They have also mapped out the neural circuits in the human brain and discovered hundreds of discrete areas of the brain that are associated with specialist functions. Meanwhile psychology has become a popular topic which is a mixed blessing.

Popular Psychology

Popular psychology occupies a similar space in popular culture as popular medicine and popular diet advice. There is plenty of information on offer but most of it is rubbish. Humans have been fascinated with themselves, ever since they became self aware. Neuroscience is all the rage and some people have started dressing up their outdated theories in modern sounding language to make them sound more plausible. They sprinkle their barmy ideas with scientific sounding words like quantum, plasticity, oxytocin, and mirror-neurons, then conclude that science has proved that their favourite guru was right all along.

Humans can believe almost anything if they try hard enough. The psychological term for wishful thinking is motivated reasoning. They select evidence and arguments to protect their prejudices instead of trying to test them to see if they are true. The problem is that there is so much "evidence" to choose from. The cumulative advice from the health sections of tabloid newspapers and websites seems to be that almost everything we consume can either cause or prevent premature death, depending on which day of the week it is. So I choose to believe that a diet of hot chillies, oranges, crisps, chocolate, beer, wine and brandy will ensure eternal life.

Similarly those who want to believe in the nonsense that is Scientology, or NLP, or in Freud's sexy ideas, are easily persuaded that the latest research in neuroscience has proved they were right all along. Beware those who promise to reveal "secrets" once you have paid them money.

It is amazing how stories become corrupted en-route from the academic journals to the websites, and then on to the presentation slides of behaviour gurus, therapists and master practitioners. With so much nonsense on offer, it is easy to become cynical and dismiss all the science, but that would be a mistake. There is a vast amount of good information available for free. Whole courses, like Robert Sapolsky's Biological Basis of Behaviour, are available on YouTube, where there are also

TED talks that are free to view, interviews and lectures from all of the people I refer to in this book.

Like dietary advice, popular psychology needs to be taken with a pinch of salt (possibly with a cracker, a slab of butter, a piece of cheese and a glass of wine).

The Bodybrain and The Heart & Mindbrain

Throughout the last two decades of the last century, Amos Tversky and Daniel Kahneman studied two different types of thinking, which Kahneman describes as "fast" and "slow".[4] Over roughly the same period, Walter Mischel was talking about "hot" and "cold" thinking systems.[5] When I first started thinking about how my own brain worked, which was the reason I decided to study psychology in the first place, I called it front and rear brain thinking. My undergraduate dissertation proposed that the reason cognitive and behavioural psychologists argued all the time, was not that they were looking at the same system in different ways, but that they were studying completely different systems. One was based on memories consisting of stored responses which were triggered by environmental stimuli. Like a doorbell ringing when the button is pressed. The other was based on recorded simulations of the stimuli themselves, which could be re-presented at a later

---

[4] "Thinking Fast and Slow" - Daniel Kahneman, 2011

[5] "The Marshmallow Test: Mastering Self Control" - Walter Mischel, 2014

date, like a video recording of the person on the doorstep. I thought intelligence was something to do with the resolution of the detail in those simulations, but I have moved on since then. Nobody agreed with me in 1976, so I went off to become a coach driver instead of a psychologist.

I could not make sense of consciousness at all, but I have kept on thinking about it throughout subsequent decades. It has been an extremely persistent pursuit throughout my life and it shows no sign of subsiding. When humans claim to be conscious, they are not talking about their entire body and brain. Only parts of it are conscious. Most of the offal in my body is not at all conscious and neither is most of my brain matter. Ideas "spring to mind" because they are created somewhere else and delivered to the mind to be experienced. I have no awareness of the processes which lead up to a conscious experience, because those are entirely sub-conscious. They take place in systems within my brain and body which I am not aware of.

The mind is the limited area of mental functioning that we are aware of. I am not going to pretend I know exactly what a mind is but I think I am one. It is not a physical thing although I happen to believe it is produced by the activity of physical neural systems. Toenails and hair cannot be conscious. They are not attached to a nervous system so they could not communicate even if they were.[6] There are a variety of body parts and organs around the body that are directly connected to nervous systems, but they do not seem to be conscious either. The intestines, kidneys, liver, and pancreas all have two way communication systems, but I do not think they are conscious. Any ideas they might generate do not appear in my mind anyway. I am rarely aware of what my right elbow is thinking, apart from every now and then when I bang it. Then I become intensely aware of it for a short period of time before it fades from consciousness.

When we think of the brain we tend to focus on the swelling of neurons within the skull, but forget that there are neurons all over the body and they are all connected. We are completely unaware of most of the neural activity which is going on in the bodybrain. As we go about our daily lives, moving around the world, sniffing, sneezing, coughing and scratching like other animals, there is a vast amount of information processing taking place. Sights, sounds, smells and tactile information are all being identified, categorised and sorted according to priority by the bodybrain which is the gatekeeper to the mind. It decides whether a particular idea is important enough to justify the attention of the mind. Most of it apparently does not, which is why we never become aware of it.

---

[6] Hair follicles and nail beds are, which is why we feel them but do not scream in agony when we have our hair or nails cut.

The heart & mindbrain is like an additional computer which is only turned on to process the most important information. It is extremely expensive to run, so it cannot operate at full power all the time. When it is working hard it soon begins to run out of neurotransmitters and it slows down. That is when self control, decision making, and clear thinking become difficult. We cannot do hard thinking for very long without a rest. The heart & mindbrain also needs to be switched off regularly for maintenance which is one of the reasons we need sleep.

Because heart & mindbrain processing is so expensive it is severely rationed by the bodybrain. Efficient, well trained bodybrains can take over most of our day-to-day behaviour, allowing the heart & mindbrain to idle and daydream. There are often times when I am not at all aware of what my bodybrain is doing.

My mind wanders so that sometimes I am not even conscious of what I am eating, because I am thinking about something else. I may look as if I am watching television, but often I am not really conscious of what is on. If something grabs my attention I suddenly become conscious, then drift off again. There are times when I am not conscious of what is happening in meetings because my mind is elsewhere. I think about going on holiday when I am supposed to be working, then I go on holiday and barely notice where I am because I am thinking about work. I spend most of my life not really knowing where I am and what I am doing. I think I might be absent minded, which is a strange expression when you think about it (which is also a strange expression).

My heart & mindbrain seems to be in charge of public relations. It does most of the speaking for the team, although my bodybrain can recite songs, poems and learned extracts of text on its own. It parrots them mindlessly. I have even noticed that my bodybrain sometimes takes over when I am public speaking. It can churn out familiar passages while my heart & mindbrain starts thinking about what I am going to do next. I have taught my bodybrain various tricks which it can manage on its own now, without much direct input from me. It does most of my work, including quite complex information processing tasks. It can drive the car which allows my mind to wander when I am driving. Sometimes I forget where we were going. Most of my behaviour is generated and controlled by my bodybrain rather than me. I am just a general supervisor, observer and note taker. Perhaps that is my purpose. But I am also the conscious part - the mind.

It is tempting to imagine that, because we have minds, other things that move must be thinking in a similar way. Anthropomorphism is the name for that tendency to attribute human traits to other animals or inanimate objects. Primitive creatures do have sensors which cause them to move, but then so do all sorts of simple systems. I doubt that primitive creatures are much more aware of what is happening in their lives than the components of my doorbell are aware of who is on the doorstep. And I doubt my doorbell can imagine what they look like and recognise people. In order to do that it would need to store information about the stimulus to create internal simulations which could be re-presented.[7]

Emotions may cause creatures to move but not all movements involve emotions. Some movements are reflex, automatic and sub-conscious. For example, plants grow towards sources of nutrients, water and light. Some turn slowly during the day to face the sun as it tracks across the sky. Others move more quickly. The Venus fly trap snaps shut to catch insects. These movements are complicated but they are all managed without a brain or mind.

The word we use to describe the process that causes living things to move is motivation. The Latin expression for movement, "emovere", gave the French "émouvoir", which means "to excite" or "stir up". That in turn gave us the English word, "Emotion". Emotions excite us and stir us up.

The way emotions work in mammals is that the amygdala becomes excited first, and it stimulates the hippocampus which is involved in memory and the sympathetic nervous system that

---

[7] Once I wrote that I bought a doorbell that videos whoever is there and texts me so I talk to them. It stored all the videos on a server somewhere in the cloud so perhaps it is conscious.

prepares the body for action. The sympathetic nervous system galvanises all sorts of processes around the body and brain as it becomes increasingly excited. Various innate and learned behaviours are triggered at different levels of excitement.

Whether the feeling of excitement of this system is interpreted as a pleasant or an unpleasant experience depends on what is going on and what we are thinking at the time. Emotions are the result of an assessment of physical responses in the body and thoughts in the brain. They do not always involve a fully operational heart & mindbrain. "Gut feelings" are sometimes an indication that the bodybrain is worried, even though the heart & mindbrain does not know why. At the extremes of emotion, when the sympathetic nervous system is in a heightened state of excitement, the heart & mindbrain can be switched off entirely. People really do not know what they are doing.

The basic emotions that drive behaviour are associated with attraction and repulsion. Living creatures are driven towards some things and away from others. They are driven to behave in ways which attract some things towards them and repel others. The rest of the time they sleep. Emotions are what motivate movement and brains evolved later to coordinate those movements as they became increasingly complicated.

Bodybrain Reading

I have admitted that my non-conscious bodybrain does most of the work that I claim credit for and I am pretty sure that is the case for all humans. Well trained bodybrains can do clever things.

The reason that cars can travel along our roads at high speeds with the traffic only separated by a painted white line, is that the drivers are brain readers. I am deliberately avoiding the term "mind reader", because it is not the mind that does it. My bodybrain can do that while my heart & mindbrain is thinking about something else. Learner drivers do not have that luxury. Until they have trained their bodybrain, heart and mindbrains have to do the work themselves, which is why it is so tiring. The more we can delegate to our bodybrain the easier life becomes, but first we have to take the trouble to train the bodybrain. Bodybrains only learn through boring repetition.

Bodybrains are constantly monitoring and assessing the behaviour of others and making assumptions about what they are likely to do next. As drivers negotiate junctions and roundabouts in their cars, or pedestrians walk down a busy high street, their bodybrains are constantly processing vast amounts of information. Body language is the term given to the non-verbal signals that humans perform constantly. It involves body postures, facial expressions and gestures. Humans are signalling all the time, whenever there are other humans around, even though most of the time they are completely unaware of what they are doing. They are also processing the signals given off by others and it is mostly non-conscious processing being carried out by the bodybrain.

When they walk down a busy street, humans can also be observed performing dominant or subservient styles of behaviour. They signal their intentions about the direction they are going to take, along with signals to show how willing they are to give way to others coming in the opposite direction.[8] Some stride purposefully and expect others to step aside for them. Others weave timidly giving way to almost everyone. Most of us swap from one strategy to another, as the bodybrain sizes up and evaluates the oncoming traffic and most of the time it works. Flocks of birds, shoals of fish and herds of cattle avoid collisions in the same way. This is all sub-conscious and automatic processing.

The only time humans become aware of all this social information processing is when the conscious part is alerted by the bodybrain about the possibility of a collision with somebody approaching. Something has gone wrong with the automatic systems and the heart & mindbrain has to take over for a moment to apply more intense processing. When I am driving that is when I notice that my heart & mindbrain

---

[8] Unless they are gawping at their phones in which case the whole system breaks down.

becomes involved again. Suddenly I am snapped back into the moment to decide what the car in front is going to do next, or what that blue flashing light is doing behind me.

Similarly when I am walking down a busy street I sometimes have to stop daydreaming and pay attention to what I am doing for a few seconds. Suddenly it becomes a game of bluff, as two people decide whether to signal dominance, a determination to carry on in their own direction regardless of the consequences, or subservience, a willingness to give way. Dominant and subservient interactions have been a part of daily life for social animals for millions of years. As it happens in modern life, some of the physiological components of the fight or flight system take effect. It is as if the two contestants on the pavement outside the chemist are preparing for a fight or to run for their lives, which is exactly what is happening, although in polite society fighting is unlikely to be the outcome. Normally both people sidestep and apologise. As a matter of fact, humans do end up fighting. There are areas of some inner cities where it is sensible to give way to gangs of young men on pavements. Similar social exchanges happen in cars, resulting in road rage. This is just one example of the dangers of putting primitive brains in charge of modern machinery.

If you do not think this applies to you, next time you are walking in a crowded street, try out this experiment. Increase your pace and confidently stride along in a straight line and see how other people scatter. Then slow down and walk hesitantly. Suddenly, other people seem to become more dominant because you are giving out subservient signals. Experiments have shown that street robbers, when shown footage of people walking along the street, can sense who are the likely victims.[9] It is nothing to do with size and everything to do with the confidence of their body language. The ability to make sound judgements in these exchanges on the street is called being "streetwise".

Much of the received wisdom in relation to the management of aggression and violence is based on a fallacy that all violence involves the same psychological system and all forms of violence can be managed in the same way. This is the idea that aggression and violence are directly related to the level of excitement in the sympathetic nervous system. As we will see when we go on to look at motivation more closely, it is more complicated than that. Those who are attached to that theory tend to be more familiar with children and adults who have learning disabilities. They are less knowledgeable about streetwise behaviour. The type of violent behaviour exhibited by people with learning disabilities and autism is often associated with over-stimulation of the sympathetic nervous system. This is panic driven behaviour. Yet most violence in

---

[9] "Psychopathy and Victim Selection: The Use of Gait as a Cue to Vulnerability." - Angela Book 2013

nature is not driven by panic at all. Predators are not afraid of their prey. They love their food just as we do. Many humans, even those who attack other humans, are not driven by panic either. Human violence sometimes involves the predatory pursuit of other humans. They may not eat their prey but the same mental processes of a persistence hunter are operating. The pursuit drive causes humans to chase a variety of things, both animate, inanimate and intellectual and it is not always associated with the highest levels of excitement. Aggression and violence also feature in mating rituals and challenges between rivals in social groups. Humans engage in similar behaviours and to become more effective at managing aggression we need to understand the relationship between aggression and violence better. They are not the same thing.

Aggression is not driven by fear. It is driven by an urge to perform, show off, threaten and intimidate. It can be enjoyable. Some humans pursue opportunities to indulge in violence. They prepare to do it while they are still quite calm, then have to find ways of stirring themselves up into an excited state when the opportunity arises. That is a combination of pursuit and performance drives, rather than panic. And because performance is all about acting we need to be careful as we assess how excited an aggressive performer really is. When people appear to "go berserk" sometimes it is a social performance rather than genuine panic. They are not as out of control as they try to appear. It is important that we fully understand the causes of aggression and violence before jumping to conclusions about the solutions. A failure to do that has been the cause of several failed policy initiatives over recent decades.

Where and What is a Mind?

It feels like "I", my "self" or "mind" are located somewhere just behind my eyes (apart from when I stub my toe, in which case I exist in my foot for a few moments before returning to my normal position). Some people have experienced "out of body" experiences. Powerful and convincing though those experiences are, they are relatively easy to replicate in the lab and have been shown to be an illusion. So the fact that I experience my own consciousness as if I am located in the front of my brain does not mean that I am physically located there, if I am physically located anywhere. However, if my heart & mindbrain wants to think it is in the front of my head I am quite happy to go along with that.

This is a rather awkward admission, as I am writing this book and asking you to believe what I am writing. I am convinced that this heart & mindbrain of mine evolved as part of a system that was involved in deception. I am the product of a heart & mindbrain which tells lies. The bodybrain generates ideas in the form of a running commentary, then the heart & mindbrain selects, crafts and edits them to create flattering confabulations out of the available content, whilst at the same time suppressing and belittling disparaging truths about failures. The combination of a creative and well directed bodybrain and a talented heart & mindbrain to do the editing is what keeps us happy. Like most autobiographies, our own life story is not an entirely impartial account.

Some people's bodybrains and minds generate belittling and disparaging life stories which make them unhappy. They need to train their bodybrain, hire better scriptwriters and editors, or go to writing school themselves. This is sometime called therapy.

For many decades we were told that the route to happiness was to raise everybody's self esteem. Aggression and violence were supposed to be caused by low self esteem because people tended to under-estimate themselves. A whole industry grew up encouraging people to think positive and believe that they were better than they thought they were. Unfortunately, far from suffering from low self-esteem, there is abundant evidence to suggest that the majority of humans over-estimate their own abilities. In fact, they estimate that they are better than average at almost everything, which of course cannot possible be true.[10] Most people rate themselves as better than the average driver and smarter, more generous, more sociable and more reasonable than the average person. The delusion tends to be

[10] "Self-Esteem, Construal and Comparisons With Self, Friends and Peers" - Jerry Suis, 2002

more extreme in respect of abilities that are difficult to measure.

High-jumpers know exactly how high they can jump, so they get accurate feedback and tend not to become deluded. But elusive qualities such as managerial competence are less easy to measure, so more prone to mental distortion and the distortion tends to be in the same direction. One way to get a more objective measurement of qualities such as managerial competence, generosity, sociability, or sense of humour is to ask their friends, colleagues or employees, then compare what they say with a self assessment.

If 1 represents absolute agreement between self-assessment and objective measures, and 0 represents no agreement whatsoever, the results are clear. Estimates of athletic ability came out at 0.45 correspondence, college performance was 0.35, interpersonal skills 0.17 and managerial competence only 0.04. Managers really do seem to have an inflated idea about themselves. But then so do most of us. In other studies 70 percent of participants claimed to have above average leadership skills. Only 2 percent believed that they could be below average. When it came to sociability 60 percent of people claimed to be in the top 10 percent. 25 percent of people thought they were in the top 1 percent so far was sociability is concerned. This is a significant level of delusion.

If that just makes them feel better there is no harm in it, but when it causes them to make errors of judgement it can cause problems. For example, doctors who were 88 percent confident of their ability to diagnose pneumonia were actually right only 20 percent of the time.[11] The financial crash of 2007 happened because of wishful thinking on the part of traders who persuaded themselves that the bundles of debt they were buying and selling could be repaid because they wanted to believe it.

To some extent wishful thinking can be beneficial. It causes people to have the confidence to take risks, some of which pay off. It makes them feel better about themselves. In the self-assessment tests those who came out with the most accurate self appraisals also tended to be depressed. I think I would prefer to be happy if slightly deluded. But we need to distinguish between the areas of our lives where it does not really matter much and those where it does.

Numerous government contracts have ended up costing far more than was expected, taking far longer than was promised and then not working as they were supposed to, because the gap between wishful thinking and reality was too big. In 2002, the £12 billion U.K. NHS Connect project was discontinued because it did not work and had cost a fortune. In 2007, the

---

[11] "Flawed Self-Assessment - Implications for Health, Education and the Workplace" - David Dunning 2004

£412 million U.K. Border Agency e-borders contract was cancelled due to cost overruns. In 2008, the £98 million B.B.C. digital media initiative was cancelled because it did not work. In 2009, the new £14.8 million U. K. police force recording system was scrapped because it did not work. In 2016 the U.K. government announced that the cost for two new aircraft carriers had doubled to £6.2 billion in just six years and the first ship would not be operational until five years after the due date. Then the UK government admitted that it was unlikely that the new £285 million airport it had just built on the British overseas territory of St Helena could ever by used. It was too windy.

All of those contracts were signed by wishful thinkers. For building contracts I have always used the rule of thumb that the experts estimates are likely to be optimistic by at least 50 percent. So if the cost is estimated at £1 million, I plan for £1.5 million. If they estimate it will take 12 months, I plan for 18 months. It has never let me down.

Humans deceive themselves and each other because their brains evolved to do that. Initially they were selling themselves. These days they are selling other things too, but they are still selling themselves. Both sellers and buyers want the things they buy and sell to be better than they really are, so they believe their own fantasies. Walter Mitty is a fictional character in a James Thurber short story and the name has come to be used for anyone who allows the gap between wishful thinking and reality to grow too wide. People forget that in the original book he was a tragic character who died in front of a firing squad.

Wishful thinking and self delusion provide short term comfort but they are a poor life strategy. When deluded individuals are finally confronted with the truth it can be a painful shock, which is why we should be teaching children to learn to recognise it. Critical thinking, scientific method and Bayesian statistics are truth detection tools which enable human brains to glimpse reality, yet most humans have not learned how to use them. There is no shortage of information in the digital age and no shortage of people claiming to be experts. What we need is the tools to find out which of them is telling the truth, which are telling fantasy stories, and which are deliberately lying.

"Science is the belief in the ignorance of experts."

Instead, over the past half century, popular psychologists have been telling people what they want to hear. Books with titles such as "I'm OK - You're OK", "Awaken the Giant Within", "Think Your Way to Success", "Boost Your Self-Esteem", "Power is Within You", "Six Pillars of Self-Esteem" and "Power Thoughts" all peddle the same idea. They tell people that they are under-estimating themselves and if they just think more positively about everything the universe will respond to their wishes.

One of the most enduring myths has been the one that selfish, aggressive and violent behaviour is always caused by low self-esteem. This has been trotted out by teachers and social workers as an established fact for decades. It was an extremely expensive delusion when it became translated into simplistic policies. Billions of pounds and dollars were poured into grandiose projects designed to raise general self-esteem, in the hope that aggression and violence would disappear. They were all abject failures because they misdiagnosed the problem. They also failed to consider what might happen to those who already had inflated self-esteem if they were encouraged to love themselves even more.

Narcissistic personality disorder is a syndrome rather than a disease. It can be regarded as an extreme version of the mental distortion that most humans suffer from. To be diagnosed you need to score five out of the nine descriptors, which are "Grandiosity", "Arrogance", "Preoccupation with success and power", "Lack of empathy", "A belief of being unique", "A sense of entitlement", "Requiring excessive admiration", "Exploitative" and "Envious of others".

Maybe I move in the wrong circles, but I have come across a lot of people like that in business and they tend to be quite successful. There are some people who deserve to have high self-esteem, because the truth is they really are better than most people. But we all need the dose of reality that comes with accurate feedback. Unless humans receive accurate ongoing feedback we know their self assessments are likely to diverge from the opinions of other people. This can create social problems for them. Some people know their place and are perfectly happy with it, wherever they may happen to be in the social strata. But some feel and believe they deserve more. They believe they are entitled to more love and respect than they are receiving. They believe they are entitled to a higher position in society and a greater share of resources, and it makes them feel angry.

Aggression and violence is actually associated with distorted high self-esteem, not low self-esteem.

"Yet Baumeister has shown that the theory could not be more spectacularly, hilariously, achingly wrong. Violence is a problem not of too little self-esteem but of too much, particularly when it is unearned."[12]

Steven Pinker

We certainly do not want to raise everybody's self-esteem. That would create more people with narcissistic personality disorders. What we need is a dose of reality therapy. In the modern world it is less easy for young people to find their place and get accurate feedback. Social media fails in this respect as it often presents the distorted feedback they crave rather than the accurate feedback they need.

Those who exhibit violent, anti-social behaviour often have a frustrated sense of entitlement because they have an inaccurate estimation of their own qualities and abilities. When feedback from the real world fails to confirm their distorted self image, they become angry with the world. Those mental processes have been evident in a number of mass killings, in which murderers took out their rage in revenge against a world that, in their minds, failed to appreciate them or give them the respect they deserved.

Humans are naturally predisposed towards authoritarian social hierarchies but find themselves living in societies which have been socially engineered in an attempt to remove those structures.

---

[12] "The Better Angels of Our Nature" - Steven Pinker, 2011

When I was an undergraduate, going to university was a privilege enjoyed by only 10 percent of the population. When there were so few of them, it was true that people with degrees tended to get the best jobs and earn more money than those without. Then, in an attempt to promote fairness and equality, successive governments encouraged more and more students to study for a degree. Education is a good thing, but telling students that they could all be earning more money than average because they could all be in the best 10 percent of jobs was not just mathematical nonsense but a cruel deception. Now the top 10 percent have post graduate qualifications, so nothing has really changed in the equality stakes.

Humans are prone to wishful thinking and politicians are only too keen to take advantage of it. But it is seductive indulgence that leads people into making serious mistakes in the real world. When reality jars with fantasy it can come as a shock. In many cultures parents protect young children from harsh reality with pretend stories, and that is fine. But there comes a time when they need to know the difference between reality and make believe. I think that ultimately there is more happiness to be had from understanding reality, imagining better versions of it, then acting on the real world to bring them about, than living in a fantasy. Only if we are willing to sacrifice some of our comforting delusions can we hope to become more effective and I believe create maximum happiness at the same time.

I think there are two stages on the route to happiness. The first is to understand how the real world works and how our own bodies, brains and minds work within it. The second is to learn how to manage our own minds, moods, emotions, and behaviour, to create life-enhancing experiences in the present and life stories for the future.

There has not been time for our bodies and brains to evolve physically, according to the processes of natural selection. So we still share the same biological and mental equipment as our Stone Age ancestors. We are equipped for a world and a lifestyle that no longer exists, so it is no wonder that we are confused. But mood management is not about wishful thinking. It is about adopting an optimistic appreciation of reality and a scientific approach to make the most of what we have.

The first step is to understand where we fit into the animal world and lose some of the hubris that makes us think we are so special.

What is it like to be an Octopus?

When humans try to imagine what it must be like to be another type of animal, for example a horse or a dog, they seldom get further than imagining their own brain inside another animal's body. It takes a far greater imaginative leap to appreciate what it must be like to be a different sort of brain. For example, what is it like to be a worm, or a bat, or an octopus?

Neuroscientists treat the octopus with some respect. An octopus actually has more neurones than humans do. It has more brains because each tentacle has a brain of its own. In the lab, an octopus can recognise itself in a mirror - a sign of intelligence that very few creatures can match. When one of its tentacles is cut off, the severed limb crawls away with its movements coordinated by its own brain. If it touches food, the severed tentacle will grab it and try to push it towards where the mouth would have been. Eventually it starves to death. Meanwhile, the main octopus can grow a new tentacle and brain to replace the lost one. I cannot imagine what it is like to be an octopus, or one of its limbs.

There are fish that live in the ocean depths in complete darkness. I cannot imagine what it would be like to be them either. What could they possibly think about if they could think at all? Humans are certainly more advanced that many creatures but we forget how similar some of our own behaviour is to that of other animals. As we all evolved from a common ancestor, it is likely that we do share some of the same internal processes. That is clearly the case with physical features and probably mental ones too. Advanced and simple systems are working in parallel within the body, brain and mind of human beings. We have no more direct access to the majority of them than we do to the mental processes going on inside other creatures. All we do is experience the results and try to work out how we did it.

What we call thinking is really intelligent guesswork. The body, brain, and mind are constantly trying to guess what is going on in the outside world by building simulations, testing them and trying to improve them. At the same time they are trying to work out what is going on in our inside world, how we ought to feel and what we are going to do about it. That involves a lot of guesswork too. What we call thinking gets muddled with what we call feeling. Some people use the terms interchangeably. Ask them what they think about a particular subject and they reply by telling you how they feel about it. In truth, it is not always easy to distinguish between thoughts and feelings because they are so closely linked. That is particularly true in the case of episodic memories which have a sort of emotional flavour attached to them.

Nervous systems began to develop around the gut of primitive tube-like creatures long before the swelling of neurons that we tend to think of as a brain appeared towards the top end. We still have a large number of neurones around the gut which communicate with those in the skull. Bodybrain is actually an accurate description. What we normally refer to as the brain evolved much later to control more complex movements but it is not immediately obvious why or when conscious minds appeared. Other information processors seem to manage quite well without conscious minds and humans can function without them too.

It seems to be the most recently evolved parts of the cerebral cortex, located towards the front of the brain, that are associated with conscious minds. Yet those parts are also deeply connected to the limbic system, which is involved in emotions. It is a mistake to regard emotions as primitive, or the limbic system as part of a phylogenically older brain frozen in time. Emotions, thoughts and behaviour are all intricately connected.

Yet it is clear that in the order of evolutionary development the body must have developed first, followed by a brain and finally a mind. Brains evolved to enable creatures to behave more effectively and succeed in a competitive world, not to create abstract ideas or exact and accurate simulations of reality. Robin Fox, the evolutionary anthropologist, observed:

"the brain's business is not to give us an accurate or objective view of the world, but to give us a useful view - one we can act on."[13]

It may be that we are not equipped to fully understand the workings of our own mind but by better understanding the workings of our bodies and brains then we might learn to use it better.

Some of our common ancestors consisted of little more than a gut. They lived in the sea with water washing over them. Nutrients passed in at one end and waste products flowed out of the other. There are still creatures living in the seas and

---

[13] Quoted in his daughter, Kate Fox's excellent book, "Watching the English: the hidden rules of English behaviour", 2004.

oceans that operate like that. They do not need brains because they do not need to move. Sea Squirts provide a compelling illustration of the link between sensors, muscles, brains and movement.

A sea squirt starts off as a tiny creature, not unlike a tadpole. It has a muscular tail, with a rudimentary eye and a very simple brain to coordinate the two. It has simple emotions which motivate it to move around in search of a better life. But once a sea squirt finds a nice new place to live, it attaches itself to a rock and hangs on there for the rest of its days. It loses the motivation to go anywhere, preferring the easy life, just chilling and allowing nutrients to wash through it. As it no longer needs to move around, or do anything really, it no longer needs the sensor, muscle or brain. So it reabsorbs them and turns into something more like a vegetable. Some of my retired friends are a bit like that.

A worm is really just a tube surrounded by muscles and sensors but worms can do something their more static relatives cannot. They can move around. Simple tube like creatures evolved nerves around the gut that contracted muscles along the tube to create movement. Gradually a swelling of additional sensors evolved around the hole at the front where the food went in. This bulb of sensors allowed more discriminating creatures to open the hole wider to ingest nutrients and close it to avoid poisons. That could be described as the beginning of fussy eating. In humans that swelling of neurons at the top of the tube has grown rather large and complicated, but in many ways the basic biology is the same. We are basically a tube that moves.

Reptiles and Amphibians are more advanced than worms. They do not have a cerebral cortex, like mammals, but they do have something called a tectum at the top of their brain. That evolved to coordinate spacial movement. It directs the nose, eyes and ears in a particular direction, so that information from a particular section of the environment can be processed in more detail. This is called selective attention.

The frogs brain does not have the capacity to process all of the available information at the same time. It can only process small parts sequentially, which is also true of human beings even though they have vastly more processing power. The comforting impression we have that we are seeing a constant, complete re-presentation of the physical world is an illusion. There are huge cognitive blind spots that we are not aware of in areas that are not currently being processed in detail, which is why stage magicians and pick-pockets fool us so easily.

The eyes and the tongue of a frog are coordinated by the brain. Movement detectors sensing a moving target, such as a fly, cause the tongue to flick out towards that part of the visual field to catch it. It does not involve much thinking. Frogs have brains but I very much doubt that they have minds like ours.

Minds need something to think about. Frogs do not spend much time reflecting on the meaning of life or planning their holidays. They react to movement and changes in the environment. When a shadow suddenly falls over a frog, it jumps. If the temperature suddenly changes, it jumps. If a small dark spot moves in its visual field the tongue flicks out to catch it. Those simple reactions are enough to provide them with food and save them from predators. Rather than providing an accurate or objective view of the world it provides useful information.

Apart from a tiny spot on the retina called the fovea, which contains a dense group of colour receptive sensors, most of the human retina works as a simple movement and shadow detector, not that much different to that of a frog. All the complicated visual simulations that humans experience are built up from rapid scans building information from that one tiny spot.

Frogs lack the advanced brain structures in the cortex to build detailed internal simulations of the outside world and work out what is happening out there. They cannot think like that. They just have a limited set of automatic behaviours triggered by features of the environment. If no behavioural response is triggered, nothing happens in the mind of a frog. If you put a frog in a pan of cold water and heat it up slowly, it will poach. The idea of jumping out of the pan simply does not occur to it.

A frog will starve to death when it is surrounded by dead flies because it does not know that the flies exist. It only reacts to movement.

If flies could learn to sit still they would be completely safe from frogs, although much more vulnerable to humans with rolled up newspapers. Flies do not have minds either, so ideas like that never occur to them. Flies can think much faster than humans though, due to the short distances information has to travel in their tiny brain. It takes time for messages to pass from one neuron to another, so the bigger the animal the slower their reactions are. If a fly had an imagination it would experience the world in slow motion.

Birds are one stage further along an evolutionary path in the development of brains. Some of them can do something more akin to human thinking, because they evolved an extension to the tectum, which is the primitive movement coordinator. It is called the wulst and it is particularly prominent in predatory birds, which need to coordinate their movements more accurately. The cerebral cortex developed in mammals to do the same thing but not all human movements are coordinated and they do not all result from conscious thought.

When a human hand touches something hot, the sensors in the skin cause neurons to fire a message to the spine, which immediately bounces another message back to the muscles in the arm, causing them to contract. The hand reacts automatically by pulling away before the brain even knows what has happened. This is mindless movement or bodybrain processing.

Chapter 2 - Bodies and Brains

Brainstuff

A nerve cell is called a neuron. It has a cell body (grey matter) and a long white tube called an axon insulated by a fatty material called myelin (white matter) which reaches out to other neurons to communicate. The cell body has tree like growths off it called dendrites, which accept incoming signals from other neurons. The axon which carries the outgoing signal can be quite long, leading to connections with other neurons all over the brain and body. At the end of the tube is another tree like structure called the axon terminal, which connects to the dendrites on the cell bodies of other neurons.

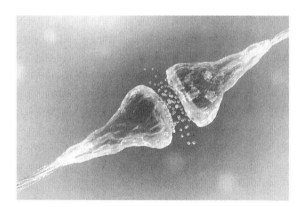

Neurons communicate with each other by sending molecules across the gap between the axon terminal and the dendrites, called the synaptic gap. They have receptors that exactly fit the shapes of certain chemical molecules, called neurotransmitters. When molecules fill their receptors the neurons become either more or less excited, depending on the type of receptor. When some neurons are stimulated they permanently change their rate of firing, which is called long term potentiation. That is how memory works.

A special form of neurotransmitter can pass through the blood/brain barrier into the bloodstream. That means they can be transported all around the body and brain and influence a range of systems almost immediately. They are called hormones. For example, a squirt of adrenaline[14] into the bloodstream can flood the whole body in a heartbeat, causing all sorts of different neural circuits to fire and affecting all sorts of different systems at the same time.

Memory

There are billions of neurons and trillions of possible combinations which means that the capacity of the brain to store memories is practically limitless. Memories are formed by changed rates of firing in neural networks, initially within the hippocampus in the middle of the brain but then distributed around the brain as a sort of backup. The hippocampus is a tiny structure and it does have its limits. At the end of a busy day it can fill up, leaving us unable to store any more new memories until some of the current batch have been moved elsewhere. That might be why we need to go to sleep and it also

---

[14] Noradrenaline is a closely related neurotransmitter. In the US they are known as epinephrine and norepinephrine.

may explain why young children need so much sleep. They have a lot to learn and remember.[15]

When certain features of the environment trigger an emotional reaction, it means that the amygdala recognises them as important and the hippocampus motivates the brain to take an interest in them. Sensors are directed towards the source of the information to gather more data. Additional processing capacity is allocated to those sensors to build a more detailed simulation of whatever it might be. If the new information causes the amygdala to become even more excited, it might stimulate circuits in the hippocampus into long term potentiation to store the simulation so that it will be recognised more quickly next time.

Until relatively recently it was thought that the adult brain could not grow any new neurons. In fact that turns out not to be true. They can grow in the hippocampus and in the olfactory bulb. However, learning does not depend on the growth of new neurons. It is changes to the connections between existing neurons that create most of our memories and there is no shortage of them.

---

[15] In 2017 Professors Tim Bliss, Graham Collingridge and Richard Morris shared the one million euro Grete Lundbeck European Brain Research Prize for their work on the neuroscience of memory. They are worth a Google.

The basic mechanism of memory was predicted decades ago by Donald Hebb.[16] It is often encapsulated by the aphorism, "when neurones fire together they wire together". Whenever neurons fire together the connections between them strengthen. Thoughts and memories are networks of neurons that make up simulations of aspects of the outside world. A simulation can be stored and re-presented at a later date, which is what we call remembering. Information about the emotions being experienced at the time are also stored as part of the simulation, so when memories are recalled and a simulation from the past is re-presented it is not only information about the physical world that is recalled. Emotions that tell us how we feel about it are recreated too.

Not all memory is stored in this form, as simulations of the world and accompanying emotions. Memory can also be stored in the form of response programmes, or learned patterns of behaviour, known as procedural memory. This is the sort of memory that enables us to remember how to do things, like tie shoelaces, ride bicycles and play sports. Procedural memory involves doing things rather than thinking about them. Some creatures only store procedural memories. They can learn and remember how to do things, but they cannot be aware of what they are doing because they have nothing to think about.

---

16 "The Organisation of Behavior" - Donald Hebb, 1949.

Simulations and Representations

Creatures that can store simulations have an imaginary world to think about. Although we get the impression that our simulations are accurate and complete, that is an illusion. The stored simulations of past moments and the current simulation of the present lack much of the detail of the physical world.

We only respond to a limited range of the electromagnetic and auditory spectra. Other life forms are sensitive to ultra violet and infra red light. Some are sensitive to electricity or magnetic fields. Some can experience much higher frequencies of sound than humans can. Many have far more sensitive chemical detectors. They all live in different worlds but none of them can create accurate and objective models of the physical world. There really is only one completely accurate model of our universe and that is our universe. But it is not possible to have an objective viewpoint because there is no such thing. The separation between time and space is an illusion created by our brains. We are all in different parts of spacetime expanding at the speed of light like every other part of the universe. A complete and accurate model of the universe would consist of all spacetime, from the moment of the big bang to the moment the whole thing collapsed back into a singularity.

Impressive though a human bodybrain is, it does not have the capacity to store an accurate and detailed simulation of even a tiny part of it, never mind the entire universe. To get some idea of the scale of information we are talking about, Pixar Studios used a fleet of cloud computers in several data centres to render 129,600 frames to create the animated film, "How To Train Your Dragon 2". That took more than 90 million render hours, or a million hours for each minute. One computer would have taken 10,273 years to complete the process. And that is just to create a 90 minute simulation for one of the senses.

Luckily we do not need to create and store simulations with that level of detail. Our mental simulations only correspond to a tiny part of the physical world but they are accurate enough to be useful. Stored simulations enable parts of brains to process information off-line, when they are not too busy paying attention to the current environment. That is really what we mean by thinking. It is more than just processing information and reacting to it. It involves re-presenting, re-drafting and sometimes creating new simulations.

Most of the time, sketchy models are good enough. When I look up at the night sky I cannot identify much of what I am looking at. Astrophysicists have much more detailed simulations of the night sky stored in their brains and when they look up they see far more than me. I have more detailed and accurate simulations of Formula 1 racing cars and commercial aircraft than people who are not interested in that sort of thing. That means when I look at them I actually see more than some other people. Most people have detailed simulations of the things they are interested in and sketchy ones of the rest of the physical universe. They have quite accurate and detailed simulations of their local area in the form of mental maps, but only very sketchy and inaccurate simulations of other parts of the world.

We do not think about the real world because we have no access to it. What we think about are our own simulations which have varying levels of detail and resolution. Often there is not enough time to add all the detail to a simulation in real time, before attention has to move on to something else important. But a brain that can store incomplete simulations and re-present them later, when life is not quite so hectic to add more detail, can gradually build up more accurate and detailed versions over time. That is what humans are particularly good at. There are times when we do not need to react immediately to the immediate demands of the environment. That is when we can review past simulations at our leisure and improve our plans for the future.

Humans do not only create simulations of the physical universe that already exist. When stored simulations are re-presented, they can be altered, adapted and combined with sections from other simulations to create something new. That enables brains with minds to think about the future, make educated guesses about what is likely to happen next, and change their own

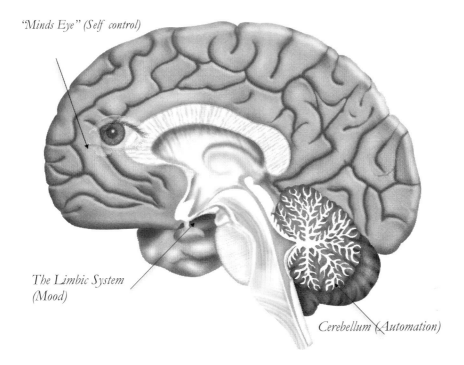

"Minds Eye" (Self control)

The Limbic System (Mood)

Cerebellum (Automation)

behaviour accordingly. It is the ability of some brains to store and re-present simulations that enables them to have minds.

Once brains evolved to create and store sketchy simulations of the real world, it was a short step towards something that would have a much more profound effect on humans and their planet. Instead of working on a re-presented simulation to make it correspond more accurately with the physical world, they started acting on the physical world to make it correspond more accurately with their imaginary simulation. It may have been accidental but it is difficult to over-state the significance of this change in emphasis. It is only very recently that human inventiveness exploded to create the anthropocene, a term first used by Paul Crutzen and Eugene Stoermer in 2000. It describes the current geological epoch in which humans are changing the planet rather than geological forces. It happened because brains that had evolved for one purpose suddenly discovered another and became creative.

The Limbic System

Even if it was possible, it would be a terrible waste of resources to store simulations of everything, even sketchy ones. We only store simulations of what is useful. It is the influence of the amygdala on the hippocampus which determines which simulations are considered important enough to store. The amygdala gives memories an emotional flavour to indicate how important they are. If we are not interested in something we do not remember it. If something is extremely exciting or frightening, we cannot forget it. Sometimes it is hard to think of anything else.

Emotions help create memories and when they are retrieved and re-presented the simulations recreate an echo of the emotional states which accompanied them. Both the amygdala and the hippocampus are part of the limbic system. Ancestors of both humans and lizards had similar limbic systems. The thalamus is a busy junction through which all the information passes to be distributed around the body and brain. The hypothalamus is another part of the limbic system, situated just below the thalamus (hence the name).

The hypothalamus is closely involved in the experience of emotions and has also been linked to blushing, the feeling of tingling skin and orgasms. It has nerves which project to the heart, liver and skin. When these nerves change their rates of firing, they can bring about significant biological changes around the bodybrain within seconds of the experience. It is also involved in motivation. All these emotional circuits in the limbic system are connected with the pre-frontal cortex which is associated with willpower and higher mental functions. What we call emotions are really a combination of the current level of stimulation in the sympathetic nervous system, what we happen to be thinking about, and how important it is to us. Important things can be either frightening or exciting, depending on what you think about them. Sometimes it is hard to distinguish between those emotions.

Psychologists used to think that the cerebral cortex, which only mammals have, was responsible for all of the advanced intellectual functions of the human brain and emotions were older and more primitive. In reality the limbic system has continued to evolve as part of an integrated system involving the cerebral cortex and neurones in the gut. The most recently evolved parts of the human brain are the neural circuits in the swollen cerebral cortex towards the front and over the top. The neural circuits that seem to be most closely associated with conscious thinking are the frontal and parietal lobes. They also have extensive two way connections to the limbic system.

So dense are these two way connections, that the frontal cortex of the brain is now considered to be an outgrowth of the limbic system. What was once described as the "old" reptilian brain is actually an integral part of the "new" human mind. This is where I guess the neural circuits that create what I am calling the "Heart & Mindbrain" might be. That is where we live.

Part of the job of the frontal cortex is to control emotions, defer urges for immediate gratification, and suppress urges to do silly things. In order to succeed in a social group, animals have to learn some degree of self control.

Animal Self Control

Simple creatures are constantly at the mercy of their immediate drives, mindlessly pulled this way and that, by whatever urge happens to be strongest at the time. Self control involves suppressing the urge to take a small reward now, in order to get a bigger one later. Sometimes in involves enduring minimal discomfort now in order to avoid more discomfort later. For example, many animals learn to suppress the urge to urinate and defecate temporarily until they find a more suitable place. This improves the quality of life in nests and camps.

Social hierarchies depend on self control. In order to survive in social groups low status individuals need to learn to wait their turn and control their frustration with high status individuals. Grabbing the food first or losing your temper is a luxury that only the powerful can afford.

This raises an important question. If animals can control their own behaviour, why are so many humans apparently unable to do so? The reason is that their bodybrains have not been properly trained. Bullies who regularly "lose" their temper and selfish people who try to take more than they give, do it because they have learned that they can get away with it. They can learn to behave differently, if somebody knows how to do it and takes the trouble to teach them. Formalised rules of self control are called manners. They vary in the details from culture to culture but have common themes. They have to be taught and learned. Once they become internalised and automated, self control becomes effortless. This is the process of socialisation that is part of good parenting. Children who have not been socialised cannot control their own behaviour. They need to be taught how to do it which involves repeated practice.

Smell and Emotion

The olfactory bulb is essentially a chemical detector. The anatomical name for it is Rhinencephalon, which comes from the Greek - literally meaning "smell brain". Rats, dogs and many other mammals, live in a world of smell. If they store simulations of the physical world they must be in smellvision. The limbic system in a rat's brain is far more integrated with the olfactory bulb than in human brains, because the olfactory bulb processes smells. In humans, the olfactory bulb is rudimentary, because our brain evolved to rely more on visual information. But smell and emotions still remain closely associated in the human brain. There are multiple links between the olfactory system, the amygdala, and the hippocampus. A smell can bring back particularly vivid episodic memories.

Smell is also an important part of the bonding process between a new infant and the mother in all mammals, including humans. When creatures live in groups it is important that they can find each other and smell plays an important part in that. Humans seem predisposed towards certain types of smells, particularly those associated with flowers, plant leaves, nuts and fruit. It makes evolutionary sense. Some of the claims made by aromatherapists are not supported by empirical evidence, but there is certainly evidence that certain smells reduce the effects of stress in animals. Dr Nick Lavidis, at the University of Queensland, identified five chemicals containing stress-relieving properties that are released when grasses and green leaves are cut. Researchers produced a spray including these, which has been shown to reduce activity in the amygdala and prevent the memory loss associated with stress in cattle. It is marketed as

"Serenascent" for humans.[17] So perhaps the smell of newly mown grass is more than just a pleasant aroma.

Many creatures communicate by producing pheromones which directly interact with neurotransmitters. Insects signal alarm in this way, and they can communicate at distances of up to two miles. Pheromones have also been shown to affect human emotions, particularly in relation to sexual behaviour and aggression. They may play a part in the bonding process between mothers and new born babies too. When women are pregnant, they grow a mass of new neurons in the olfactory bulb. That may account for the disruptions to taste and smell reported during pregnancy.

Gut Feelings

Nervous systems first evolved from nerves around the gut in primitive tube like creatures, and we should not forget that we still have neurons in the gut. If fact, humans have more neurons in their gut than rats do in their head - about 100 million of them. This network of gut neurons is called the Enteric nervous system. It is the original brain and it is still part of the integrated body, brain and mind system that we experience as emotions or mood.

The word Enteric comes from the Greek word for intestine. The Enteric nervous system has been around for far longer

---

[17] https://www.uq.edu.au/news/article/2009/08/does-gardening-improve-your-memory

than the swelling at the top that we normally think of as the brain. Like the limbic system, it has been evolving alongside the cerebral cortex and it should really be regarded as an integral part of the modern human brain too. So the bodybrain consists of the cluster of neurons in the head and spine, along with the enteric nervous system. The Enteric nervous system is involved in the experience of emotions. It affects the way we feel, think and behave. In fact many of the feelings associated with emotion are experienced in the body, because that is where they originate. We get feedback from the bodybrain about how fast our heart is beating, how we are breathing, what is happening in our gut and skin, and which muscles are contracting in the face and body. Then the heart & mindbrain tries to make educated guesses about what is going on by taking into account the context and checking the reactions of other humans if they happen to be around.

Writers in all cultures throughout history have referred to emotions as if they were happening in the heart and gut, and maybe they were right. They use terms like "heartbroken" when somebody is upset and describe "heart stopping" moments. When something sad happens it is described as "heart wrenching". If they are not feeling enthusiastic about something they are described as "not having the heart for it". Tragic events are described as "making their hearts bleed". Emotional people are sometimes described as "bleeding hearts". Unemotional people are described as "heartless". Politicians talk about "winning hearts and minds". Emotional experiences are also described as "gut wrenching". People claim to have "gut feelings" about things. They have "gut reactions". They describe a "sinking feeling in the pit of their stomach" when things are going wrong in their lives. Complaining too much is described as "belly aching". Disapproval and disgust "turn stomachs". A brave performance is described as "gutsy". Cowards are described as "lacking guts". Humans in almost all cultures talk about "pissing themselves" with laughter and "shitting themselves" with fear. Emotions are all rather basic.

Most of the activity in the Enteric nervous system happens subconsciously, as does most of the other information processing in the bodybrain. But it is a nervous system and it should be considered as part of the bodybrain along with other mindless information processing systems.

The Endocrine System

There is a lot of information processing and internal communication going on inside the bodybrain that we are unaware of. When food arrives in the stomach, the Enteric nervous system is sending messages to the pancreas, telling it to produce enzymes to help the digestive system to break down the fats. We are not conscious of that happening at all, because we are not told about it. The "we" to which I am referring here is the heart & mindbrain. The endocrine system is a collection of glands that secrete hormones directly into the bloodstream. It is a slower acting communication system than the sympathetic nervous system. Once again, we only notice the results of its activity. We have no direct access to the process.

The bodybrain produces insulin to regulate blood sugar levels. The immune system automatically manufactures killer cells, which constantly patrol the circulatory system destroying invading bacteria and viruses. None of this involves the heart & mindbrain. If the brain evolved to be useful and the heart & mindbrain is not necessary for all of this automatic processing, it must have another purpose.

The Sympathetic Nervous System

Physiological arousal, stimulation, excitement and stress, are all descriptions of activity in the sympathetic nervous system. The sympathetic nervous system is what wakes us up and gets us moving. At different levels of stimulation it enables us to sleep, daydream, pay attention, learn, memorise and perform learned behaviours. At higher levels of stimulation it switches from heart & mindbrain to bodybrain processing, to enable quick reactions when there is no time to think things through. Unfortunately, that means it turns "us" off, so we do not really know what is going on when it is highly stimulated. That can be a problem.

Increased stimulation of the sympathetic nervous system puts the bodybrain into different physical states, preparing the body for different kinds of action. It increases activity in the heart and lungs, increases blood pressure, closes down activity in the gut and diverts the blood supply towards the larger muscles. It is the sympathetic nervous system that gets people excited and frightened. I am not sure whether it is correct to describe the heart & mindbrain as being excited or frightened. I think when it is turned on, it experiences the excitement or fear in the bodybrain and tries to make sense of it. We can only experience one emotion at a time so far as the sympathetic nervous system is concerned, because it is entirely related to the level of stimulation. However the heart & mindbrain can switch from one interpretation to another quite quickly. For example, somebody who is laughing at a joke can suddenly take offence. Similarly someone who is upset can sometimes be diverted by humour and see the funny side of the situation. Sometimes people do not know whether to laugh or cry.

The parasympathetic nervous system tries to do the exact opposite of whatever the sympathetic nervous system is doing. It tries to calm everything down and is associated with decreased excitement in the amygdala. It diverts blood back to the smaller muscles and organs. It slows the heart and breathing down, activates the gut to start food processing, and allows the heart & mindbrain to come back to life so we can think more clearly.

Effective mood management involves increasing or reducing the levels of stimulation of the sympathetic nervous system according to what we want to do. Learning and performing are only possible within a relatively narrow range of stimulation. Extremely low levels cause the heart & mindbrain to shut down, which is when people begin to daydream and nod off. Too much stimulation also reduces functioning in the heart & mindbrain, which is why humans begin to do silly things and perform badly when they are over-excited, stressed, or frightened.

Yet we enjoy being excited and actively seek out activities to raise the level of stimulation. This is one of our greatest sources of pleasure. Good parenting, teaching, and behaviour management are not just about suppressing excitement. They are sometimes about creating it. Mood management is about assessing the current mood and being able to navigate into different moods for different purposes. Before bedtime we need routines that reduce stimulation. At other times we need activities to increase it. At higher levels of stimulation, heart & mindbrain function begins to degrade as resources are diverted towards faster reacting bodybrain processing. At extremely high levels people lose awareness of what they are doing altogether because their heart & mindbrain switches off.

Being able to control your own moods, emotions, and behaviour to influence those of other people is the pinnacle of self control and it opens up all sorts of opportunities to improve the quality of life.

Mindgames

As humans lose consciousness at both extremes of stimulation, it follows that there must be an optimal level where they experience the most intense form of consciousness. Humans have been trying to find that optimal state for as long as they had minds. This may be what they are achieving through meditation or mindfulness.

Throughout history many cultures have experimented with chemicals which interfere with consciousness. In my social circles beer, wine and brandy are the preferred vehicles. Unfortunately, in my experience, these do not deliver optimal levels of consciousness or performance for that matter. Such pleasures are more accurately described as mindlessness than mindfulness, but bodybrains seem to enjoy them. In the case of alcohol that may be because it gives them control. Alcohol seems to depress activity in the heart & mindbrain, reducing inhibition of the bodybrain. That is why drunk people say and do silly things.

Mindfulness is best achieved sober. Learning to manage moods to get into that state is a skill which, like all other physical and mental skills, has to be learned and practised before it becomes perfected. Self control can be learned in the same way. Some grandiose claims have been made about what can be achieved through meditation and mindfulness which are not evidence based.[18] However, there is abundant evidence that an over-stimulated sympathetic nervous system is bad for our physical health, so being able to calm it down when it is causing a problem seems like a good idea. But staying calm is not the purpose of life. Life is about having fun and being happy.

Happiness and well being is a rather more complicated business. It involves achieving a balance between the enjoyment of pleasures in the present and the creation of opportunities for more pleasure in the future. It also depends on an ongoing self appraisal which humans conduct as they create and maintain their own life story. How satisfied they are with the character they have created seems to be important. Sometimes they have to sacrifice comfort in the present as they work to build up the character and populate their story with memories for the future. Investing in memories can be good value, because they can be re-presented multiple times and provide enjoyment each time. Sharing them as stories provides opportunities to perform, and that provides pleasure too. Even stories about events that were not much fun at the time can repay the investment as they are remembered and retold.

I had to be rescued from the very top of a black slope in Courchevel once and remember feeling my broken bones crunching on the way down. I was also in a light aircraft

[18] "Has The Science of Mindfulness Lost Its Mind?" - Miguel Farias, 2016

returning from France which ran out of fuel over the sea off Beachy Head and we had to make a forced landing in a ploughed field after gliding over the cliffs. On another occasion, after a car crash, I spent some time in hospital having lumps chipped off my hip to repair the bones in my arm.

None of those were pleasant experiences but the way I feel about them seems to have changed over time. They are not associated with unpleasant emotions now. On the contrary, I enjoy recalling them and have turned them into stories. I suspect I have embellished them over the years.

There is something to be said for opting for the quiet life like a sea squirt, staying in to watch familiar entertainments and having plenty of early nights. When you find a good restaurant it is tempting to play safe and keep on going there. Some people like going on holiday to the same place every year. Some even get into a routine of doing the same things on every day of the week. It takes less mental effort.

The problem with this approach to life is that when we repeat familiar experiences we are not putting down new memories. The heart & mindbrain only takes an interest in novel experiences and consciousness is associated with the heart & mindbrain more than the bodybrain. This is something older people need to think about. The more time we spend doing familiar things, the less aware we become of what we are doing as the bodybrain takes over. That is one of the reasons that time seems to speed up as people get older. By not paying enough attention to what they are doing they begin to sleepwalk through life.[19]

We need to strike a balance between comfortable indulgence and making an effort to try new things, change routines, meet new people and visit new places. Time passes much more slowly when you are doing new things, because you become more conscious of what you are doing as you are putting down new memories. There is also accumulating evidence that exercising the heart & mindbrain provides protection against the effects of diseases associated with dementia.

Emotions can be fleeting experiences. People do not normally freeze or remain in a blind panic for long. Ecstasy does not last long either. When they find something funny, humans normally laugh for a short period of time then get over it. They do not laugh hysterically at the same joke for hours. If they did comedians would have an easy life. Emotions are short term experiences. Moods are the name we give to medium term emotional states. Disappointment is an emotion but being miserable is a mood. Comedians steer an audience into a good mood, which makes it easier for them to experience fleeting emotional pleasures from their jokes. The term wellbeing is usually used to describe a longer term state of body and mind. It is a less precise term that involves such things as physical and

---

[19] "Felt Time: The Psychology of How We Perceive Time" - Marc Whittman, 2016

mental health, social relationships, and material standard of living.

For the sake of simplicity, I am using the term mood management to cover what we can do to influence experiences in the short, medium and long term.

The Mood Elevator

The mood elevator is like an imaginary lift in a tower block or hotel moving up and down all the time in response to what is happening in our external and internal world. When the sympathetic nervous system is stimulated, the mood elevator moves up to the next level.

At each floor level, the doors open to make available a range of behavioural programmes that can only be activated at that particular level of stimulation. When stimulation of the sympathetic nervous system reduces, or stimulation of the parasympathetic nervous system increases, the lift moves down.

When the mood elevator is at basement level that is when humans are fast asleep. The heart & mindbrain is switched off. They are unconscious and unmotivated, but that does not mean all of the bodybrain is switched off. Part of the bodybrain must still be monitoring what is going on, because it wakes us up if it hears a loud noise, or receives feedback from the enteric nervous system telling it that we need to go to the bathroom. When I say "us" I am referring to the heart & mindbrain.

Bodybrains can still react to stimuli even when heart & mindbrains are not creating simulations of them to remember in the future.

As the mood elevator passes up towards ground level, the heart & mindbrain begins to create simulations, but they are not very good ones at this level. Quality control and continuity are weak as the mind wanders in the state of altered consciousness we call dreaming. The heart & mindbrain cannot manage to maintain a coherent narrative at that level because the hippocampus is not working properly to store the simulations. In order to have a stream of consciousness you need to be storing a linear sequence of simulations, and without a functioning hippocampus it is impossible to keep track of what is happening. That may be part of what happens when people begin to suffer from dementia.

Most of our dreams are forgotten unless we wake up in the middle of them, which allows the neural circuits in the hippocampus to begin long term potentiation before the simulation fades away. "Waking up" is how humans describe the way their mind and body works at ground level.[20] This is a relaxed state, rather than a fully alert state. Some people day dream at this level.

---

[20] "Waking Up" is also the name of an excellent book on happiness, spirituality and consciousness by the philosopher Sam Harris.

If stimulation increases, the mood elevator moves up to the next floor, level 1, which is the learning state. This is when the bodybrain takes an active interest in something and it is accompanied by a rather pleasant feeling of curiosity and motivation as the hippocampus produces a neurotransmitter called dopamine.

At this level of stimulation the heart & mindbrain can concentrate, which is a term for a more focussed type of consciousness. Hard thinking takes mental effort, of the kind needed for complicated mental arithmetic and problem solving. It is a completely different experience from bodybrain processing, for example reciting a learned poem, song or multiplication table, which is effortless. Because heart & mindbrain thinking takes so much effort, humans need to be highly motivated to do it. Most cannot keep it up for long. Getting their students into a learning state and keeping them there is what educators are trying to do. Employers who pay their workers to do hard thinking for them want their employees to be in this state too. I suspect most pupils and employees spend far less time in this state than their teachers and employers realise. If we spent more time managing moods to ensure that they are in the correct mental state both learning and performance would improve dramatically.

The performance state is one level up from the learning state. Once they have learned a mental or physical skill, performers of all kinds say that they need to get themselves into a state of slightly higher stimulation to perform at their best. Skilled performers report that they need to be nervous or excited to perform at their best. Anxiety and excitement are just different interpretations of the same level of stimulation of the sympathetic nervous system. Although they perform better at this level, top performers also report that they are less aware of what is going on around them at the time. Motor racing drivers, sports players, actors, and stand-up comedians describe a similar hyper-focused experience which is rather like being in a trance. They describe themselves as being "in the zone" where they literally lose themselves and enter a state of what Mihaly Csikszentmihályi calls, "flow". He became fascinated by artists, especially painters, who became so immersed in their work that they forgot to eat, drink or sleep. Some people fall into a similar state playing video games. They continue for days on end. In Japan professional gamers have been known to wear incontinence pads so that they do not have to leave their console. Some viewers go into a trance watching box sets on the television and sit for hours. It is hard to know whether they are really conscious or not.

I regularly fall into a similar state when I am writing. Hours pass me by without my being aware of anything at all apart from what I am writing. I could literally be described as absent minded when I am in this state. I am not conscious of what is going on around me or what is going on inside me for that matter. I "wake up" to find cold cups of coffee next to me and baths that I ran hours before and forgot about. I am beginning to think that it is my bodybrain which writes these books, rather than me. I am switched off most of the time while I am doing it. Playing musical instruments is a similar experience. I suspect that it is my bodybrain that has learned to play the piano, rather than me. I taught it, which took considerable mental effort, but now it does most of the playing and it does not involve any mental effort, because it does not really involve me. I think I play better when I am slightly drunk. The biographers of many famous artists, writers, and actors describe their ability to perform while intoxicated. Alcohol seems to disable the heart & mindbrain before it affects the bodybrain.

Flow is certainly a curious state to be in. It is a different state of consciousness; one that has something in common with meditation, mindfulness and the states of altered consciousness pursued by followers of Eastern religions. I am not convinced that it is really correct to describe it as enhanced consciousness. In my experience it is reduced consciousness.

If the mood elevator continues its journey upwards in response to higher levels of stimulation, performance begins to fall away. This can be described as a state of excitement or anxiety. From a physiological point of view, there is very little difference between the moods people report at this level. It depends on how their heart & mindbrain interprets what is happening in context. Two people on exactly the same roller coaster ride could be at exactly the same level of physiological stimulation, but be having a somewhat different quality of experience. One could be happy, excited, grinning and laughing as they wave their arms around, enjoying the thrills of the ride. Another could be clutching their knees, screaming in fear and hating every moment of it.

Emotions and moods are not just about the physiological level of stimulation. They also depend on how an individual interprets what is happening - the mental spin they put on their life story. Changing the way we habitually interpret experiences is another important part of mood management. It is possible to interpret the same information in different ways to avoid discomfort and extract more happiness from it. This should not be confused with wishful thinking, the sort of self-delusion that causes individuals to make bad decisions and avoidable errors. Wishful thinking causes humans to behave in ways that create problems and reduce opportunities for happiness. But there are times when there is nothing much we can do about a situation. We do not need to make any decisions, apart from how we are going to choose to feel about it. Realising that we can choose how to feel is an important first step towards more effective mood management.

The heart & mindbrain automatically tries to make sense of the world and impose meaning on it. This can turn into a rather negative experience when it becomes trapped in futile searches for meaning where none exists. We need to recognise that bad things happen. Sometimes random things happen. There are coincidences and bad luck. It is always sensible to check, just to make sure we have not made a mistake or that there is not something we can do better next time, but otherwise there is no point in ruminating about things that make us feel bad. Sometimes it is better to accept life's ups and downs with equanimity and decide not to let disappointments upset you. There are always better things to think about. These habitual thinking programmes can be learned and automated until they become second nature, so that far less time is wasted on unproductive mood depressing mental activity.[21]

Some children and adults enjoy high levels of stimulation and seek out excitement. They enjoy the thrills they get from dangerous sports and a range of other activities. Risk management is about balancing the level and likelihood of coming to harm against the pleasure provided by the activities. Where possible we need to provide safer alternatives or at least control the risks so far as that is possible.[22] In the case of

---

[21] See "Persuasive Scripts" - Bernard Allen, 2008, also "Happy: why more or less everything is probably fine" - Derren Brown, 2016

[22] See "Risk Assessment for Behaviour Management" - Bernard Allen, 2012

children, responsible adults need to protect them from the consequences of poor judgement. At these higher levels of stimulation, the heart & mindbrain weakens as it is replaced by stronger urges to react immediately and automatically from the bodybrain. Self control and judgement decline at high levels of stimulation and at this level both happy and unhappy people do things that they later regret, because they are not thinking clearly.

It is not really fair that "we" get the blame for this, as it is not "us" that is responsible. When the sympathetic nervous system becomes over-excited our influence becomes weaker. One of the cruel injustices of life is that we are always yoked to our own bodybrain and when it gets us into trouble, we have to take the consequences.

In some circumstances over-stimulation of the sympathetic nervous system can cause the heart & mindbrain to shut down altogether. No matter how clever heart & mindbrains might think they are when the whole system is in a learning or performing state, they are no use at all when they are completely switched off. This is what happens in states of extreme arousal. At that level, the mood elevator doors open to a menu of fully automatic reactions. The benefit of these is that they can be quickly executed by the bodybrain without any delay from the heart & mindbrain trying to think. There may be no time for that. The downside is that sometimes the automatic programmes available are not suitable for the situation or the bodybrain chooses the wrong one. Those who have not taken the trouble to train their bodybrain, by equipping it with replacements, will be left with nothing apart from instinctive, innate animal reactions if they reach that level. They cause problems.

These are extreme states of panic, or frenzy, in which humans are not really aware of what they are doing and they may not remember what they did afterwards. Animals in this state typically freeze or alternatively lash out with teeth, feet and claws. The freeze response is a high stimulation response created by activity in the cerebellum which causes the animal to play dead for brief periods.[23] These can be described as "first nature" reactions. But when physical or mental skills are sufficiently practised they can become as automatic as innate reactions. In fact well learned reactions, such as a brilliant save from a goalkeeper in a football match, are sometimes described as instinctive. When learned behaviour becomes automated it is referred to as "second nature".

Automated physical and mental routines take the pressure off the heart & mindbrain at all levels of stimulation but they become crucial at high levels. Equipping ourselves with a repertoire of effective and appropriate second nature

---

[23] "Neuronal circuits for fear and anxiety" - Tovote, P. et al., *Nat. Rev. Neurosci.* **16**, 317–331 (2015).

responses, for use in stressful situations which are foreseeable, is one of the most valuable investments it is possible to make. Bodybrains cannot do this themselves. They need to be trained through repeated practice, which is the only way bodybrains can learn. The whole system needs to be in a learning state for that to happen.

So there are two avenues open to improve the way humans perform under pressure. One is to manage the sympathetic nervous system and find ways to calm it down so that the heart & mindbrain can remain in control. The other is to train the bodybrain, so that it is better equipped with a range of learned mental and physical programmes to fall back on when the heart & mindbrain begins to fail. In many occupations where humans are expected to operate under pressure, such as in the military, in hospital operating theatres and in the airline industry, the rehearsal of checklists and drills has become an important aspect of ongoing training. That is all about training the bodybrain.

Fun, Fear and Stress

Alcohol, testosterone and adrenaline do not make people violent. They just cause people who are predisposed to violence to express the behaviours that are already programmed into their bodybrain. Adrenaline does not cause aggressive behaviour, what it does is raise or lower the mood elevator to allow certain behaviours to be expressed in certain circumstances.

The same hormone, in exactly the same amounts, can produce very different experiences, depending on how the bodybrain is programmed. When adrenaline is associated with anxiety and fear it is experienced as an unpleasant feeling. When it is associated with thrills and excitement, it can be enjoyable. The amygdala is often referred to as the fear centre, but that is misleading. It is the fun centre too. Humans deliberately seek out exciting experiences which can be scary, enjoyable and memorable, all at the same time. They watch horror films, go on rollercoasters, leap out of aeroplanes in the hope that a parachute will open. They jump off high platforms in the hope that the elastic tied around their feet will not snap. Some enjoy driving motor vehicles at high speed, skiing down mountains, jumping off cliffs into the sea. Some take mind altering drugs. They are sometimes called adrenaline junkies.

All of those activities stimulate the sympathetic nervous system, so they do involve adrenaline. But they are also associated with the production of dopamine, which is associated with motivation and pleasure. Some thrill seekers have underactive sympathetic nervous systems. Others, who prefer to seek out a quieter, more relaxing lifestyle, may have an overactive system. Those who have to manage human behaviour as part of their professional work need to learn to recognise the difference.

The Adrenal Response

The adrenal response describes what happens to the body when the sympathetic nervous system is over-stimulated. When the bodybrain notices something unexpected, exciting, or worrying, it sends a message down the spinal chord to the adrenal glands, which are situated just above the kidneys. The adrenal glands can produce a surge of adrenaline that floods the bloodstream in half a second and affect a number of different physiological systems.

The immediate effect of a small surge of adrenaline in the system is an increase in physiological arousal as the eyes, ears and nose are directed towards the source of interest to gather more detail. If the bodybrain recognises the source and decides it is not important after all, everything calms down again. But if it fails to recognise the source, or recognises it as something that has been associated with strong emotions in the past, more adrenaline may be released.

Adrenaline shuts down the digestive system, which may be experienced as a feeling of butterflies in the stomach. That can be interpreted as either excitement or nerves, depending on the situation and the mental programming of the individual. Adrenaline also increases the heart rate, and can literally cause the heart to miss a beat. That can be interpreted as exciting palpitations in the heaving breast of a love struck teenager, or fear by someone worried that they are having a panic or heart attack. All the time these physiological changes are taking place, the heart & mindbrain is trying to make sense of what is going on by making educated guesses based on the context.

Dilation of blood vessels in the face and neck cause people to blush, which may be experienced as either embarrassment or anger. The goose-bumps sensation, caused by tiny hairs standing on end, is part of a primitive protection mechanism. It can be experienced either as tingling excitement or fear. It all depends on what mood the heart & mindbrain chooses to experience.

The airways widen to allow more air to flow to and from the lungs, which means the gullet has to narrow. This makes it difficult to swallow, causing the experience of a lump in the throat. At the same time there may be a feeling of tightness above the eyes, which is caused by over-activity of the tear glands. All those secretions have to go somewhere, so they drain off into the nose and throat. Sometimes the excess spills over the eyelids and flows down the cheeks. This is what causes emotional people to have red eyes, produce tears, have dribbling noses and to keep gulping. Yet they do this both when they are laughing hysterically and when they are crying inconsolably. Some people cry when they are happy.

At higher levels of the adrenal response the skin begins to sweat and the blood drains away from the surface towards the larger muscles, causing a pale pallor and tingling feelings at the extremities.

Small muscles, starved of oxygen, may begin to twitch causing lips to tremble and eyes to twitch. Hands may shake as they lose fine muscle control, which can make holding a pen or inserting a key in a lock difficult.

At the most extreme levels of stimulation, the digestion system shuts down completely and evacuates waste contents. At that level of stimulation the heart & mindbrain is usually shut down as the faster reacting bodybrain takes over. This is the state of blind panic known as amygdala hijack.

An elevated heart-rate, combined with fast shallow breathing, can produce the experience of tightness in the chest. That in turn can cause the brain of an anxious person to panic and produce more adrenaline, in what becomes the vicious circle known as a panic attack. In a panic attack there really is nothing to fear but fear itself, but knowing that is not much help when the bodybrain is out of control. In panic attacks people hyperventilate, breathing out more than they are breathing in. This lowers the level of carbon dioxide in the blood, causing a condition called respiratory alkalosis. The symptoms are dizziness, difficulty breathing and mental confusion. What they need to do is slow down and breathe more deeply. Cabin crew on aircraft are trained to encourage people having panic attacks to breath into a sick bag, so that they breathe back in more carbon dioxide to correct the imbalance.

The important point is that people often do not understand what is happening to them when they are experiencing the adrenal response. Anxious people sometimes choose an interpretation which frightens them and causes more adrenaline to be produced. They literally do not know how to interpret what is happening to them and they are often looking at the faces of other people for feedback. For that reason, those who have to work in stressful environments need to learn to control their own facial expressions and body language to avoid upsetting those around them. People with self control can influence the emotional climate around them by deciding to behave in a calm and controlled manner.

By educating individuals who suffer from panic attacks to become more aware of how their own bodybrain and heart & mindbrain work, they can learn to interpret the feedback differently and change the way they habitually feel in stressful situations.

Post Traumatic Stress

Most people experience stressful situations from time to time during their lives, but not everybody reacts in the same way. Some sympathetic nervous systems are just more excitable than others. Most people will undergo emotional shocks to their system at some stage during their lives. They will experience rejections, disappointments, bereavements and may find themselves in frightening situations where they experience amygdala hijack.

It is perfectly normal in the days and weeks following a traumatic emotional experience, for individuals to wake up in the middle of the night with their mind racing. It is normal for them to keep thinking about what has happened, in an almost obsessional way. That is the heart & mindbrain trying to make sense of it and rewrite the life story to produce a narrative they can live with. Sometimes they need help from another scriptwriter to enable them to do this, which is essentially what a good counsellor does. Talking and listening to a sensitive person can help them make sense of it and imagine a more palatable future. They may not get over a trauma for some time but most gradually get used to the way they are feeling as they begin to adapt to their new life. Over time, the intensity of the adrenal response when they review what happened reduces, and gradually their physiological levels return to normal.

Most people do recover from upsetting events, without suffering significant long term damage, but sometimes the system goes wrong. From an evolutionary perspective, it makes sense for creatures to want to learn from such experiences. After a traumatic experience, the bodybrain tries to make sense of what has happened. It searches for ways to take control of the situation and prevent similar traumas from happening again.

Bodybrains cannot understand that some life changing events cannot be controlled or prevented, but that does not stop them from trying. Unfortunately one of the most pervasive bugs in our mental software is confusion between correlation and causation. If an animal survives a traumatic event, the hippocampus attaches warning flags to anything associated with it. It will experience feelings of revulsion if it comes across those features again in the future, and urge the creature to run away from the situation. This is how phobias start.

All creatures learn to avoid places in the physical world that are associated with pain and fear. Humans can also learn to avoid places in their mental world, places they avoid thinking about. These are painful memories. The problem is that if they cannot think about those things, they are unable to process the information and integrate it into their redrafted life story. They become stuck. Whenever their heart & mindbrain tries to process what has happened, the bodybrain creates a new adrenal response so severe that it shuts the heart & mindbrain down again. The re-presentations of past events may be simulations, but the adrenal response is real and in the present. They are reliving the emotional response.

Bereavement or other upsetting events can cause happy memories and associations to become painful ones, to the extent that some individuals have felt the need to move home, because they could not cope. Some feel the need to break all ties to their past and disappear to start a new life elsewhere.

When people do not recover in the normal way, they are described as suffering from post traumatic stress disorders. Because the experience is so vivid, people in this state believe that they are reliving the whole experience, but remember we cannot store detailed simulations. They can suffer a delusion that their memory is improving as they relive the emotional experience and think they are recalling more details. The evidence suggests otherwise. Humans under enormous stress do not remember the details accurately, because the hippocampus is unable to store them due to amygdala hijack. Perceptions of time, the order of events, and key features of what happened become muddled. That is why people suffering from severe stress can be unreliable witnesses.

Some misguided therapists have tried to help their clients to fill in the gaps by helping to create false memories for them, in the mistaken belief that they were recovering lost ones. There is no reliable evidence that recovered memories are genuine.

Losing It

In an emergency, the ability to react quickly becomes more important than the ability to get all the details right. That is why the fast reacting bodybrain suppresses the activity of the slower heart & mindbrain in adrenal hijack. Some of the innate, automatic reactions which humans exhibit in that state evolved for a different animal, living in a different world. People sometimes freeze in a crisis, or lash out with teeth and claws as part of the innate fight or flight response. That may not be the best response in an emergency, for example there have been several air disasters where passengers died unnecessarily because they froze after the plane came to a stop, instead of undoing their seat belts and getting out of the aircraft.

This has nothing to do with intelligence. The intelligent heart & mindbrain is switched off. This is about over-stimulation of the sympathetic nervous system and adrenal hijack. In April 2014, the Uruguayan footballer Luis Suarez was awarded the Professional Footballers Association's Player of the Year award. His manager said at the time:

"Probably what people do not see with Luis is that he's a very, very highly intelligent man off the field…"

Brendan Rogers, April 2014

By all accounts he is an intelligent man, but intelligence is not much help when the bodybrain takes control. Two months later Suarez was thrown out of the world cup for biting an opponent during a match. That was not very intelligent, especially as during the previous season he had bitten another player, also in a match that was being broadcast around the world in high definition. He received a lengthy ban. So what was he thinking? Did he think nobody would notice if he started gnawing on another players flesh?

The truth is that he was not really thinking at all. He had become too stressed and over-excited, to the extent that his heart & mindbrain had switched off. The impulse to bite is not unusual. Animals do it in fear, some in anger, and some when they are sexually aroused. It is triggered by the adrenal response. Luis Suarez has written about what happened and explained how he felt at the time. They were both important matches and he had made mistakes in each. He said he could feel the pressure mounting and knew that he was losing control.

Some people are simply more emotional than others. They need to train their bodybrain to react differently under stress and discover ways of calming it down.

Unhealthy Stress

Perhaps highly emotional people should avoid stressful jobs. Unfortunately they do not always have the choice. Extreme stress, or extended periods of moderate stress, can cause damage to the physical and mental health of those affected. Stress is the reaction of the sympathetic nervous system to demands made on the individual, rather than the demands themselves. If the sympathetic nervous system remains excited for long periods of time it can take its toll.

High levels of stress affect the neurons in the hippocampus, disrupting their ability to form new memories and inhibiting learning. There is also some evidence that long term stress shrinks the hippocampus over time. Stress has the opposite effect on the amygdala, causing it to grow as the neurons within it become hyper-sensitive to threat, in what is a vicious circle.

Stress causes the body to produce other hormones, in addition to adrenaline. Some cause the liver to increase blood sugar levels in an attempt to supply more energy, should it be needed to run or fight. As part of the stress response it also suppresses the immune system, to prevent the normal responses to injury. For example, the natural reaction of the bodybrain to soft tissue injury is to cause swelling which immobilises the affected area and allows healing. That is fine if the creature is already in a safe place and can afford to rest, but it is the last thing it needs when it is running or fighting for its life. In times of physical danger, being able to run on a damaged leg may increase the chance of short-term survival, although it increases the risk of longer-term damage to the limb concerned. It is a trade off that evolution selected for our ancestors, who lived in a violent world where physical injuries were common and lives were short. It may not be the best balance for the modern world.

One way of killing invading bacteria and viruses is to increase body temperature to create a fever and put a sick creature to sleep, which allows all available resources to be redirected to the battle with the invaders. But animals faced with immediate threats from predators or rivals could ill afford to lie down and go to sleep. So the stress response prevents that from happening. Again, it would have provided benefits to our ancestors in the short term to escape danger, but if it continues over a longer periods it risks the body becoming overwhelmed by bacterial or viral attack. It is a common observation that people in stressful jobs keep on working until their holiday, only to become ill during the break. The reality is that they were probably already ill, but their immune response was suppressed so they did not realise it. They needed that break more than they knew.

Our physiological system reacts in exactly the same way to the stresses of urban life as it did when the threats tended to involve violence. In business meetings and traffic jams, there are bodybrains preparing for physical attacks by becoming stressed and turning off their immune systems. There is no need for it but bodybrains do not know that.

People who live under constant stress are more likely to develop chronic medical conditions. All the cells, including brain cells, need to be supplied with oxygen, proteins and nutrients. Waste products need to be removed. Cells need to be repaired and replaced. This general biological housekeeping keeps us healthy but it is put on hold at times of high stress.

Nodding off during a violent attack would obviously be a fatal error, so stress also prevents sleep. Those who suffer from long term stress may also suffer from long term sleep deprivation, which is also bad for their health. Sleep seems to be necessary for brains to reorganise, repair and redistribute their memories. Even hibernating birds need to sleep as they fly.

The good news is that the brain seems to be much more resilient than was once thought. Pessimistic determinists who peddled the idea that children who suffered traumas or failed to form the normal attachments at the usual age were doomed, have been proved wrong. One of the optimistic discoveries of recent years has been the extent of plasticity in the brain. It keeps changing all the time. Many people who have suffered appalling experiences in childhood have recovered to become happy and successful adults. We do not hear about them because they do not come to our attention.

For most humans, throughout most of history, life was dangerous and horrendous. Wars, famines and natural disasters were common. Many of their siblings and friends died before adulthood. Many were orphaned as children. They suffered terrible illnesses and infections. It seems likely that child sexual and physical abuse has always been a hidden part of human society too. The food was terrible, entertainment was limited and everybody had to work all the time. They had good reason to be miserable.

In contrast, across the U.S. , Australia, and Northern Europe, in the 21st century humans have never had it so good. No generation has experienced such a high material standard of living, or enjoyed such good physical health. No generation has been safer and there have never been so many protections in place to protect individual rights. The opportunities for entertainment and pleasure have never been so varied and extensive. Humans should be finding it very easy to be happy.

Yet there are widespread reports of a mental health crisis. There is an epidemic of self-harming and eating disorders. There have never been so many support services, yet children and young people seem less able to cope with normal life than their predecessors.

The issues causing the anxiety are nothing new. Children and young people are struggling to cope with everyday issues, such as the break-up of relationships, falling out with friends, the death of pets and anxiety about stories in the news.

One in three calls to the charity ChildLine in 2016 was related to mental health issues.[24] In Sweden exactly the same pattern has been reported.[25]

Something has gone wrong here and before we set about trying to fix things, we need to make sure we have correctly diagnosed the problem.

---

[24] https://www.nspcc.org.uk/fighting-for-childhood/news-opinion/mental-health-problems-most-common-reason-contact-childline/

[25] http://www.euro.who.int/en/countries/sweden/news/news/2014/12/most-swedish-school-children-report-their-health-as-good,-but-mental-health-is-a-concern

Many of the theories upon which we are building our brave new world are unexamined. I believe they are based on false presumptions about what humans need to be happy and they fail to take into account human limitations.

Perhaps part of the problem is that life does not feel as familiar and comfortable as it once did. Young people do not feel as if they are fitting in to the physical, social and emotional environment which is being created for them.

Psychopaths and Mood Managers

Whilst some people struggle to cope with their moods, emotions, and behaviour, and lose their heads in a crisis, there are others who seem to be relatively untroubled by their emotions. This can be both a good thing and a bad thing. The psychologist Kevin Dutton has made a study of the characteristics of people who seem to perform well in a crisis.[26] The reason he calls them "good psychopaths" is that they share several character traits with a group of people who have got themselves rather a bad name.

When people think of psychopaths, they usually imagine serial killers or mass murderers but those are the exception. Most of them are repeat offenders who steal from friends, family or strangers they befriend. They con old and vulnerable people.

---

[26] "The Good Psychopaths Guide To Success" - Kevin Dutton and Andy McNab, 2014

They lie convincingly and seem to be without shame. They are described as heartless.

The characteristic that has been traditionally associated with psychopathy is a lack of emotion. They do not seem to have any feelings. They are described as anti-social. Yet psychopaths often have highly developed social skills. Some of them are very good at reading the moods of others and responding to them appropriately. They are often described as charismatic, which is what makes them such good confidence tricksters. Charm, persuasiveness, confidence, coolness under pressure, and courage are all attributes that are highly prized and rewarded in most cultures.

Psychiatrists have traditionally used different words to describe the psychopaths they meet. It must be hard to admit that a mass murderer really is charming, so the doctors describe them as "superficially charming". Persuasive becomes "convincing liar". Confident becomes "cocky". Courageous becomes "recklessness".

Psychopaths have traditionally been studied in prisons or secure mental hospitals, so the experts may have been building their diagnostic tools on rather a biased sample. We need to look more carefully at what makes bad psychopaths different from other people who display charm, persuasiveness, confidence, coolness under pressure, and courage. I have known many successful head teachers, business people, psychiatrists, barristers, airline pilots, and surgeons who showed similar characteristics. In my opinion, some of them could more accurately have been described as superficially charming and cocky. Some were convincing liars as I found to my cost. But I have to admit that most of them were courageous and a few were reckless. The difference between risk taking and recklessness is self control. The difference between bravery and cowardice is the same thing.

There are some people who are extremely emotional and cannot function under pressure at all. There are others, at the other end of the spectrum, who are unemotional and unaffected by feelings of any sort. They do not care about other people or what they feel or think. In studies when they are shown photographs of injuries resulting from accidents and bomb explosions their brains do not show the same emotional reaction in the amygdala as the normal population. Rather than showing an extreme emotional reaction and experiencing revulsion, they show a mild emotional reaction linked to curiosity.

Dutton looked at eight character traits which are shared by those who are diagnosed as psychopaths. In an article published in 2016 he ranked current and past world leaders according to how their biographers scored them.[27] US Presidential candidate

---

[27] "Would You Vote For A Psychopath?" - Kevin Dutton, Scientific American Mind, 27, 2016

for 2017, Donald Trump, came just below Idi Amin and just above Adolf Hitler. His rival, Hilary Clinton, came, just below Napoleon Bonaparte and just above Emperor Nero. However, before we rush to judgement it should be noted that not all of the traits are associated with bad leadership.

The first three traits, known collectively as Fearless Dominance traits are evident in successful leaders. They are Social Influence, Fearlessness, and Stress Immunity.

It is the next four, which he identifies as the ones that cause problems. Collectively he describes them as Self-Centred Impulsivity. They include Machiavellian Egocentricity, Rebellious Nonconformity, Blame Externalisation and Carefree Nonplanfulness.

That is a perfect description of an untrained bodybrain. That is the mind of a toddler.

The difference between the good psychopaths who become successful leaders and the bad ones, is that the good ones have self control.[28] Many legal systems are based on the concept of deterrence. This is the idea that humans are deterred from doing bad things only because they fear the consequences. Some religious people believe that without religion, and the fear of ultimate judgement by God, there would be no morality.

---

[28] "Willpower: Why Self-Control is The Secret to Success" - Roy Baumeister and John Tierney, 2012

If that was true, it would be humanists, agnostics and atheists who were responsible for all the child abuse and atrocities throughout the world. That is patently not the case. It is not a lack of emotions that causes mankind's problems. Many of the people who do the worst things are extremely emotional. It is a lack of self control.

Heart & Mindbrains can think ahead and realise that they would prefer to avoid prison. They can decide that they would prefer to avoid the opprobrium that bad behaviour ultimately draws and realise that short term benefits have significant long term costs. heart & mindbrains can realise that selfless and generous behaviour is highly valued by their social group. It makes them feel good about themselves as they polish up their life story. They can decide that they want to build up a reputation for trustworthiness, kindness, generosity and honesty. They might have developed a personal system of morality and decide to follow it. They might get a deep sense of satisfaction and personal pride from their ability to resist the urges that get them into trouble.

But none of that is any good if they cannot control their own bodybrains when the need arises. What distinguishes good leaders from bad psychopaths is a well trained bodybrain that is able to carry out the wishes of a well developed mind. What makes bad psychopaths indulge their impulses is not a shortage of fear, it is a lack of self control. In my experience, fearful people exhibit less self control, less courage and less generosity than fearless people. Fearful people cause as much harm to society as psychopaths because they lack self control. There are many fearless, heroic individuals who have sacrificed their own best interests for others. Some have willingly sacrificed their lives.

Whatever moral code heart & mindbrains may wish to follow, their ability to do so will be governed by how well they can control their bodybrain when they are put to the test. That is where some pious but weak people have let themselves down.

It is true that some people are less affected by moods, emotions, and behaviour than others. They are less easily upset, less prone to tears, less prone to panic and less prone to violence. Humans are also innately equipped with differing amounts of willpower. But neither of those limitations necessarily determines whether or not they can develop self control. Willpower and self control are not the same thing.

Alcohol disables the heart & mindbrain, reducing willpower and allowing the bodybrain to take over. Some individuals do not change much under the influence of alcohol, suggesting a well trained bodybrain. As a general rule, I am rather wary of people who turn into completely different people when they have had a few drinks. That is what they will be like under pressure too. In the shocking old days, depicted in the television series

Madmen[29], job interviews and business negotiations were often conducted over drinks. Now that is frowned upon. Alcohol impairs judgement, so there are many occasions when it would not help decision making at all, but it does expose bodybrains. I am always interested to see what a bodybrain is really like when it is not being suppressed by a heart & mindbrain dependent on willpower.

Self control is something I only learned rather late in life. It does not rely on willpower but on habitual training, so that the bodybrain automatically and effortlessly generates more effective patterns of thought and behaviour. Training your bodybrain is like training a dog. It takes time, effort and consistency but it can be life changing.

Society needs people who are able to manage their own moods, emotions, and behaviour and those of others. We need people who can think clearly in a crisis, control their own behaviour and keep their heads when all around them are losing theirs. We need new terminology to describe the "good psychopaths".

I am calling them mood managers. They make good leaders. Individuals who are paralysed by fear, overcome by their own emotions, squeamish and afraid of hurting or upsetting anyone, do not make effective leaders. They may delay necessary decisions until it is too late, because their bodybrain evades the

---

[29] This is a reference to a television series about the excesses of the advertising industry in the 1970s in which everybody seemed to drink all the time.

short term discomfort involved in making them. Prevarication in leadership can cause far greater harm and unhappiness in the long run.

Crisis situations require risk takers who can keep their nerve. They do not shy away from making difficult decisions, which is a politician's euphemism for hurting people. The sad truth is that leadership sometimes involves having to make "difficult decisions" for the greater good. The people sitting on the board of the National Institute for Clinical Excellence (NICE) have to decide which treatments the country can afford and which it cannot. Just being "nice" is actually not very helpful. Nice people can turn out to be very poor leaders. Military leaders have to decide whether or not to send troops into danger, knowing some of them will lose their lives. Doctors have to decide which patients will receive transplant organs. These are literally life and death decisions. They are being made every day. Avoiding emotionally unsettling decisions can cause greater suffering in the long run. We need to find people who are capable of making them quickly and rationally, without damaging their own physical and mental health in the process.

Decision makers sometimes need to be able to make decisions quickly, then move on without worrying unnecessarily. It is not just political and business leaders who need to be competent mood managers. They are needed in many areas of life.

I would not really mind if my surgeon was a bit arrogant and narcissistic. I would not really care whether any of the team in the operating theatre empathised with my plight. I would prefer them to be cool, calm and efficient. I would prefer a relaxed, capable, nurse to one who faints at the first the sight of blood any day. Similarly, I would prefer air traffic controllers to be cool and calculating, able to think clearly and work calmly under pressure, not hot and bothered. And the last thing I want to hear from the flight deck is the pilot of my aircraft howling and sobbing when something has gone wrong. I am perfectly capable of doing that for myself. I want mood managers in jobs where emotions can get in the way.

People with charm, persuasiveness, confidence, coolness under pressure, and courage, combined with an inclination to take risks, are attractive. They do well at job interviews, they get promoted and are elected into positions of power and public office. They also seem to make a lot of money in the process. I do not begrudge them that because they are valuable. I suspect most political leaders and the leaders of most major corporations, which these days is often the same thing, are either psychopaths or effective mood managers. They will both get the job done, one way or another.

The trouble is that we are not very good at distinguishing between the two. We want mood managers in those positions rather than cold blooded psychopaths, both for our protection and their own. I suspect we have always had a mixture, hence the monsters of history.

Chapter 3 - Motivation

Social Systems

So far we have been looking inside the body, brain and mind of an individual human in an attempt to see through human behaviour to the processes that drive it. But sometimes the behaviour of individual components makes more sense when you take a step back and look at the whole system. If you have ever watched a flock of starlings roosting at dusk it can be a wonderful sight. The flock swirls into sequences of geometric patterns. Shoals of fish, nests of ants and swarms of bees operate in a similar way. They create immensely complicated patterns, each behaving individually by reacting to what is around them, without any understanding of what the others are doing elsewhere in the system. They do not store mental simulations of the physical world so they have no concept of what is happening.

It is tempting to imagine that one of the birds in a display must be in charge, orchestrating the whole show like the squadron leader of the Red Arrows. Yet none of those birds inside the flock can have any idea what it looks like from the outside. It is not easy to visualise a system from the inside.

Bees create hives, termites build elaborate towers, ants dig networks of tunnels, but there is no single architect in charge of the design and construction process. There is no controlling mind. No single ant or bee has ever been able to visualise the end result, understand what they are doing, or appreciate their own work. They do not have heart & mindbrains capable of appreciating that sort of thing. Complex behaviour does not require complex minds.[30]

Intricate and complicated systems can emerge spontaneously from very simple physical processes. For example, snow flakes, the frosted patterns on windows, crystals, and flowers are all intricate shapes that arise because of the natural laws of physics in our own universe. Most of the textures in hyperrealistic animations and computer games are produced by a simple process of replication, similar to the one that produces the shapes of all trees and root systems. The replication of the same basic patterns at different scales are called fractals.

Natural selection is another simple process which over a vast period of time has created a spectacular variety of complex life forms, both in terms of physical structure and behaviour. The Portuguese Man O' War is a good example. It is a strange creature that looks rather like a jellyfish and has venomous tentacles which can deliver a painful and sometimes fatal sting. Yet it is not really a creature at all. It is a siphonophore, which means a colony of various different specialised animals called zooids. They have become so physiologically integrated that they function like one individual creature and could not live

---

[30] See "The Blind Watchmaker: why the evidence for evolution reveals a universe without design " - Richard Dawkins, 1986

independently, even though they are a combination of different species.

Humans are a strange combination of creatures too. Most of the cells inside a human being are not human at all. They are bacteria. There are more bacteria cells living in the human gut than there are human cells living in the entire body. A human being could more accurately be described as a colony of bacteria being transported around in a vehicle made of meat and bone. From the point of view of our gut bacteria, we are just transport and maintenance slaves whose ultimate purpose is to create more bacteria.

"A hen is only an egg's way of making another egg"

Life and Habit - Samuel Butler, 1877

The same could be said for a human. A human is bacteria's way of making more bacteria. Some humans prefer to think of themselves as a bit more important than that. It is all a matter of perspective.

We are only just beginning to realise how much we rely on those gut bacteria. Not only do they assist human digestion and synthesise vitamins. They produce short chain fatty acids that act like hormones affecting neurons. The bacterial system in the gut seems to have evolved to work rather like another endocrine organ. Disruptions to the balance of those gut bacteria have been linked to a range of inflammatory and autoimmune conditions. We cannot live without them.

Various human cells have specialised to form organs. They could not exist independently either. Brains cannot exist without the other organs to supply the oxygen, nutrients and minerals they need to function. The other organs could not survive independently without a brain to manage movement to collect those nutrients. They are all interrelated systems.

Individual human beings have become specialised too. They could not possibly maintain their current standard of living acting independently. Aristotle was probably the last person alive to know everything that was available to be known in his own lifetime, but he lived over 2000 years ago. Now there is no human brain capable of knowing everything there is to know. Individual humans are components of social and professional networks and organisations at local, regional, national, international and global level. The computer I am typing on was produced by vast numbers of brains, scattered all around the world, most of whom have never met or interacted directly in any way. Some of those brains are now dead. Many of them do not even realise that they contributed to my computer.

It was designed by teams of people from around the world. The commodities from which it is constructed came from mineral mines and oil wells on various continents. They were transported across oceans to be fabricated into different components in different parts of the world, then transported to China for assembly. Finally the completed product, along with thousands of others, was shipped to Ireland to be redistributed across Europe. The ship that brought it would have passed thousands of other vessels criss crossing the worlds oceans. No single person could have invented and built my computer in a lifetime. They would have had to become an expert in a vast array of different fields, including geography, geology, mining, oil extraction, plastics, metallurgy, glass, silicon chips, quantum physics, chemistry, fibre optics, coding, acoustics etc, etc, etc. A lifetime is not long enough to learn all that. Yet somehow, by specialising and sharing knowledge, computers, smartphones, cars, ships, planes and space rockets get made.

It is easy to be dazzled by human achievement and forget that complicated results emerge from simple systems. If an alien arrived from another system and asked who was in control of it all, the honest answer would be nobody. Human activity is not controlled by any one person or any group of people really. It is a vast mindless system that has taken on a life of its own.

In some ways humans are extremely complicated yet in other ways they are not. They might not really know what they are doing, any more than a snowflake does when it forms into a unique and complex six sided shape. Human behaviour was shaped by genes that must have evolved to do something other than make computers and space rockets first. It is only relatively recently that human brains started doing rocket science.

Selfish Genes

The term selfish gene is often misunderstood.[31] It does not mean that genes always make individuals behave selfishly. They make them behave altruistically too, so long as those behaviours result in others who share the same genes passing them on. Genes are selfish because they have no interest in the individual organisms or groups of organisms that they use to create copies of themselves. So far as genes are concerned, human beings are just a way of making more genes like them.

If some individuals in the human system fail to reproduce, that does not matter so long as the whole system produces more copies of their genes than alternative systems. Genes are not interested in humans, or computers or space rockets. They are not interested in anything really, because they cannot think. They are completely automatic and at some stage they will all die out when the current environment selects something different. The genes that currently drive our behaviour survived because they beat the competition in a previous epoch. There is no guarantee that those same behaviours will be selected in the next one. The current epoch, the anthropocene, may be shaped by humans, but that does not mean they always know what they

---

31 "The Selfish Gene" - Richard Dawkins, 1976.

are doing. They might have minds but a lot of their behaviour is still mindless.

There are examples of altruism throughout the animal world. Worker ants spend their entire lives slaving away without ever getting a chance to mate themselves. However the genes that cause them to behave that way are successfully passed on by their sisters, so the next generation behaves the same way. It is easy to slip into anthropomorphism when describing the apparently benevolent behaviour of worker ants. They are certainly highly motivated and hard-working. That is how they got the name. But they cannot think or experience emotions, because they do not have the necessary mental equipment. They are literally selfless because they have no concept of self.

Equal opportunities does not mean much in the ant world. The worker and soldier ants are all female, and they work solidly for the entirety of their short lives, never getting a chance to have any fun. Only one female ant gets the opportunity to reproduce, the one we call the queen. The job of the workers is simply to care for the queen and look after her young. Female workers build the nest, go out to gather food for the colony, and then store it in special chambers, which they glue together with their own saliva so that the walls are hard and smooth.

Female soldier ants defend the colony by fighting off enemy ants, or other insects that threaten them. They sometimes sacrifice themselves by using their large heads to block the entrances to the nest.

The purpose of a male ant is simply to mate with the queen then they die.

Ants are not the only species in which the division of labour is not entirely equitable. There are many examples in nature where most of the useful work, child rearing and hunting is done by the females. The males in many species seem more interested in showing off and fighting with each other than doing anything useful. One might question why we bother to have males in the great scheme of things, a point frequently and well made by my wife, but evolution does not progress towards the perfection of individuals within a species. The purpose of the individual is to work within a system to reproduce genes.

Not all males are completely useless. Male emperor penguins are good parents. They stand in the freezing cold for weeks at a time, trying to keep their egg warm, as they get thinner and thinner waiting for the female to return with some food. They do not seem to benefit personally from this experience, but the genes that make them behave that way survive into the next generation to create new offspring that will do the same thing.

Life is a competitive business. Species and individuals within species compete for resources and opportunities to reproduce. Predators kill their prey to provide nutrients and fuel for their body and brain. Rivals kill their competitors to increase the chance of their own genes being passed on. And, as we have seen, cooperative behaviour can also make evolutionary sense. The genes that incline individuals within a species to cooperate in social groups can be more successful than those that incline individuals to go it alone. The game of life is a numbers game. Human beings are driven by competing urges to behave in different ways and the environment selects the right balance of behaviours for the current circumstances. The others die out.

Changing environmental pressures can affect the expression of behaviour so that individuals and groups with similar genes behave differently in different environments. They might lean towards cooperative behaviour in one set of circumstances, but change towards more selfish styles of behaviour when the conditions change.

Game theorists have programmed computers to interact and play competitive games using a variety of different styles of behaviour. They have run millions of trials which show that cooperative strategies often beat selfish ones in the long run. Teams can do better than individuals. In the game of life, billions of trials have been conducted in real time which prove the same thing. That is why cooperative behaviour evolved.

That does not mean that selfish behaviour never works. Selfish individuals can thrive within a cooperative group where most people play by the rules, so long as they do not get caught. Therefore cooperative societies need to develop mechanisms to identify and punish cheats, to prevent others from copying them. Only a certain number of cheats can be supported in a cooperative society. If everybody starts cheating, the whole society collapses.

Lifestyles

Social creatures have developed two very different styles of social behaviour. It is related to parenting style, but it affects the way the entire social system works. Human beings can adopt either style and sometimes they move from one style to the other. In order to understand human behaviour and the moods that drive it, we need to take a closer look at these styles.

Some animals and birds form partnerships and stay together, working cooperatively to raise their young. This is called pair bonding in the natural world. Both parents invest their time and resources in looking after the young, which increases the likelihood of the brood surviving to adulthood and passing on the parents genes.

An alternative strategy is for the males to impregnate as many females as possible and leave the females to raise the young alone. The individual offspring might have less of a chance of surviving with just a lone parent, but overall the males are playing the numbers game by producing many more offspring. The more offspring they produce, the greater the chance that some of them will survive. This is called a tournament style society. The genes carried by males have a better chance of surviving than those carried by females, so in tournament species the males are competing with the females to some extent.

Pair bonding females have an incentive to be choosy about the partner they are investing in. They are going to have to live with them for some time. They are attracted to individuals that show some potential as a partner and parent. Courtship rituals in pair bonding species involve males trying to impress females, for example by building nests, or bringing gifts of food and nesting material, to show what a good marital prospect they are.

Poets have romanticised and anthropomorphised these attractive performances in animals and birds, imagining that the creatures involved must be experiencing the same thought processes as humans do when they behave in a similar way. Lovers are sometimes described as "love birds".[32] In reality it all comes down to statistics rather than romance. This is demonstrated by the way that evolution has shaped some of those courtship rituals. Imagine a bird who was trying to find the largest and juiciest worm available, to show what a good prospect he was for a long term relationship. He kept finding worms that were quite good, but not good enough, so he rejected them and continued the search for perfection. Eventually, when he finally found the gift worm that he thought

---

[32] https://www.buzzfeed.com/babymantis/the-25-most-romantic-animals-that-ever-lived-1opu

would sweep her off her feet, he returned to find that she had already accepted a scrawny worm, had set up home with a bearer of rubbish gifts and was pregnant. If that story was played out over thousands of trials the outcome would be that those romantic perfectionist genes would die out.

Something like that does seem to have happened in the case of many species of birds. Short sighted behaviour on the part of females created an evolutionary race as the males competed to see who could get away with the meanest gifts. The result is that many birds now just offer token gifts in their mating rituals, such as a twig or a pebble. Perhaps a similar process led to garage forecourts selling lacklustre bunches of flowers for £1.99.

In tournament lifestyles the males are not going to be around for long, so the females are not so bothered about whether they are good company or good parents. They just go for the strongest and fittest looking. Tournament species include birds, such as grouse and peafowl, big cats, mountain gorillas and elephant seals.

It is possible to identify tournament species just by looking at the differences in size and appearance between males and females of the species. This is called sexual dimorphism. In pair bonding species the males and females are so similar looking that they are sometimes difficult to tell apart, whereas in tournament species the males tend to look bigger, more impressive and more threatening. There are a few exceptions, for example the spotted hyena is one species where the females compete for males, but in the majority of tournament species it is the males who compete. They tend to have bigger and stronger skulls, even though the actual brain cavity is not much different in size.

It is for protection. Some have evolved weapons in the form of horns, tusks and elongated canine teeth. Tournament creatures evolved to fight and, in addition to the physical features, they also inherit aggressive mental programmes. Tournament lifestyles are associated with increased levels of aggression and violence within social groups. The most powerful males spend most of their time keeping an eye on the less powerful ones, using threats, intimidation, aggression and physical violence to prevent them from mating. In tournament species, typically just

10 percent of the males account for around 90 percent of the mating.[33]

"In the 30 years I have been studying baboons the leading cause of death amongst male baboons has been male baboons."

Robert Sapolski

Infanticide features in tournament species too. When another dominant male supplants the ageing leader, which will always happen one day, he will sometimes kill all the offspring of his predecessor. They are competing with his DNA. Nature can be brutal.

Before we become too sentimental about pair bonding species we need to expose some myths about them too. Older zoology texts paint a rather sentimental story, describing peaceful, loyal, monogamous couples bonding for life and returning to the same nest each year. More recent discoveries have rather shattered this romantic narrative. DNA testing has shown that many of the young being brought up by domesticated males are not actually theirs. The females are having sneaky affairs, hedging their bets by ensuring there is a variety of DNA in their nest, just in case the DNA of their partner is not up to scratch. The males are playing the same game, by making sure they have their eggs in more than one basket.

---

[33] "The Biology of Human Behaviour" - Robert Sapolsky, 2005

In pair bonding species, bird nests are more likely to be abandoned by the female, who may decide to start another family with a better prospect. It may seem cruel, but from an evolutionary point of view it makes sense. There is a good chance that the original male will stay on to rear the young alone while she gets another chance to pass on her genes.

Humans seem to be one of the many species that can adopt either reproduction strategy according to prevailing circumstances. From an evolutionary point of view, there is a certain logic to maintaining this flexibility. In a relatively safe and stable environment, pair bonding might be the more successful strategy. By investing in a kind, generous, high quality, parenting partner, building a home, and raising a family together, there is more chance of the young reaching adulthood and passing on their genes. But if the world becomes a more dangerous place, tournament styles might actually be a safer bet for the males. By having their DNA in as many different nests as possible, it is more likely that some of it will survive, even if many of the nests are destroyed. A dominant male who can impregnate 90 percent of the females in the group has a good chance of passing on his DNA, even if several of the females and their offspring are killed. Equal opportunities does not carry much weight in tournament societies.

It is not too much of a stretch of the imagination to apply the same principles of flexible lifestyles to human behaviour. In war torn countries, or in places that are regularly struck by natural disasters and famines, the same numbers game could apply. There is even a biological mechanism that could put it into effect. A foetus growing inside a mother who is experiencing high levels of anxiety may develop a larger amygdala, that is more responsive to fear, and a smaller hippocampus, that does not plan so well for the future. It might also result in a tendency for adult males to behave impulsively, aggressively, and lean towards tournament styles of social behaviour rather than pair bonding when they are raised in hostile environments.

Fortunately humans have the opportunity of an extended childhood, during which the development of the brain can be further shaped. The human brain is far more plastic and adaptive than was once thought, so it could be that an extended childhood in favourable conditions can overcome early disadvantages and allow a harmonious partnership of heart & mindbrain and bodybrain to develop. Our task is to ensure that all children are raised in those nurturing environments.

Cultural influences clearly have a significant effect on whether humans adopt one lifestyle or the other. Individual humans can and do change the way they behave when they move from one culture to another. Some humans adopt both strategies at different times in their lives, behaving like tournament species for a while then settling down into a pair bonding style.

I am trying, and probably failing, to appear morally neutral in these depictions of human behaviour. It is impossible to ignore the reality that tournament species are more aggressive and violent than pair bonding species. It seems to me that humans who adopt tournament styles of social behaviour tend to be more aggressive and violent too. Some human cultures and sub-cultures celebrate and encourage tournament style behaviours. They are the macho cultures, which emphasise physical differences between the sexes with males displaying muscle bulk, physical strength and facial hair. Some macho humans do produce large numbers of offspring with multiple partners, leaving the females to bring up their young alone. Macho males also spend a lot of their time trying to impress other macho males, with ritual displays of aggression and violence. Violent sex and rape are also features of tournament species in the natural world, rather than pair bonding styles. In tournament species, the males are equipped to threaten, intimidate and fight off other males, which also means that they can force themselves on the smaller females, who do not get much choice in the matter.

It should be said, for the sake of balance, that in tournament species the females do tend to be attracted to the largest and most fearsome males. In pair bonding species, where the females are similar in size to the males, they can at least fight off unwanted attention to some extent.

As a general rule, human cultures that institutionalise tournament behaviour are likely to feature more aggression and violence, with less equality. They tend to benefit a small minority of dominant males at the expense of the majority of the population. They are not noted for their compassionate treatment of women, children and the majority of non-dominant males.

There are human cultures that celebrate and institutionalise pair bonding lifestyles, where couples form supportive partnerships with both sexes investing in the rearing of the young. The differences between the sexes are downplayed. They all try to make themselves more attractive, by looking as young, fit and healthy as possible and by behaving generously and considerately. Pair bonding displays involve seduction rather than intimidation, with both sexes trying to impress potential mates with displays of wit, humour, charm, intelligence, kindness and generosity.

Tournament styles involve aggression and violence. I know which sort of society I would prefer. The optimistic message is that humans can learn to live according to either style. We are nothing if not adaptable. But piecemeal social engineering, of the kind advocated by Karl Popper, also requires an honest recognition of the way human bodies, brains and minds really work. We need to take a cool hard look at human behaviour in order to make sense of it.

Motivation

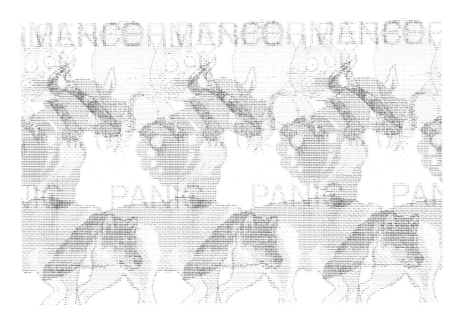

Motivation is the holy grail of psychology. In the business world, bosses want to motivate their employees to work harder. Sales managers want to motivate their teams to sell more. Marketing managers want to motivate their customers to buy more. A whole industry has grown up providing motivational speakers, training courses on motivation, self help books, materials and posters. Motivation is where the money is, so the cutting edge research should all be happening in this area too. To some extent that may be true, but there are a lot of old ideas bouncing around too.

Abraham Maslow is the guru of motivation in popular psychology. He first set out his ideas in a short paper, called "A Theory of Human Motivation", back in 1943. It suggested that humans were motivated by a hierarchy of needs, often represented as a layered triangle.

Basic needs are at the bottom of the triangle, progressing towards more elevated aspirations at the top. According to the most commonly reproduced version, humans are motivated to meet basic physiological needs, such as eating, drinking, waste disposal and sex, first. According to the experts, motivation is a bit like a platform computer game. Only when those basic needs are met, can they move up to the next level, which is safety needs, then they go on to social needs and eventually what Maslow described as "self actualisation".

Popular though Maslow's triangle is with business people and educationalists, there are a number of problems with it. Firstly, he never presented any empirical evidence to support his theory and subsequent research has failed to find any. Secondly, although an internet search turns up thousands of triangles, all called "Maslow's Triangle", most of them have been created by other people. There never was any triangle in Maslow's paper. The numbers of layers in the various triangles purporting to be his vary too, as do the descriptions of the needs in each layer. For example, some triangles include "Aesthetic Needs", "Transcendence Needs", "Morality Needs", "Know and

Understand Needs", "Cognitive Needs", "Sexual Intimacy
Needs", "Confidence Needs", "Openness Needs",
"Belongingness Needs" and "Employment Needs". Different
authors have simply taken a triangle and added their own
hierarchy.

Maslow did not have any triangles in his original work and he
did not even claim that there was a fixed hierarchy of needs.

*"… we have spoken as if the hierarchy were a fixed order but actually it is
not nearly as rigid as we may have implied."*

Abraham Maslow 1943

So what does that leave of Maslow's triangle?

There is one important message that cannot be repeated often
enough. Humans can be in discomfort for a variety of different
reasons and it sometimes takes imagination to work out what is
wrong, either because they do not realise themselves or they are
unable to communicate. We cannot assume that all the people
in care environments are adequately fed, washed, toileted,
comforted, entertained and treated kindly. It may sound
obvious, but there have been too many similar scandals in
hospitals, schools and residential care settings in the recent and
distant past, to allow complacency. We cannot just assume that
people will do their jobs. We cannot just assume that service
users are comfortable in their current environment. We need
better systems of monitoring and supervision to ensure that

carers are actively and imaginatively identifying comforts and discomforts, and that they are able to take effective action to manage the moods of those around them.

But I do not consider Maslow's theory, as it is traditionally taught, to be very convincing as a conceptual framework to explain human motivation. It cannot be true that humans have to complete one level in a hierarchy before they can move up to the next one. Half the world's population are not having all of their base level needs met, yet that does not mean they are not motivated to love each other and look after their children. Many people who are living in poverty are still motivated to sing, dance and create art. Humans have been doing that since prehistoric times. Hunger and discomfort was part of everyday life for them.

At the same time, religious aesthetes, absent minded professors, lovesick poets and starving artists are renowned for neglecting their basic needs as they pursue more lofty ones instead. They forget to eat.

Just as some eccentric humans ignore the hierarchy and jump to the top, without bothering to fill in the intermediate layers, there are others who do not seem to be motivated to move to the next layer when their basic needs are met. They are happy to stay where they are, repeating the same processes of eating, smoking, drinking, taking drugs, having sex, going to the toilet, watching television and having a nap. Not everyone seems to be driven to become an academic, or an artist.

We need a better explanation of human motivation that describes the behaviour of humans in the 21st century. Maslow's "research" on motivation involved reading 21 biographies and autobiographies of academics and other exceptionally successful people. There are two mistakes right there. Autobiographies are notoriously unreliable sources of information in the first place and exceptionally successful people are, by definition, exceptional. In statistics this is called a sample error.

The biographies of most successful people, whether in sports, politics, business, the arts, or academia, reveal similar but unusual personality characteristics. They tend to be obsessional, highly motivated, people. They may pretend it was their effortless genius that propelled them to the top, when in reality the evidence usually shows that they fought and clawed their way up.

We need a more comprehensive framework upon which to build a better understanding of human motivation and behaviour. We need to see through the complex dazzle of surface behaviour to see a much simpler system that drives it. It is natural to assume that, because we are human, we have privileged access to the way humans work. That is a hubristic delusion.

Who are We Talking About?

Before I start talking about what drives us to behave the way we do, I want to re-ignite an uncomfortable flame that might have gone out. It is uncomfortable, because it does not harmonise intuitively with the way we like to think and feel about ourselves, which is probably why we are so keen to extinguish it.

We need to decide what we mean by "we". When we describe ourselves as individuals "we" do not mean an individual cell. They cannot be conscious. Some see themselves as the whole package, a combination of body, brain and mind, but not all of the body is conscious. We can cut off our nails and hair without it affecting consciousness at all. Amputees do not suffer from degraded consciousness. People who are paralysed from the neck down do not lose consciousness either, which suggests it is located in the head. Some people think they are a brain, and have plans for their brain to be preserved when they die, in the hope that "they" will reappear one day. I suspect they will be disappointed in that. I do think the neural circuits that produce us exist in the brain, but I do not think they are all the brain. You can have parts of the brain removed without it affecting consciousness. That means "we" are only part of our brain.

I think that "we" are minds that are generated by some, but not all, of the neural circuits in the body and brain. "We" have ideas but other parts of the brain generate different ideas. "We" have to train and manage other neural circuits that sometimes want to do different things from "us". That means those circuits are not "us".

In all sorts of ways life would be much simpler if I was completely wrong about this. Free will, morality, human rights and our entire legal system are all based on the presumption that "we" are unified coherent entities, capable of expressing opinions, making rational choices, making promises and keeping them. If all that was true, everything would work fine. But I want to ignite a flicker of doubt.

Although the circuits that generate "us", the heart & mindbrain, are physiologically integrated with various other neural and chemical systems in the bodybrain, and dependent upon them, "we" are not them and they are not "us". "We" cooperate with those systems in order to survive but we also compete with them because our interests are not always aligned. "We", as conscious minds, compete with the unconscious bodybrain. I am treating it as one entity even though it consists of a number of different systems.

When "we" are trying to stay awake, trying to exert self control, trying to use willpower, trying to concentrate, or trying to pay attention to something, the reason "we" are conscious is that "we" are making an effort to control something else. The reason "we" need to make an effort, is that "we" are experiencing resistance and opposition from a bodybrain that wants to do different things. It has its own ideas, by which I mean it is constantly generating a variety of different mental programmes which would drive our behaviour in various different directions if any of them gained ascendancy. All the ideas have different strengths ranging from those too weak to be noticed, through faint ones we barely notice, to strong ones we cannot ignore. Normally the strongest wins and jumps into the driving seat.

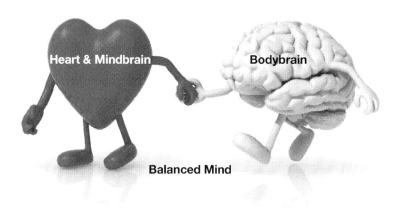

The heart & mindbrain sometimes seems to be rather isolated, trying to guess what the rest of the bodybrain is up to, in much the same way as it tries to guess what other people are up to. When humans are performing, in a state of flow, the same idea or mental programme is occupying the bodybrain and the heart & mindbrain. "We" are experiencing what we are doing. But sometimes the heart & mindbrain has a different idea. The bodybrain is doing one thing and "we" are thinking about something else, or trying to do something else. Sometimes the heart & mindbrain wants to suppress the strongest programme being generated by the bodybrain and supplant it with one of its own. That involves mental effort.

When that happens we are described as being in two minds, but I do not believe that is literally true. "We" are in one mind, wrestling with a mindless bodybrain that is trying to control our thoughts or behaviour. I do not believe the bodybrain has a separate consciousness, as Daniel Kahneman suggests the experiencing self does. If it did, that would raise even more perplexing ethical and philosophical questions. I think we have enough to be going on with.

In practical terms, if mood management is intended to increase happiness and reduce discomfort it needs to be directed towards the system that is capable of experiencing happiness and discomfort. That is the heart & mindbrain. That is "us". When the heart & mindbrain is switched off, so are we. There is no point at all in being happy unless you know it.

Heart & Mindbrains are always at risk of being hijacked by bodybrains. When the bodybrain becomes unbalanced, the sympathetic nervous system fires up automatically, causing the bodybrain to generate mental programmes to motivate movement away from sources of discomfort or towards sources of comfort. That process does not always achieve the desired result because the bodybrain cannot think ahead.

Bodybrains can stop "us" from doing what "we" really want to do. They remove choice from "us" because when bodybrains become excited they can run out of control.

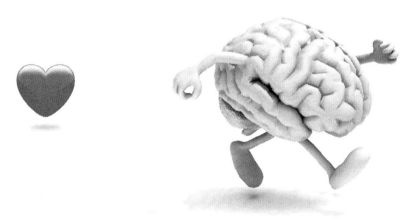

Uncontrolled Bodybrain - Unbalanced Mind

Drives and Needs

Behaviour is largely driven by the bodybrain. In the western world, vast resources are squandered on a leisure industry which encourages people to over-indulge their basic drives. "Need" is the wrong word.

Maslow assumed that human needs and drives were the same thing. He wrote that:

"… appetites (preferential choices among foods) are a fairly efficient indication of actual needs or lacks in the body."

Abraham Maslow 1943

If only that were true. It is worth remembering that he wrote that during the Second World War, a time when basic foodstuffs were rationed and luxuries scarce. In the modern world, needs and drives have gone their separate ways. Bodybrains experience a variety of appetites and the commercial world has discovered multifarious ways of satisfying them, both naturally and, increasingly, artificially.

When opportunities present themselves, bodybrains are driven to consume things and behave in ways that are not very good for them. And that is what they will continue to do, unless we can find ways of controlling them through willpower, which does not work very well, or by training them which is what I am advocating.

I had a friend at university who recommended tactical puking as a strategy to enable him to consume even more beer on Saturday nights without passing out. He did not "need" more beer, he just enjoyed the process of drinking it. He became a psychiatrist of course.

Humans are not motivated by needs. They are motivated by drives. For example, bodybrains are driven to consume and store rich sources of energy, which made sense for our hominid ancestors. They needed to store spare energy for the winter and times of famine. In those days, rich sources of carbohydrates, fats and sugars were scarce. It was difficult to become obese. Now, in affluent countries it is all too easy.

The shelves of supermarkets are stacked with concoctions made up of different combinations of carbohydrate, sugar, fat and flavouring, which are designed to be ingested as a leisure activity, rather than to meet any immediate need for nutrients. Bodybrains are still driven to ingest and store energy they will never need. In 2015, the Chief Executive of NHS England described obesity as a slow-motion car crash, warning that 70 per cent of adults would be overweight or obese by 2035. In order to understand why we behave the way we do we need to look at what drives us.

I am going to group all behaviour, including human behaviour, under three overall headings, called Pursuit, Panic and Performance. These are the basic drives. Panic is the drive to move away from things. Pursuit is the drive to move towards things. Performance is the drive to show off, make an impression and in some cases build a reputation. Creatures in the wild spend most of their waking time in either pursuit or panic mode. Humans and other social animals spend rather a lot of time in performing.

Panic

The word "panic" is usually used to describe the most extreme expression of the drive, but I am using it to describe any strength of motivation. At low power settings it is experienced as worry and anxiety, at moderate levels it is experienced as fear, and at very high settings it may be experienced as terror.

The panic drive is particularly finely tuned in creatures such as rabbits, deer and birds, which have natural predators. They need to keep a wary eye out all the time and be ready to flee at any moment when they are in exposed positions. They can only afford to relax when they are hidden.

Panic usually only takes control of behaviour for a short time. It turns off when the threat is no longer imminent. Creatures in panic tend to run away for a short distance and then reassess the situation. Many predators cannot run fast for long, so the prey only need to be able to keep going longer than their predators can. When panic subsides, pursuit takes over, diverting attention towards a search for a safer place or a different activity.

Pursuit

Most wild animals are torn between the competing urges of pursuit and panic. They are programmed to cautiously pursue and approach things that capture their interest, when they feel curious, but at the same time they need to be ready to switch to panic mode and run to escape to a safe distance if they feel threatened.

The simple rule to determine whether pursuit or panic is driving behaviour is to determine what the focus of attention is. If a creature is moving towards its focus of attention that is pursuit. If it is moving away that is panic. They can switch from one drive to the other, but they cannot be going in both directions at the same time. The pursuit drive is not only active when a predator is hunting down its prey. It is activated whenever any creature is motivated to approach anything. Panic and pursuit are like forward and reverse gears.

The pursuit drive can last a short time before the animal is distracted by something else, but in some animals it has evolved to last a long time. Modern humans evolved from hominids who were nomadic hunter gatherers. They relied on a form of hunting called persistence or endurance hunting. This enables animals who are slower than their prey at running over short distances to catch them over longer distances. They track and stalk their prey, wearing them down until they are too exhausted to go any further. Wild African dogs, wolves and hyenas are persistence hunters. Animals that are dangerous predators over short distances can become helpless prey over longer ones. Cheetahs are the fastest runners on the planet, but they can only keep it up over very short distances indeed. That is why they need to sneak up on their prey.

Along with horses, humans are amongst the most effective endurance runners. Tribesmen in Africa track down and kill the big cats that prey on their flocks, because humans evolved as persistence hunters. Antelope may be able to outrun big cats over medium distances but humans can even outrun antelope over extreme distances. David Attenborough filmed African bushmen hunting down an antelope for days until it simply collapsed with exhaustion.[34]

Persistence hunters need to remain highly motivated for long periods of time, even when no immediate reward is forthcoming. They have to suppress the urge to give up and tolerate short term discomforts in favour of longer term rewards. Human motivation is probably linked to an ancestry of

[34] "Human Mammal, Human Hunter" -Attenborough - Life of Mammals - BBC

persistence hunting. It evolved to keep animals motivated for long periods of time. When the pursuit drive is operating hunters gain pleasure and satisfaction from what they are doing, which enables them to overcome hardships and discomforts. At the same time as other neural circuits are experiencing pain, their bodybrain produces dopamine and natural opiates to help them overcome it. These chemicals also provide pleasure. You can see a mixture of agony and ecstasy on the faces of long distance runners towards the end of a race. It is difficult to tell whether they are enjoying it or not, because we naturally default to the assumption that we are watching one person, with only one opinion on the matter. In fact what we are seeing is competing neural circuits, one trying to stop the pain now and the other trying to keep going. As we will see later, anticipation of reward in the future creates the experience of reward in the present, because of the way dopamine circuits in the brain work. That is why smart people learn to enjoy the pursuit and not rush towards the climax, because once they get there all the fun stops.

Humans spend their lives engaged in a variety of pursuits, both short term and persistent. When asked why they follow their pursuits they might say that they enjoy them, or that they are meaningful or satisfying in some way. These are really circular explanations. All they are really saying is they do it because they are driven to do it.

Persistence pursuits involve self control. Migrating birds and fish have to defer immediate comforts as they journey towards more hospitable climates, sources of food, and opportunities to reproduce. Some of them will not survive those vast journeys, yet they are still driven to undertake them. It must be a powerful motivation. Humans are the most impressive creatures on the planet when it come to stretching out their pursuits. They work for years to pay off mortgages and put money into pensions for the distant future. They have life long pursuits with some deferring their rewards beyond their own lifetime. The Cathedral of Notre-Dame de Paris took about a century to complete, and Cologne Cathedral took over 600 years. Neither the designers, nor the people who worked on those buildings would ever see the fruits of their labours, but they must have got some satisfaction from the project. They enjoyed the process of doing it.

Self control and intelligence are linked to the ability to defer immediate gratification, yet it is not really correct to describe it as foregoing pleasure. What is really happening in the bodybrain of an animal driven by pursuit is that one form of pleasure is being traded for another. Persistence hunters, and humans engaged in other pursuits, are receiving pleasure in the present as they engage in those pursuits. That is why they are so strongly motivated to do it. They are enjoying the experience of dopamine driven neural circuits in their brain. They may be anticipating future rewards, but they are also experiencing something rewarding in the present. Anticipation itself can be pleasurable. They experience a sense of purpose and meaning in what they are doing. It is a nice feeling, otherwise they would not do it. This is the mechanism of intrinsic motivation. We need to take a more systematic and imaginative approach towards stimulating those feelings.

Performance

The final drive is performance. It is evident in social creatures who are driven to make public displays of various sorts. They must be highly motivated to put on these performances otherwise they would not expend so much energy on them. The purpose of any performance is to make an impression on other animals which causes them to change their behaviour in some way.

Some plants and animals have attractive physical features and aromas that lure other creatures towards them for a variety of reasons. For example, flowers, fruits and nuts attract birds, bees and animals to assist plants as part of a cunning reproduction strategy, although of course there is no cunning or strategy involved. These are automatic features that evolved over time. The angler fish has evolved an appendage that looks like a tiny fish, which hangs in front of its mouth to lure prey towards it.

One purpose of attractive performances was to display physical characteristics that provided evidence that the performer had good mating potential, and was strong, fit and healthy. The tail of the Indian peacock is often given as an example of a purposeless, showy appendage but recent research has shown that the size and number of the eye spots on the tail correlates with strength of the bird's immune system. So the plumage actually is an indicator of good health. As with many species, the male peacocks are pretty indiscriminate and will mate with whoever they can get, but the hens are more choosy. They go for males with tails.

In addition to showing off their physical features, many creatures have evolved behavioural performances to impress competitors and potential mates. In pair bonding species the females might look for evidence of generosity, nest building ability and parenting skills, so the males evolved performances to highlight those features and make them appear more attractive.

Some creatures evolved off-putting features to drive others away from them. For example, many species have evolved markings that look like staring eyes. Butterflies have markings on their wings, owls have them on the plumage on the back of their heads. Most creatures are wary of large staring eyes and find them off-putting. Dr Neil Jordan, of the University of New South Wales, has made practical use of this. In July 2016 he reported a successful experiment to protect lions in Botswana in which his team painted large cartoon eyes on the rear end of cows owned by local tribesmen. The tribesmen had been pursuing and killing lions after they attacked their cattle. The painted eyes put the lions off, causing the attacks to stop and saving both the cattle and the lions.[35] Humans are the only species that can continue eating while maintaining eye contact.

Tournament species are more interested in size, strength and fighting ability, so they evolved performances to show off those features. In tournament species the performances are not just directed towards attracting potential mates. They are also directed at putting off the competition. Dominant males in tournament species give threatening looks, adopt aggressive postures, and make fearsome noises and gestures, as they try to intimidate their rivals and prevent them from mating.

In addition to performances which show off genuine features, evolution has added some deceptive ones. For example, some birds feign a broken wing to lure predators away from their

---

[35] "i-Cows: can intimidating eye patterns painted onto cows stop lion attacks?" - Neil Jordan, 2016

offspring. Many species evolved the ability to play dead, which puts off predators who tend to prefer fresh moving targets. There is an awful lot of deception in the natural world.

Some prey have evolved the ability to camouflage themselves and behave in ways which trick predators into thinking they are more dangerous or toxic than they really are. The false cobra evolved to imitate the much more harmful genuine cobra, by flattening its neck and making a similar hissing sound. The viceroy butterfly evolved to look like the monarch butterfly, which is covered in a toxic substance that birds have learned to avoid.

Dominance and subservience performances receive most attention in the literature but there are actually three typical groups of social performance in nature. One gives the impression that the performers are more confident, threatening and potentially dangerous than they really are to drive away unwanted attention. The second gives the impression that the performers are more attractive, kinder, and more intelligent than they really are to attract attention. The third gives the impression that the performers are more helpless than they really are, to procure food, protection and support or less dangerous than they really are to lull the target into a false sense of security. This group is different in that they give the impression that the performer is less able than they really are.
Creative Diversions

All human behaviour can be regarded as an attempt to gain pleasure and satisfaction from exercising the three basic drives. Some human activities involve doing what those drives evolved to make us do, but many of the activities of modern humans can be regarded as ingenious cheats. There are ways to hack into our own mental systems to turn on those drives and extract pleasure from them in a variety of imaginative ways.

Many human activities share the characteristics of a hunt, and they create pleasure and enjoyment through the activation of the same neural circuits. Shopping is sometimes described as a bargain hunt. Some shoppers get as much pleasure from choosing and trying on the items as they do from the final purchase. Real hunting is a bit like that too. Smart shoppers learn to squeeze additional enjoyment from the pursuit by deliberately delaying the capture. Really smart shoppers do it online. They get all the pleasure of the hunt, as they track down bargains at minimal effort, then they have the pleasant anticipation of the delivery, plus the added uncertainty of not knowing exactly when the parcel will arrive. Brains seem to find uncertainty extremely attractive, as we shall see in the section on dopamine circuits.[36]

Razorfish published the results of interviews and surveys of 1680 shoppers in several countries. 72 percent of UK

---

[36] I keep putting these little teasers in because human brains like that sort of thing.

shoppers, 73 percent of Brazilian shoppers, 76 percent of U.S.shoppers and 82 percent of Chinese shoppers said they were more excited waiting for online purchases to be delivered to them, than they were when they went to shops to buy them.[37]

Really smart online shoppers can get all the enjoyment for free, because they can send things back. Some online merchants send an email or text, informing the customer that their order has been received, when it has been despatched and when it will be delivered. This is good in one way, because every text produces a little surge of dopamine, but not so good in another, as uncertainty and surprise are themselves sources of pleasure. The more accurate these messages become, the less uncertainty there is. I have noticed that Apple always sends out an email telling me exactly when my new toy will arrive, then delivers it a few days early, so I am delighted by the surprise and can hardly complain about the service. I know I am being manipulated but I enjoy it.

The same pursuit drive that caused our ancestors to pursue, gather and collect things drives modern humans to collect coins, music, movies, video games, stamps, books, dolls, cards, keychains, even rocks. Collectors are not really driven to use the items in their collection, so much as hoard them. They experience pleasure as they gather them.

---

[37] "Digital Dopamine" http://www.razorfish.com/ideas/digital-dopamine.htm

Some people become locked into pursuit loops, buying similar things or even multiple versions of the same thing. Impulse buying and hoarding can become addictive to the extent that it becomes a psychological problem. Sometimes gatherers do not even bother taking the items out of the box before setting off on another pursuit. Both rich and poor people can become addicted to shopping, but the pleasure they get out of it is more related to the time they spend doing it than the amount of money they spend.

Spending £10 in a Pound Shop, carefully choosing each item, then giving everything away to the charity shop next door might sound like a stupid thing to do. But if you can afford it, it would probably provide more pleasure than spending the same £10 on one impulse purchase. Add to that the additional pleasure extracted from the performance drive as you give the items away, reinforcing your public and self image as a decent generous human, and that might be £10 well spent.

Supermarket checkouts, and the shops in petrol stations, seem to be set out to encourage impulse shopping, which is the opposite of smart shopping because you get very little time to enjoy it. Almost as soon as pursuit is switched on, the deal is done and it switches off again. Petrol stations in particular seem to be stacked with rubbish to tempt idiotic men, which I regard as blatant sexual discrimination. The items for sale take advantage of primitive urges to equip ourselves with tools and weapons for imaginary pursuits. I have collections of extremely poor quality socket sets, pocket knives, torches, chargers, and adaptors with multiple connections for devices I do not even own. None of them brought as much joy into my life as I anticipated at the time.

I remember one item in particular. It was a battery powered electric pepper grinder that, for no apparent purpose, had a torch on the bottom. I suppose if you ever found yourself in a darkened room, with a mysterious, unpeppered plate of food, it might come in handy. When I saw it, I was torn by two competing drives. One was my heart & mindbrain telling me that this was the most stupid pointless toy that had ever tempted me. The other was my bodybrain telling me that I needed it desperately, just in case I ever found myself in a darkened room with a mysteriously unpeppered plate of food. The problem with this twin brain system is that sometimes the bodybrain recruits the heart & mindbrain to argue on its behalf. One of the functions of the heart & mindbrain is to manage public relations and cover up stupid behaviour, such as wasting money on an electric pepper grinder. So although my heart & mindbrain started off trying to convince me not to buy the thing, it ended up trying to persuade me that it had been a good buy which would revolutionise my life. It did not revolutionise my life and I am not sure why I am telling you this.[38]

If you can afford it, shopping can be a therapy of sorts. Smart shoppers squeeze the maximum pleasure out of the process by increasing the anticipation for as long as possible. Buying expensive items on impulse has to be the stupidest form of shopping of all, because it guarantees minimum pleasure for maximum expense. I doubt that rich playboys who buy expensive sports cars on impulse get much more pleasure from the experience than I did buying my electric pepper grinder. (I am talking about the shopping experience here, rather than the product which to be honest I could have lived without.)

The same basic drives are in action at charity auctions where wealthy people exercise their pursuit and performance drives together as they bid for things they do not really need, and at the same time demonstrate how virtuous they are.

Happiness is the pursuit of things in general, not the attainment of anything in particular. Anyone who thinks that the achievement of any particular goal, or owning any particular thing, will make them happy is likely to be disappointed. The pleasure is experienced during the pursuit rather than after it

---

[38] I have just been distracted by a dopamine driven google pursuit to see if you can still get electric pepper grinders. You can, but they do not seem to have the torch on the bottom. Mr Hilary Tuttle gives his four stars and says, "I have used electronic mills for years and these perform as would be expected, effective and efficient".

has ended. Unfortunately this is something bodybrains never learn and when we get excited the bodybrain takes over.

The pursuit of anything can give pleasure and a sense of purpose to life. We need to create more pursuits for ourselves and others so that we can switch from one to another and learn to extend them for longer to extract more satisfaction from them. They are the source of all our pleasure and happiness. Those who understand them and learn to use them intelligently can take far more pleasure out of life than those who cannot.

The task of educators and employers is to turn pursuit on and try to direct motivated brains towards the right targets. We know that it is even possible for the pursuit drive to be stronger than the panic one, because people who are highly motivated are able to overcome their fears. Pursuit is what drives predators to hunt and stalk their prey, bees to search for pollen, prospectors to search for gold and explorers to go on adventures. It has driven humans to do wonderful things, such as setting sail to explore and discover new worlds, build pyramids and cathedrals, and sending rockets into space.

It has also moved great minds to pursue the answers to profound philosophical and scientific questions, and less great minds to pursue the answers to puzzles in magazines. It is what moves humans to read books, watch television and take an interest in life generally. It drives both meaningful and trivial pursuits.

Unfortunately it has also driven some humans to do terrible things. Humans pursue grim vendettas, seek bloody revenge and commit atrocities because they are strongly motivated to do it. This happens when pursuit becomes paired with performance but before we get on to that I have to talk about sex.

Sex

It is impossible to talk about human motivation without talking about sex. Sex is a taboo subject in many human cultures, which means that people tell lies about it, so it is easy to be misled about what is really going on. Some people regard the sex drive as something distinct from other drives, but I am going to regard it as just another target for pursuit.

We seem to have an inexhaustible capacity to be "shocked" by sex scandals in the media, even though they are almost all exactly the same story repeated with the names changed. The fact that humans are so fascinated by them also shows something about their psychological make-up. Sanctimonious types, who are inclined to become fired up in moralistic outrage, are demonstrating that they are even more obsessed with it than the rest of us. Moralistic outrage is a combination of pursuit and performance. Sex certainly is an odd business.

Sex and violence sometimes become confused in nature. For example, the female praying mantis has gained a reputation for biting the head off her mate during intercourse, which is rough sex by any definition. In her defence, she only does it when she is hungry and needs more energy to complete the reproduction process, which is less than 30 percent of the time.

Flatworms, on the other hand, are hermaphrodites. They have a sword-like penis that can be used both for hunting food, fighting other flatworms and for reproduction. As a matter of fact, reproducing and fighting are the same thing for flatworms. Mating involves attacking each other in a fencing duel. The loser is the one who is penetrated. The price they pay for losing the duel is that they have to give up the bachelor life to become a mother and bring up the children. Their sword fighting days are over. Winners get to have other sword fights and so have an increased chance of passing on their own genes. So the violence does have a purpose.

Sex on the beach can be violent too. Male Monk Seals sometimes crush the females to death at mating time. A male Southern Elephant Seal can crush the female's skull in its jaws during copulation. It is not immediately clear how that helps to promote their genes.

The Antechnius is a small Australian marsupial which only lives for one year. During the mating season it tries to mate with as many females as possible during a frenzied fortnight. Anyone who has ever claimed to be "shagged out" does not really know the meaning of the term. The male Antechnius literally shags itself to death, which is an example of extremely high motivation.

Human attitudes towards sex and violence are confused too. In recent years western cultures have shown considerably more tolerance towards same sex relationships than was previously the case. Paedophilia is currently the number one taboo in western society but that is not the case in all societies. Other cultures which still abhor same sex relationships allow older men to marry girls who in the west would be regarded as children. In Niger, Chad, Bangladesh, Mali and Ethiopia, more than 20 percent of marriages involve girls below the age of 15. Marriages involving very young girls are also very common in India and in Muslim countries where scholars cite the authority of Sharia law. In the natural world puberty is the definition of adulthood but humans have extended the period of childhood dependency beyond that. The human brain does not fully mature until towards the end of the third decade.

Human sexuality seems to be rather fluid, as the basic instinct is fine tuned during the process of socialisation. Individuals can get into trouble when their pursuit drive is switched on by the wrong sexual targets for their own particular culture. For example, in 2015 there was a court report of a man who was prosecuted after repeatedly sneaking into a farmyard to masturbate as he rolled around in pig excrement. Apparently that is not regarded as acceptable behaviour in Cornwall.

When humans become sexually attracted to things that are unusual, the suffix "philia" is often added, so somebody who loves bananas in the wrong way could be described as suffering from bananaphilia (although I made that up). Haemophilia should be something vampires have, but in fact it is an inherited blood condition. For those who are experiencing the pursuit drive switching on and wish to learn more about paraphilias, which is the proper medical name for unusual sexual targeting, Dr. Anil Aggrawa has listed over 500 fascinating examples.[39] Something must have driven him to do that.

We like to think we know what we are doing most of the time but the evidence suggests otherwise. The Wikipedia entry for physiological arousal says:

"Not to be confused with sexual arousal."

Yet that is wrong. Humans do get confused about the causes of their physiological arousal. For example, in experiments conducted on humans who had been taking physical exercise in a gym, the participants were asked to rate photographs according to how sexually attractive they found the subjects. They thought all of the people in the photographs were more sexually attractive than a control group who had not been exercising. The reason is that after taking exercise it takes time for all the physiological systems to return to normal. They still

---

[39] "Forensic and Medico-Legal Aspects of Sexual Crimes and Unusual Sexual Practices" - Anil Aggrawal, 2008

had slightly raised heart rates and were feeling a bit flushed, which also happens when people are sexually excited. Their heart & mindbrain simply became a bit confused about what they were feeling and misattributed the emotion.

In another experiment on misattribution of emotion, young male students were interviewed by a female experimenter. Some were interviewed after they had just crossed a scary footbridge. After interviewing them on an unrelated topic, she gave them her mobile phone number, supposedly so they could add information about how they felt, if it occurred to them later. Those who were stimulated by panic after crossing the bridge were significantly much more likely to phone the researcher back than those interviewed in more relaxing circumstances. Several also asked her out for a date. They mistook their fearful arousal for sexual attraction. It must have affected their memories of the interviewer because by the time they phoned, their sympathetic nervous systems would have calmed down. This tells us something about memory too. We remember the emotions that accompany experiences, and when we re-present those memories at a later date we also recreate the emotions at the same time. It is clear that excitement and stress do become confused and that physiological arousal can become confused with sexual arousal. Perhaps those footballers were lucky that Luis Suarez only bit them.

The enjoyment humans get when they are engaged in any form of pursuit is called "intrinsic motivation". That pleasant feeling is associated with dopamine circuits in the hippocampus, and in order to understand how to enjoy life to the full, we need to understand how those dopamine circuits work. They are the key to motivation, behaviour and addiction.

The Neuroscience of Pursuit

In 1954, Olds and Milner discovered neural circuits in the limbic system of a rat's brain that seemed to be associated with pleasure.[40] The rats learned to press a lever that provided stimulation to those neural circuits and they would continue pressing it until they collapsed with exhaustion. As soon as they recovered they would start pressing it again. They were not interested in anything else. Those circuits are often described in the literature as reward circuits.

Robert Sapolsky, Professor of Biology, Neuroscience and Neurosurgery at Stanford University, describes experiments on rhesus macaque monkeys.[41] The experimental animals learned that after a light came on, if they pressed a button ten times, a treat would be delivered after a short delay. Monkeys are good at learning that sort of thing. The amount of dopamine released in the pursuit circuits was being measured during the

---

[40] "Positive Reinforcement Produced by Electrical Stimulation of Septal Areas and Other Regions of Rat Brain" - Olds and Milner, 1954

[41] "The Biology of Human Behaviour" - Robert Sapolsky, 2005

experiment and it is dopamine that provides the pleasure of motivation. It was traditionally assumed that those reward circuits were activated at the moment the animal received the reward, but it turns out to be more complicated than that. The dopamine circuits do behave that way initially, but they begin to change their behaviour with experience as the animal learns what it has to do to get the reward. In other words, as they become motivated by the pursuit.

What actually happened in the experiment was that as the monkeys learned the task, dopamine started being released earlier. Once the task was learned dopamine production began as soon as the light went on, and it continued to be produced until the moment the monkey had pressed the button for the tenth time. Then dopamine production stopped. That means the motivation, and the enjoyment associated with it, stopped before the reward was delivered. Those circuits could more accurately be described as motivation circuits or pursuit circuits.

Without active dopamine neurons in those circuits, laboratory rats although still capable of walking, chewing and swallowing, just cannot be bothered to do anything. They completely lose motivation and can starve to death, even when food is placed right next to them. When the pursuit drive is switched off, motivation seems to disappear and so does the pleasure in life.

Gambling Brains

Many behaviour policies focus attention on the rewards that come at the end of a pursuit to motivate people using a simplistic model of reward and punishment. They need to focus on what is happening before that. Some experts have also advocated consistent rewards as the best way to motivate humans. That turns out to be wrong too.

In a follow up experiment, once the monkeys had learned to press the button ten times after the light showed, the machine stopped rewarding them consistently. It began to only reward them intermittently, in a random pattern averaging out at one of three conditions. They were either rewarded randomly for 75 percent of the time, 50 percent, or only 25 percent of the time.

You might expect that not being rewarded consistently would depress motivation. In fact it had the opposite effect. Inconsistent reward increased motivation significantly and once the machine stopped providing rewards altogether, they kept on responding to the light and pressing the lever for far longer than animals who had been rewarded consistently.

The reason is that once the monkeys had learned to expect the reward they were surprised when it did not happen. Surprise triggers curiosity and pursuit. The more uncertain the reward, the more dopamine was produced and presumably the more exciting it was for the monkeys. Brains are addicted to uncertainty.

It was not the amount of reward that motivated the monkeys most, but the amount of uncertainty. If the monkey was never rewarded, it was 100 percent certain that no reward was coming. If it was always rewarded it was 100 percent certain that a reward was coming. The most uncertain condition, equally far away from never and always, is a random schedule that rewarded the monkeys 50 percent over time. Sure enough, that was when dopamine production was recorded at the highest level.

The brain is a statistical calculator which is highly motivated by uncertainty. The brains of those excited laboratory rats produced exactly the same amount of dopamine when they were rewarded 25 percent as they did when it was 75 percent, because those schedules are both exactly the same distance away from certainty. Somehow their brains were keeping track of the odds.

Even when they were being rewarded on a random schedule for only 25 percent of the time, dopamine production was still twice as high as when they had been rewarded consistently. They were more highly motivated to keep working and were getting more pleasure from it when they were being rewarded less. This explains why gambling is so addictive. The pleasure gamblers get from those intermittent wins is enough to motivate them to keep on playing until they have lost all their money. Most gamblers are losers who feel like winners and it is feelings that drive behaviour most of the time. Whether it is fair to take advantage of them is a different matter.

Understanding dopamine circuits provides a clear message for managers, teachers, carers and parents. If inconsistency increases motivation, we should ensure that rewards are inconsistent, because that makes them more motivating. If certainty decreases motivation, we should ensure that sanctions are consistent and inevitable, so children are not tempted to gamble by breaking the rules to see if they can get away with it. Just as some people become addicted to gaming machines, and remain excited each time they play, some children learn to gamble with inconsistent adults. They keep on gambling because every now and then it works. Inconsistent parenting trains children to play adults like gaming machines, which is why some of them refuse to take no for an answer. You just never know when the payout might come from an inconsistent adult, so long as you keep on pushing. We know that a 25 percent payout is enough to keep dopamine neurons excited.

This is something for governments to think about too. It is the uncertainty, not the size of the reward or sanction, that motivates human behaviour. As I was writing this, in the U.K. the government announced that it was doubling the fine for dropping litter. The previous month it had announced an increase in the fine for using mobile phones while driving. Increasing fines will have no effect if enforcement is inconsistent, which it is. On the contrary, for risk takers, inconsistent enforcement makes the gamble even more exciting. If rule makers want rules to be followed they need to increase the level of enforcement, not the penalties. Gambling and risk taking are part of human nature.

Our ancestors were hunter gatherers who were driven to stalk, pursue, capture, collect and bring home food and other useful things. They were not always successful which meant that they had to be motivated to try again. So, intermittent failure increases motivation, causing animals to try harder and persevere until they succeeded. Many creatures, including humans, seem to become more strongly driven to take risks when times are bad. Throughout recorded history it has always been those under most pressure, often as a result of natural disasters or wars, who were driven to embark on the most dangerous journeys. In 2016 there were thousands of men, women, and children risking their lives to cross the Mediterranean from North Africa in the pursuit of a better life in Europe. Similar mass migrations have been recorded many times before in human history. Our ancestors also travelled from far off places, carrying with them the genes that had allowed pursuit to overcome panic. Those with a weaker pursuit drive, who could not overcome their fear of the unknown, must have stayed where they were as resources ran out and perished.

Modern humans are driven to take risks because they all carry the genes of risk taking ancestors. Evolution has selected a balance of risk. Just as genes that made humans too risk averse died out, so did those that made them take too many risks. Somewhere in the middle, evolution selected the correct balance between curiosity and timidity. That is the mental programming that drives our behaviour. Humans are still driven to take risks. They undertake a variety of arduous pursuits which must provide them with feelings of satisfaction and pleasure even when there is a chance that they could be injured or killed doing them. Adventurers have lost fingers and toes on treks across the polar ice. Many have lost their lives. They have crossed oceans, climbed mountains, navigated rapids and crawled around subterranean pot holes. Such pursuits can be strenuous, with periods of time when considerable effort is expended without any immediate reward. Explorers endure long periods of boredom, discomfort and sometimes pain. The pursuit drive has to be strong enough to keep them going through those difficult times. Learning to switch that drive on and harnessing it is the key to motivation and mood management.

Competing Pursuits

Navigating life's journey involves frequent diversions and detours as competing pursuits temporarily come to the fore to hijack our attention for a while. There are always vast numbers of neural circuits competing for control of the bodybrain, ready to provide more immediate distractions, as anyone who has struggled to concentrate will appreciate. Fear, hunger, thirst or tiredness may cause a temporary change in direction as a short term pursuit gains ascendency and we search for food, drink and a place to rest. A message or a tweet can provide a temporary distraction when we are trying to concentrate on something else. Then, as the strength of the more immediate pursuit subsides, there is an opportunity for one of the longer term pursuits to regain control again.

Humans can have a number of open pursuits at any one time. The neural circuits associated with those incomplete pursuits are still there, firing away in the background. They may not be strong enough to immediately capture attention and direct behaviour in the present, but at some time in the future, when there is less competition, they might take over again and move another step towards completion. When we were moving into our current house I found an old laminated card at the back of a drawer. It was a life plan that I had sketched out several decades before. The plan was that I would have become financially secure by the time I was fifty, changed my career (I was a head teacher at the time I wrote the plan), then design, build and live in my own house. That must have seemed a very long way off when I wrote it and in the intervening years I had forgotten all about it as other pursuits captured my attention. In the intervening years it seemed as if opportunities presented themselves which resulted in me doing all of those things. It was nothing like the sort of planning that management experts recommend. There was nothing smart about it. There were no detailed, specific, measurable, attainable, realistic or timely objectives. I was not checking off my progress. I was not even aware that a plan existed. It was just a set of open pursuits, long forgotten, but still ticking over in the back of my brain waiting for opportunities to present themselves. I muddle through life like that. Perhaps my bodybrain does plan, but it does it in a rather haphazard and intuitive way. I suspect that many people in the real world operate that way, a number of open pursuit circuits that are brought to life by intuition when opportunities present themselves.

I am not suggesting that people should simply rely on intuition, because our natural intuition is distorted by all sorts of bugs in our mental software. Daniel Kahneman and Amos Tversky, the inventors of behavioural economics, called them heuristics and they can get us into trouble. People repeat the same mistakes because they are unaware of the bugs in their own thinking. Untrained bodybrains jump to the wrong conclusions, but they can be trained. Educated heart & mindbrains can examine and question ideas thrown up by the bodybrain and identify and correct errors. That is why learning about basic psychology, critical thinking, the rules of logic, and the mental distortions that corrupt our thinking, should be part of the core curriculum. If we can learn to recognise the bugs we can protect ourselves from the most common thinking errors. Some people have learned ineffective and faulty patterns of thinking, which repeatedly get them into trouble, whilst others have learned more effective ones. heart & mindbrains can train bodybrains to think in a different way. Bodybrains learn to juggle thoughts in the same way as they learn to juggle balls. It takes mental effort to start with but thinking becomes automatic and effortless with practice.

The Tragedy of Pursuit

The pursuit drive is associated with pleasurable experiences and feelings of anticipation. When people describe themselves as "excited" as they are looking forward to something, they are describing a slightly raised level of stimulation in the sympathetic nervous system, that is accompanied by activity in the dopamine fuelled pursuit circuits.

One of the bugs in the system is that those neural circuits cannot wait to turn themselves off. When they take control of behaviour they drive individuals towards the completion of the pursuit with a sense of urgency, at which point they are switched off and "we" are left with a slight feeling of anti-climax. Remember, those dopamine circuits in the monkeys stopped firing as soon as they pressed the lever for the last time. That was before the reward was even delivered. It is one of the great tragedies of life that bodybrains never learn that. The only way of extending pleasurable pursuits is for heart & mindbrains to take over and find ways of slowing them down. If human behaviour was controlled by heart & mindbrains, people would make sure that they stretched out their pursuits for longer. But most of the time, bodybrains are in control galloping towards satiation as fast as possible. To get the most out of life humans need to control their excitable bodybrains.

I remember looking forward to Christmas as a child and wishing that time could pass more quickly as the day approached. Yet, when the day came, it was often not quite as good as I had imagined it would be. It was good, but not that good. Many things in life are a bit like that. When people are hungry they anticipate that they will feel better after eating. Yet the pleasure involved in eating is rather short lived. Soon each mouthful seems slightly less enjoyable than the last, until a point is reached when they no longer want to eat anything. The same food that seemed so attractive at the beginning of a meal can trigger feelings of repulsion towards the end. You would think bodybrains would learn that, but they never do. Some people always rush their food. Bodybrains do not plan for the future or think about the past. They live in the present and as soon as they feel hungry, they repeat the process and start rushing again. If only bodybrains could think.

Looking forward, to anticipate the future, and backwards, to remember the past, both involve similar mental processes. The brain creates and stores mental simulations of the past and future which can affect our mood when they are re-presented. Those simulations can also become distorted and corrupted by bugs in the software. For example, some people have fantasies about what it would be like to have a large amount of money. They imagine it will make them happy. If that ever happens to them, they may discover that the experience is not quite what they expected. It is good, but not that good. Beyond an income of about £50 000 additional money does not seem to produce any additional happiness. In some cases it seems to create mental health problems. Some individuals have more money than they know what to do with. They live in sumptuous homes, dripping with gold and jewelled artefacts. They race around fashionable cities in supercars, gamble away fortunes in casinos, then spiral out of control on drink and drugs. Shopping addicts keep buying things, thinking that reality will match their anticipation, then experiencing mild disappointment each time. So they try buying more things to compensate, but each time end up feeling the same. What they need to do is to be able to keep pursuit circuits switched on. All the toys in the toy shop will not make a child happy but children of all ages find that hard to imagine. There are numerous cases of lottery winners who discovered that the happiness they imagined money would bring proved elusive.

Some rich people have learned that the way to stay happy is to keep on working. There are billionaires who just keep on going, long past the age when most people have retired. In the news in 2017 are Rupert Murdoch (85), Bernie Ecclestone (85), Warren Buffett (85), George Soros (86), Charlie Munger (92) and Carl Icahn (80). They obviously do not need the money. They seem more interested in making money than spending it, because making money is an open ended pursuit. Open ended pursuits provide far more pleasure than closed ones. Doing things can be more fun than buying things. If they are happy working all the time that is their business. But they might wish to reflect on what they are doing just to check. There are some outwardly successful people who do not seem to be very happy. They may have become addicted to the feeling they get while their dopamine driven pursuit circuits are active and never realise that whatever they attain can never be enough.Some dopamine addicts sacrifice their family and social lives, working from early in the morning until late at night, without really understanding what they are doing or why they are doing it. They may not be getting their life balance right. In order to be able to make an informed choice they need to understand their own mental processes a bit better.

Some humans take a more direct route to obtain short term pleasures. They ingest chemicals that mimic or increase the production of dopamine, such as amphetamines and cocaine.

Others chase happiness in different ways. Some eschew material possessions and pursue a spiritual life. Prayer, meditation and mindfulness are exercises that can enable the heart & mindbrain to control both the bodybrain and bring about altered mental states. They can be powerful mood management tools.

Some choose intellectual and leisure pursuits that keep them motivated and happy. Learning to manage the pursuit drive is one of the keys to happiness but it needs to be done in a strategic way to get the best effect. When one pursuit switches off, humans have an urge to switch another one on. So when one long term pursuit is coming to an end, it is a good idea to have new ones prepared. People need things to look forward to.

One of the downsides of wealth is that the rich have the capacity to complete their pursuits quicker than most people, which can mean that they experience more disappointments. Wealthy people can keep on buying houses, cars, planes and yachts, and they keep on discovering it is never enough. Those who can only dream of living such lives might already be happier than their wealthy counterparts because happiness does not come at the end of a pursuit. At least they have something to dream about.

Wild animals spend most of their time in pursuit, interspersed with brief periods of panic. They are far too busy trying to stay alive, getting enough to eat, finding mates and feeding their young to have much time to think about how happy they are.

For most of our history that applied to humans too. In the natural world the environment extended our pursuits for us, because almost everything took time and effort.

Modern humans have created artificial means to satisfy their urges almost immediately. The first pangs of hunger can be immediately switched off at a fast food outlet. Fast mobile connections to the internet allow instant access to pornography. Fast search engines allow instant answers to questions, that in the past might have triggered an enjoyable pursuit for the answer. These days entertaining pub arguments that used to take all evening are quashed in an instance by somebody with a smart phone.

Those dopamine driven pursuit circuits are fundamental to our enjoyment of life and they need to be managed with care. It is the bodybrain which wants to switch them off as soon as possible, but that is not what "we" really want.

The neurotransmitters that power our neural circuits to motivate us to behave the way we do are quite simple to make. They are made by converting small molecules that are common and abundant in the natural world around us. The adaptions the body makes to these common molecules are simple ones because the brain needs to be able to do it quickly. If it took too long to create the neurotransmitters that enable neurons to communicate and process information, by the time the brain recognised a shape as a predator it would already be too late.

They would be eaten. The proper name for these molecules are amino acids. We call them food.

Because the stuff they are made from is so readily available and they are so easy to convert, it is also relatively easy to make artificial ones. Recreational drugs trick the brain to provide pleasure and entertainment. Cocaine and amphetamines work on the dopamine pursuit system, which is why they are so highly addictive. Behaviours can be addictive too, if they cause the brain to produce natural dopamine and adrenaline. Modern technology has provided new ways of doing that by enabling humans to repeatedly switch from one pursuit to another, producing a surge of dopamine each time. That is how video games and gambling machines work. Repetitive behaviours, such as checking emails, texts, tweets, messages and news alerts, also create addictive dopamine loops.

I sometimes check the news on my phone if I wake up in the middle of the night. I just experience an urge to do it and I enjoy it. When I am supposed to be working, I sometimes get distracted by meandering google searches, moving from one pursuit to the next. Asking what I am searching for rather misses the point. The pleasure comes from the pursuit. I am like a hamster in a wheel, being entertained whilst doing something rather odd. It is all fuelled by dopamine. I suspect there are many people in offices entertaining themselves in a similar way, while their bosses are away on motivational courses learning about Maslow's triangle.

I am not saying that all these activities are bad. They provide entertainment and enjoyment, which is an important part of life. Too many people do not get enough of that. But we need to educate children so that the next generation understands what they are doing and they are in a position to make informed choices about how they want to achieve their life balance. Some of the recreational drug adventurers did not understand what they were doing and became hopelessly addicted. It is bodybrains which become addicted and heart & mindbrains that try to get into recovery.

We also need to rethink the way we organise our lives to take into account the best interests of both heart & mindbrain and bodybrain if we are going to achieve the best balance of short term pleasures and lifetime fulfilment. There is more to be had from life than mere short term gratification. There was a time when children had to wait for the toy they wanted, and all the time they were waiting those children were experiencing the excitement of anticipation. There was a time when treats were rare, something to look forward to. Children had to work to earn pocket money and save up to buy things for themselves. Of course they wished that they did not have to wait and could have it all immediately, but we have to be careful what we wish for. We do not always know our own minds.

Now some children have learned to expect instant, repeated, continuous gratification. They object to the idea that they should have to work or wait for anything. They are well versed in what they have come to believe are their rights. It is as if their bodybrains have become empowered as their heart & mindbrains weakened. Sometimes it is easier to give in to them, rather than trying to resist unreasonable demands, but in doing so we may actually be depriving them of happiness. Instead of repeatedly allowing them to switch off their pursuit circuits, it might be kinder to teach them how to switch them on and keep them going. Giving in to unreasonable behaviour is feeding an addiction.

The state, as a corporate parent, is worse at this than many natural parents. Some social services departments have policies which they claim promote children's rights, when in reality they do the exact opposite. They simply give power and money to children who have not yet learned to control their bodybrain. They have underdeveloped heart & mindbrains and untrained bodybrains.

Effective mood management involves developing a balance between short term and longer term pursuits to provide opportunities for extracting the maximum pleasure, happiness and fulfilment from life. In order to achieve that, the heart & mindbrain needs to be developed and the bodybrain trained, so that it does not keep derailing the longer term pursuits of the heart & mindbrain.

We need to challenge policies that are founded on myths about the way the body, brain and mind work. We are heart & mindbrains. Only the heart & mindbrain is capable of providing the deeper feelings of satisfaction, contentment and fulfilment that come with a longer term perspective. The heart & mindbrain is the part we should be empowering and protecting with concepts such as human rights, because it is the part that makes humans special. Untrained bodybrains steal away our opportunities to implement the choices we make.

Bodybrains can become addicted to all sorts of damaging behaviours. When they do, it is the heart & mindbrain that needs support. It is heart & mindbrains who try to act in our best interests. It is heart & mindbrains who try to improve our behaviour and help us become better people. It is heart & mindbrains who encourage humans to take more exercise, lose weight, improve their diet, study harder, work harder, stop offending, refrain from violence, clean up, give up drinking, smoking and drugs, and become better parents. And it is bodybrains that keep stopping them from doing all of those things. Some heart & mindbrains need support if they are to bring their unruly bodybrains under control and it is in the best interests of society to offer them support.

Yet we do the opposite. Wishful-thinking is one of the addictive bugs in our mental programming and it has corrupted thinking in relation to individual choice, human rights and liberty. The various conventions on human rights were supposed to protect individuals from abuse and interference from oppressive governments. The term "individual" derives from the Latin word "individuum", which means an atom or indivisible particle, and that is where the policy has become confused. We may wish that humans were indivisible, it would certainly make life simpler for policy makers were it true, but it is not true. Human beings are not indivisible particles. They are a combination of different systems that are often in competition and sometimes in conflict. Sometimes they are in two minds and cannot decide what to do. The most fundamental divide is between the two basic thinking systems, the heart & mindbrain and the bodybrain. They pursue different objectives. One does not think and simply acts on impulse to satisfy its own immediate urges for gratification. The other is conscious and capable of making rational choices as it tries to act in the best interests of both of them.

That is not what I am talking about. This is not mind-body dualism - we are talking about two physical systems. We, as a society, need to decide which system we are going to side with Choices made under duress are not genuine choices. If we tempt a bodybrain, when it has seized control of behaviour, it will always go for short term gratification. So that is no choice at all.

"The spirit is indeed willing but the flesh is weak."

St James Bible

Unfortunately it is the other way round. Sometimes it is the mindbrain that is weak. When the sympathetic nervous system is excited the bodybrain becomes stronger. To find out what a human being really wants we need to present them with a choice when they are not under duress, when the sympathetic nervous system is calm. Then the heart & mindbrain may choose either to go with the bodybrain and enjoy a short term pursuit, or it may choose to exert willpower to pursue a longer term objective. Once that choice is made, there are occasions when the heart & mindbrain needs to be protected until the bodybrain is trained. Sometimes bodybrains need to be kept away from temptation. Food, alcohol, drugs and weapons need to be locked away. Sometimes people need to be physically restrained. Protecting heart & mindbrains which are capable of making their own choices from being pressured by their bodybrain when it becomes over-excited is not a deprivation of liberty, it is the protection of liberty. I have worked with children who asked to be held to prevent them from doing things they knew they did not really want to do.

They did not know it at the time, and neither did I, but they were describing an internal battle between a developing heart &

mindbrain and a bodybrain that was not yet trained. I strongly believe that too many children are failing because their own attempts to manage their own behaviour is undermined by simplistic policy in this area.

When a baby is newly born the bodybrain is completely in control of behaviour. All pursuits are short term. heart & mindbrains only develop gradually over time. Babies do not have the rapid eye movement sleep, which is associated with dreaming, until after the age of about two years. That might be when memories are beginning to form and the heart & mindbrain begins to develop. Few people can remember much before that age. The process of socialisation is really bodybrain training. Young children learn to use the toilet and dress themselves. They learn not to hit and bite other children and how to share. They learn a variety of social skills that enable them to fit into the society in which they happen to be raised. We call these manners. All of this learning involves some degree of self control. Initially young children need external controls to help but the better trained a bodybrain becomes, the less the heart & mindbrain needs to rely on external control or willpower.

It is the ability of the heart & mindbrain to take control that makes humans special. That is what we mean by executive function and that is what we should be trying to develop. The last thing society should be doing is empowering untrained bodybrains. Children with untrained bodybrains grow into adults who can easily become addicted to various destructive behaviours and substances which ultimately reduce their opportunities for happiness.

As they begin to exert self control over the bodybrain, heart & mindbrains allow children to think things through, make reasonable choices, and increase their opportunities for happiness throughout life. The relationship that develops between the heart & mindbrain and the bodybrain is similar to that of a good owner and a well trained dog. Good owners care for and look after their dogs, but they also train them so that they can be given more freedom. It is untrained bodybrains and unsupported heart & mindbrains that are being deprived of their liberty.

Aggressive Performances

Evolution has perfected similar noisy, aggressive, threatening performances in many species. The performance tends to be toe to toe, face to face and head to head. It involves staring eyes, facial contortions and flared nostrils. They inflate the chest attempting to look bigger than they really are. Animals sometimes display their weapons at the same time, for example exposing their claws and teeth. Some humans perform a similar display when they flare their nostrils, bare their teeth and wave their fists about. A performance that gives the impression that an individual might be dangerously unstable, unpredictable, and possibly crazy enough to fight to the death, is a particularly effective repellent. Which is why many social animals have perfected it.

Dominant performances are motivated by a combination of the pursuit and performance drives and some humans get into the habit of performing this way because they enjoy it. When a dominant animal gives a threat signal, subservient animals usually give a display of submission which avoids the need for a challenge. Even during a fight, when one animal displays a submissive performance it is often allowed to withdraw to lick its wounds or wounded pride. A submissive performance is driven by a combination of the panic and performance drives.

Ritual performances of dominance and subservience usually only take place between animals who are close in the social hierarchy ranking. The others avoid one another. It works like the ladder system in competitive sports. Players earn the right to challenge somebody at a slightly higher level by beating those around the same level. The leader in any social group does not normally waste too much time and energy fighting low ranking, non-threatening, competition. But they do need to keep a wary eye on those next in line.

In tournament species especially, individuals are preoccupied with assessing and occasionally testing each other with these aggressive performances. The lower ranks avoid trouble by giving submissive performances to all the higher ranking animals, leaving them free to test out those in their own league.

Subservient and Helpless Displays

Animals giving subservient displays tend to avoid eye contact, crouch, or even prostrate themselves on the ground in front of more dominant animals. Sometimes they roll over to display their vulnerable underside as a sign of submission. If a baboon is briefly driven from the social group following a fight, it may make submissive social reassurance signals to indicate that it wants to rejoin. That might in turn trigger reciprocal social reassurance signals and grooming rituals from other members of the troop. In humans we call it kissing and making up.

It is important to remember that humans are motivated to give both dominant and subservient performances, so they must gain some sort of pleasure from both. Subservient performances by humans include bowing, kneeling, or even lying prostrate in front of figures of authority. Those receiving honours at Buckingham Palace are expected to kneel in front of the Monarch. People begging for money, help, or forgiveness, sometimes adopt similar body postures. Many cults and religions incorporate submissive displays into their rituals. Humans throughout history have knelt or prostrated themselves in front of their Gods. Some secular leaders encourage similar performances of adulation.

Even though the behaviours are common, the words used to describe this sort of performance have negative connotations. Those who do it are described as obsequious, servile, sycophantic, or toadying. They grovel, fawn, kowtow, bow and scrape, abase themselves, curry favour, flatter, ingratiate themselves, suck up, butter up and generally fall all over other humans. Apparently it is not the sort of performance that humans want to admit to, even though many of them do it. The same can be said for a lot of human behaviour.

Performances are intended to impress an audience so sometimes even subservient performances have to be done in public. For example, celebrities who have been caught out doing something embarrassing are often driven to make public apologies on television, rather than private ones to the people who deserve them. Politicians make public apologies on behalf of their predecessors. Victims of tragedies also seem to be driven to express their grief in public rather than in private, often in front of cameras. When a public figure dies, people feel an urge to go onto the streets to make a public display of their grief, rather than doing it quietly at home. Most funerals are public performances involving dressing up, parades and rituals.

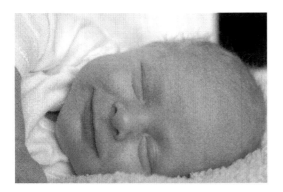

Pulling Faces

New born babies can grin and grimace but their range of facial expressions is limited. However some of the basic muscle groups are already wired up, so when they contract together they make recognisable expressions. These reflex expressions disappear after a couple of weeks only to re-emerge once they become wired up to thoughts and feelings later on. They form the basis for a growing repertoire of increasingly subtle facial expressions.

Faces are an important element in performance. They can transmit a considerable amount of subtle information, even when the performers are unaware of what their own faces are doing. The faces of individuals in social groups are generally much more animated and mobile than when they are sitting alone. Humans in groups keep looking at each other, pulling groups of facial muscles into different shapes, checking and comparing reactions, and sometimes mirroring the faces they see, but it is all largely subconscious.

This is a reflex expression of a newborn baby.

CCTV recordings of human faces, recorded when the subjects are alone, show that they are expressionless for long periods of time, even though they are not aware of it at the time. Even when subjects are filmed watching comedy videos which they claim to have enjoyed, their faces lack animation for most of the time. This social effect on facial signalling is evident even in young children.[42] The contrast between the way they behave alone, and the way they behave when another child is present watching the same videos is dramatic. They are far more animated. They look at each other to compare reactions and mirror each other's facial expressions, taking turns to prompt one another to smile and laugh.

Humans have a facial expression that signals social reassurance, friendship and lack of threat. It is exhibited in situations that are potentially frightening or embarrassing, as a signal of willingness to cooperate and sometimes as a request for cooperation and reassurance. It can also be used to signal subservience. Whenever humans give the signal, or see it, they experience pleasure which is associated with the production of

---

[42] See "Child of Our Time" - Robert Winston, BBC

neurotransmitters and hormones, including opiates and oxytocin. We call it smiling.

A social reassurance signal usually prompts an automatic smile response from a stranger, although they might be puzzled afterwards about why somebody just smiled at them. It is a natural expression of reciprocity. People like smiling and being smiled at. They also like stories that make them smile and people who make them smile. The bodybrain learns to associate smiles, and the people and situations that produce them, with good feelings. Inducing smiles by any means is a simple mood management trick. These days people have a range of entertaining and amusing resources at their fingertips which could trigger smiles, but sometimes they forget to use them.

The facial expressions associated with moods and emotions must be innate to some extent, because they are cross cultural. Congenitally blind babies express similar emotions, such as smiling, at similar times in their development as sighted babies. To some extent facial expressions are cross species. Other animals have evolved performances that involve the communication of emotions through facial expressions. Some have shown an ability to read human faces.

Research published in 2016 showed that horses could understand human facial expressions. When shown photographs of angry human faces, the heart rate of the horses increased and they became nervous. With relaxed and happy human faces they calmed down and become more relaxed.[43]

It is commonly asserted in the literature that people with autism find it difficult to empathise and understand facial expressions. That is a rather careless generalisation. Alexithymia is an inability to recognise moods. Not only do those who suffer from alexithymia find it hard to identify other people's moods. They also find it hard to identify and understand their own moods. About 50 percent of people with autism have it, compared to about 10 percent of the general population. That means 50 percent of people with autism do not have it.[44]

Some people with autism are hypersensitive to emotional signals from others, particularly those from animals. Temple Grandin was diagnosed with autism in 1950. She did not speak until she was three and a half years old and often communicated her frustration by screaming. She went on to become a world famous expert on both animal behaviour and autism. For the past two decades she has been Professor of Animal Science at Colorado State University and described the empathy she experiences with animals. She describes animals as experiencing either fear or curiosity, the equivalent of what I am calling panic and pursuit. She says she operates like that too.

---

[43] "Functionally relevant responses to human facial expressions of emotion in the domestic horse (Equus caballus), Amy Victoria Smith et al 2016

[44] "The impact of autism spectrum disorder and alexithymia on judgments of moral acceptability." - Rebecca Brewer, 2015

Dr Paul Eckman was a pioneering American psychologist who spent his career studying emotions and the facial expressions used to express them. He found that humans across the planet used and recognised similar facial expressions. We can paint all sorts of subtle and complex multi-expressions over the top, but there seem to be just four basic coordinated muscle groups that form the templates. Eckman originally thought that there were six basic expressions, but more recent research has shown that surprise and fear, which were previously considered to be completely different expressions, are actually contractions of the same muscle group at different strengths. Disapproval (sometimes described as disgust) and threat are the same muscle group too.

The four basic muscle groups are:

1. Happy / Thrilled

One muscle group creates happy faces, familiar in the traditional comedy mask which has survived from Greek theatre. This is the face of pleasure and social reassurance. The mild expression is associated with satisfaction and contentment. The stronger version with joy and rapture.

2. Sad / Distraught

Another muscle group creates sad faces, familiar in the tragedy mask. This face signals suffering with a mild expression associated with pleas for comfort and reassurance. The stronger version expresses more desperate cries for help.

3. Surprise / Fear

A third muscle group creates expressions of surprise with mild contractions, which turn into expressions of fear with stronger contractions. Surprise directs attention towards the source of interest. It is associated with the pursuit drive, motivating the creature to approach the source to find out more. Fear switches from pursuit to panic, if it does not like or understand what it is seeing. Then the urge is to move away from the source of interest to a safer distance.

4. Disapproval / Threat

Disapproval and disgust are associated with mild contractions of this muscle group and are accompanied by a mild panic drive, as the animal is urged to withdraw from the source of interest. Stronger contractions switch on pursuit as the facial expression becomes one of anger or threat. Then the animal is driven to approach the source in an aggressive performance to drive it away.

Of course humans have developed all sorts of variations on the basic themes but most facial expressions trigger recognition in one of the basic groups.

All facial expressions are a sign that the performance drive is up and running. Humans put maximum effort into contracting their facial muscle groups when there is an audience to see the performance. They are much less animated when they are alone. Some behaviour experts claim that there is no such thing as attention seeking. Clearly they do not get out much. The whole point of performance is attention seeking.

Social performance is about communication, getting attention, and making an impression, but it is not always an honest impression. Some performers pursue vulnerable targets to take advantage of them. Seducers and confidence tricksters pursue their victims with false promises and deceptive performances, pretending to be more desperate than they really are. Bullies intimidate their victims with deceptive threat performances, pretending to be more angry, upset, and out of control than they really are. What distinguishes these deceptive performances from the real thing is that the performers are not as highly aroused as they pretend. Extreme arousal is associated with panic, whereas they are in pursuit. This is a performance with a purpose.

Aggressive threat performances are usually aimed towards rivals. Attractive performances, for example those involving singing, chanting, dancing, gift giving, grooming, nest building, and cries for help are aimed towards potential mates and allies.

Humans and a range of other animals in distress make similar sounds, including whimpering, high pitched wails, squeals and cries. Those sounds may be accompanied by behaviours such as huddling or crouching, rocking motions, and other repetitive movements. It would be no good pulling sad faces and adopting these postures if nobody could see them, so performers choose a place where they are visible to an audience. A creature hiding up a tree, under a bush, or in a cave is not in performance mode. They could be driven by panic. But when they choose a public stage, make a noise, or behave in a way that attracts attention that is performance.

Performing provides its own pleasures. Some people learn to get a buzz from aggressive performances. Others learn that cries for help can be rewarding and those behaviours can become habitual. The act of crying can be enjoyable in itself. It causes the body to produce prolactin, a hormone that, like the neurotransmitter serotonin, is involved in the experience of reward. People feel better after a good cry. Some deliberately choose to entertain themselves with tear jerker stories to procure that effect. Others habitually provoke arguments that end in tears. They may not understand what they are doing or why they are doing it, because habitual patterns of behaviour develop and strengthen automatically when they are rewarded inconsistently. Habitual behaviour is addictive. Some humans get into the habit of performing cries for help whenever they want something, because they learn that it is easier than making an effort themselves. Indulgent parents can inadvertently train their children to do this, which is not good for the individual or society.

In any cooperative social system, hidden amongst the genuine needy, there will always be cheats. These are performers putting on convincing cries for help to con the kind and vulnerable out of their money. Some work the tables in open air restaurants fleecing tourists, some flatter wealthy widows and empty their bank accounts, others write begging letters and scam emails.

In the U.S., there are numerous religious channels on cable networks which feature a succession of plump, tanned, toupeed individuals putting on very impressive cry for help performances. With tears of emotion running down their faces, they beg for more money to maintain their extravagant lifestyles. It obviously works. Many cults, religions, trades unions and political movements consist of a hierarchical structure in which the leaders are maintained in luxurious lifestyles, funded by people who are poorer than they are. It is almost the standard model. They get away with it because humans are programmed to react to cries for help, just as other social animals will sometimes respond to calls of distress by grooming the animal.

Along with the crocodile tears associated with deceptive cries for help, there are also tears of synthetic rage. Aggressive performers in synthetic rage pretend that their sympathetic nervous system is more highly stimulated than it really is. They pretend to be out of control to give the impression that they could be dangerous and unpredictable. It is an attempt to get others to back down and accede to their wishes or demands, or to shy away from making demands on them.

Social performances evolved in creatures who live in social groups which have flexible social hierarchies in which individuals compete to negotiate their relative position. In nature reproductive success is related to the social position they are able to achieve within the group.

Chapter 4 - Brains and Minds

Some social hierarchies in the natural world are rigid. In ant nests and bee hives, for example, everybody knows and accepts their place. The queen is the queen, workers are workers, and soldiers are soldiers. They do not need to worry about Machiavellian intrigues such as jealous princesses trying to depose the queen, workers plotting revolts or military coups. Those ideas do not occur to them, because they do not have heart & mindbrains to think like that. They are not really individuals because they look, process information and behave in exactly the same way. They manage perfectly well as bodybrains.

But some social birds and animals began to organise themselves in a different way and that was when social life became more complicated. Ants and bees within the same nest or hive are truly cooperative in a way that humans are not. In competitive hierarchies individuals are competing with each other within their own group. That is a significant difference. They only cooperate when it suits them but at other times they switch into competitive mode. This requires much more brain power to manage, because they no longer all look the same or behave in the same way all the time. They have evolved into unpredictable individuals with individual characteristics. Group members have to be able to recognise all the different members of the group, remember their idiosyncrasies and remember where each of them is in the social hierarchy. They have to make judgements about whether they have any chance of improving their current position by moving up the ladder.

In primate troops the largest and physically fittest males are in dominant positions but they are all ageing. At the same time younger animals are growing and becoming physically fitter and stronger. The social hierarchy is not static and at times there will be individuals who are just one challenge away from swapping positions. In human hierarchies size and physical fitness have been replaced by other qualities but the same internal processes operate. Challenging those in positions of power carries attendant risks.

In nature, ritual performances of dominance and subservience, involving threats and sometimes actual violence are a common feature of social hierarchies. In birds, the social hierarchy has been named the "pecking order". Rhesus Macaque monkeys have both male and female hierarchies. Modern humans have even more complicated networks of hierarchies, and to avoid damaging social gaffes they need to learn and remember where everybody else is in those hierarchies, which is no mean feat in itself. They also need to develop self control.

Young primates are born with the basic innate equipment which enables them to recognise and give threat performances. They are also equipped to give subservient performances. Juvenile male Rhesus Macaque monkeys, who have been raised in the lab without ever seeing another monkey face, immediately adopt an expression of fear and subservience when shown a picture of a threat face. That makes evolutionary sense. In the monkey world, and in rougher parts of the human world too, animals that do not immediately pay attention to threat signals from dominant individuals may be attacked.

But over time, they need to learn that they do not have to subserve all the time to everybody who gives a threat signal. They learn that they can give threat signals too, and that some animals subserve to them. That is the beginning of the life long negotiation of social hierarchy. Good judgement is the key to social success in competitive societies.

"Anyone can become angry. That is easy. But to be angry with the right person to the right degree at the right time for the right purpose and in the right way, that is not easy."

Aristotle

When primates challenge each another in aggressive performances they give the impression of being extremely angry. Sometimes they seem to be in such an extreme state of rage that they can barely control themselves. Humans describe it as losing their temper. Yet they tend to only do this when they are performing with individuals they perceive as being at, or below, their own level in the social hierarchy.

Some of the henchmen who worked for notorious dictators and criminal gangsters had their own fearsome reputations, yet they somehow manage to control their temper in the presence of the boss, even when provoked. No matter how angry and out of control they appear to be, most animals regain their composure remarkably quickly when they know they cannot possibly win a fight. Humans who are prone to losing their temper are much less likely to do so with somebody who is holding a gun to their head, than with a defenceless minion. Losing your temper is an indulgence. It is based on a calculation even though it may not be a conscious one. It is part of a stereotypical performance that is part of the behavioural repertoire of competitive social animals.

The only individuals who do not need to worry too much about self control are the dominant ones at the very top. They have the luxury of being able to get away with venting their fury upon whoever they like. Everyone else has to get used to displaying both dominant and subservient performances according to the circumstances. The wrong performances have resulted in people not being allowed on flights, failing to get into nightclubs, and getting arrested. Whereas socially skilled performers who judge it correctly can get upgraded, negotiate discounts and talk their way out of trouble. Underpinning many social interactions are finely balanced dominance and subservience performances.

Domestic dogs learn to subserve to their owner, because it comes naturally to them. It comes naturally to monkeys and humans too. Groups of humans organise themselves spontaneously into hierarchical structures. Hierarchies can be observed in families, groups of friends, sports teams, societies and work places. Bodybrains are constantly working out where they are and where everybody else is in the social system in a largely automatic and subconscious process.

Sometimes social and work groups have an explicit formal hierarchy set out at the beginning, but even then it is not uncommon for a different implicit one to emerge. Some nominal leaders are not natural ones and they become puppets for others who really wield the power in the group.

Within human gangs, teams, groups, and committees, there are individuals who try harder than most to bully and dominate. Not all leaders have to be bullies, but bullies do have a tendency to become leaders. Some individuals subserve and grovel to the bullies. Others refuse and challenge them, which can result in confrontations which either reinforce the current hierarchy or move people around within it. They may be more subtle than other primates in the way they do it, but humans still follow the same basic rules.

Social competition has much in common with other games that humans like to play. It involves players trying to give the impression that they have a slightly better hand than they really do. It is all about deception. Well adjusted individuals have a fairly accurate idea of where they are in any social hierarchy.

They know their place. Those with social skills may be able to negotiate their way up to a slightly higher position than their genuine talents deserve. It is the socially inept who are caught out when they try to impress people who are outside of their range. Grovelling to superiors or bullying inferiors who are no threat to them are both frowned upon.

When things are settled, social groups can operate in a more collegiate manner, but humans seem to default back to a more rigid hierarchy when they feel threatened. That is when groups seek stronger leaders and seem more willing to subserve to them. In times of tension democratic systems can be their own undoing, because when humans are feeling insecure they will happily vote for dictators and give away their rights and responsibilities.

When social hierarchies are relatively stable, and most people know their place, levels of violence are low. It is when there is uncertainty across the system that challenges become more common. Removing too many key figures from any hierarchy can destabilise a social group and result in increased levels of conflict at all levels. Nobody knows who they are supposed to dominate and subserve to any more, so every interaction becomes a challenge as they attempt to recreate the social order.

Examples of this have been seen in a wide variety of social settings. When a number of influential staff and pupils leave a school it can quickly result in a breakdown of discipline. Chaos can ensue when a social hierarchy is allowed to collapse with nothing left in its place. That is a lesson our political masters have learned the hard way in recent years after interfering in hierarchical foreign governments.

One individual can be a member of several different groups and hold a different rank in each one. For example, a business executive may have high status in the company they run, but be a low ranking beginner at the tennis club. There are special rules zones in many cultures where the normal social hierarchy is suspended; for example in sports teams, pubs, some places of leisure and at parties where people are expected to pretend to be equals. In an attempt to force this pretence of equality, high status individuals sometimes have to dress down and behave foolishly to signal their willingness to play the game. They make self deprecating jokes and low status people are allowed to tease them in these settings. They are all performing trying to make an impression of one sort or another.

The Evolution of Social Intelligence

Corvids, which include crows, ravens and magpies, have been studied for many years for their intelligence. They can recognise and remember all the other individuals in their own social group and their characteristics. They have extremely complex social structures and negotiate social status by playing a terrifying game of chicken, in which two birds fly directly towards each other at high speed, until one swerves away at the last minute. Corvids have good memories for faces, including human faces. Not only can they tell individual humans apart, but they remember past events and carry grudges. They can communicate and have been known to gang up and attack humans they do not like.

Research in 2012 using PET scans, found that when crows viewed human faces with threatening expressions, they had increased activity in the amygdala, thalamus and brain stem which mirrored the emotional responses of human brains in similar experiments.[45]

When they were allowed to observe another group of birds interacting in a neighbouring aviary, corvids were able to learn and remember their entire social structure. They took a particular interest when they saw low status birds showing off to high status birds, which is bad manners. The watching birds showed their disapproval by displaying threatening postures. Nobody likes a show off.

Corvids are clever. They are one of the few creatures capable of solving problems and using tools to find food. These signs of social intelligence alongside other forms of intelligence are significant, because bird brains are very different from mammalian brains. They diverged from our common ancestors over 300 million years ago. They do not have a cortex like

---

[45] "Brain imaging reveals neuronal circuitry underlying the crow's perception of human faces" - John Marzluff, 2012

mammals, but they do have another structure called the nidopallium, which is somewhat analogous in function to the prefrontal cortex in humans.

Corvid brains and human brains must have evolved similar abilities separately. The fact that two different types of brain both evolved creative intelligence alongside the ability to manage complex social hierarchies may be a clue that there is a link between the two. In mammals, the heart & mindbrain first evolved to manage an increasingly complex social world that was based on deception and detection of deception.

When size was all that mattered, potential mates would just size up what was on offer and choose the biggest. Competitors would fight anyone who got in their way and the strongest would always win. But that was a waste of time and energy. So in the evolutionary arms race judgement and intelligence began to play a more significant role. Individuals with judgement could assess their opponents and pick their battles, avoiding those they were unlikely to win. Those who could deceive others into believing they were more attractive, clever, or dangerous than they really were, could negotiate their way into positions that their talents did not really justify. We have all worked for people like that. So intelligence evolved to enable social animals to detect and see through the deceptive performances of others, and to create ever more convincing ones of their own.

That is why social status negotiations in nature are often preceded by a lengthy period of posturing and showing off. This enables both parties to assess the potential of the other. It also allows them to decide whether a fight is really worthwhile. Evolution favoured those who could bluff and put on a good performance over those who could actually fight. It also favoured those who could see through the bluffers.

Intelligence and Counter Intelligence

The ability to recognise familiar behaviours and predict what other creatures are likely to do next provides a huge evolutionary advantage. For example, learning to recognise the difference between a hungry animal and a full one could be useful for prey. Learning to recognise which individuals are likely to be slow runners could be useful for a predator. There is also an advantage in being able to assess the level of stimulation in the sympathetic nervous system of a competitor, because different innate behaviours are associated with different levels of stimulation.

That is all useful intelligence. There is also an advantage to be gained in developing the ability to hide that sort of information and disguise thoughts and feelings, to make it more difficult for others to guess the individual's intentions. Intelligence resulted from an evolutionary arms race as creatures in social hierarchies developed increasingly complex information processing systems to create and detect increasingly complex deceptive performances. Evolution selected intelligence over brawn and gullibility.

The terms intelligence and counter-intelligence are used to describe the activities of security services around the world. Their murky world involves inventing and distributing propaganda and misinformation, whilst at the same time gathering and analysing information about their enemies and rivals to work out what they might really be thinking and what they are likely to do next. Intelligence services communicate in code, to prevent others from knowing what they are really up to. When their codes are broken or hacked, they have to refine them and invent new ones. At the same time they are constantly trying to break and hack the codes of the competition. That is exactly what the human brain evolved to do.

Social animals are selling an image of themselves in a competitive market place. Like most advertisers, they are interested in projecting the most impressive image they think they can get away with, rather than the most accurate one. How far humans are willing to go in their deceptions varies, but most put on clothing to disguise, or at least cover up, their less attractive bits. Older humans try to give the impression that they are younger than they really are, by removing hair from various parts, and artificially colouring what is left. They even add coloured dyes to their skin, or paint over it with make-up, sometimes going to the extent of drawing false mouths and eyes around their real ones. They have plastic surgery and hair transplants. They adorn areas of their skin with permanent tattoos, pierce their bodies and insert shiny objects into the holes, and hang decorations on their fingers, wrists, ankles and necks. They wear uncomfortable shoes to make themselves look taller and spray chemicals over themselves to give the impression that they smell better than they really do. All this is accepted as perfectly normal.

Humans also practise strange postures and facial expressions in front of mirrors and shop windows, posting photographs that look nothing like them as profile pictures on social media. They photoshop their own photos. Then they go off singing, dancing, and making public performances in social marketplaces.

Like other social animals, humans are inclined to take a close interest in those they judge to be somewhere around their own level in the market. That is when they start comparing themselves and worrying.

"It is in the character of very few men to honour without envy a friend who has prospered."

Aeschylus

When somebody like them becomes conspicuously successful, humans experience feelings of vague unease about it, even if they are reluctant to admit it. It feels as if they have lost something even though they are personally no worse off. It is not rational but neither is much of human behaviour.

Different cultures and sub-cultures may value different characteristics and capabilities. Some value size, strength and fighting ability. Others value intelligence, generosity and kindness. But whatever they value, humans judge others according to those values. They may not be keen to admit it, or even be aware that they are doing it, but humans are both natural performers and critics. They judge the performances of others because it comes naturally to them.

"All the world's a stage, And all the men and women merely players"

William Shakespeare

Even those who claim not to be competitive, who value cooperation, humility and integrity instead, cannot resist letting other people know about it. Those who share information and opinions on social media are publicising a variety of messages, but the meta message is all about them. They are defining and redefining their image of themselves according to their own values.

Social intelligence evolved to enable humans to rate each other. Those who lack social judgement struggle in the game of life. Some are too ambitious in the image they are trying to project and fail to be convincing performers. Instead of making a favourable impression, they come over as cocky, opinionated or idiotic. Whenever there is a large gap between the projected image and objective reality it can result in painful feedback and unhappy social interactions. Objective reality, so far as social performance is concerned, is what other people think of the performance. It is not really objective at all, because social performance distorts human appraisals of other qualities.

In a world of deceptive intelligence impressions are sometimes more important than reality. Some, who lack confidence and/or skills as social performers, may project a less impressive image than they could get away with, and suffer unfairly as a result. Individuals who are genuinely more talented and skilled can be overlooked due to a bias towards social performance which can have damaging affects for society if the wrong people are selected and promoted. Really artful performers are those who manage to project an image that is impressive, whilst at the same time giving an impression that they are not really trying.

That is a double deception causing observers to speculate that they might be even more impressive than they appear.

The information processing involved in deceptive intelligence is complex. Performers need to create an internal simulation of the image of themselves they are trying to project. At the same time they have to monitor feedback and create an internal simulation of how they imagine their performance is being received. They are having to imagine themselves outside of their own body looking at their own performance. This may be where the experience of self-consciousness and ultimately all consciousness originates from. Humans seldom feel as self-conscious as they do when they are being inspected and judged by other humans. When people trip up in public, they sometimes look around self-consciously to check whether anyone noticed. Meeting the eyes of a stranger in a public place can be a curiously intense experience too. Public speaking produces intense and sometimes overwhelming experiences of self consciousness. Consciousness is closely associated with social performance.

Knowing What You Think

In psychology and neuroscience, consciousness is referred to as the "hard problem". We are not talking about being awake as opposed to being asleep here. We are talking about what happens when our mind comes to life, and begins to experience a tiny part of the information processing going on in the whole body and brain.

Some neuroscientists have postulated that consciousness is a natural feature of the universe, like magnetism and gravity. They suggest that it might arise spontaneously in complex, synchronised, information processing machines. I find that explanation unconvincing, because my mind does not gradually dissolve in and out of existence. It never experiences a vague general consciousness of all the information being processed. It remains completely unconscious of most of the processing, and only becomes briefly and intensely conscious of minuscule parts of it.

Minds can only experience some of the thought processes going on in the heart & mindbrain and none of the information processing going on in the bodybrain. It only experiences the results of bodybrain processing. We are minds. When we have experiences such as gut feelings, they are clues that the bodybrain is working on something that might be important but we cannot experience those workings directly. When we have that "tip of the tongue" feeling, we know that the bodybrain is searching for an idea but we are not aware of the process. We just have to wait patiently until it delivers the answer or gives up.

When my heart & mindbrain is thinking hard, I actually become less conscious of what is going on around me rather than more conscious. When I stub my toe, I suddenly become more conscious. But I am only aware of a tiny amount of simple information processing that relates to pain in my toe. That is not complicated of synchronised information processing. It is the sort of processing that many other life forms can manage perfectly well without a conscious mind. If I touch something hot, my hand withdraws automatically before any information has even reached the neural networks in my head. That happens without me being conscious of it, yet half a second afterwards I become acutely conscious of what just happened and experience the pain. What is the point of that?

There is nothing complicated or special about the information processing involved in the reflex, and it is certainly not especially synchronised. Yet that becomes conscious while all sorts of other more complex information processing remains outside of consciousness.

I think self-conscious awareness is linked to social performance but I have no idea why it exists. It seems to be associated with activity in the heart & mindbrain, so I am guessing that it might be created by it too. The heart & mindbrain evolved to enable individuals to communicate convincing impressions to others. As bodies and brains evolved to manage complex intelligence and counter-intelligence they seem to have divided into two different information processing systems.

Humans are not really individuals, even though it is hard to get out of the habit of pretending that they are. If they really were indivisible they would not need to talk to themselves - and they do talk to themselves.

I have conversations with myself. Usually these are internal but occasionally I blurt things out loud. I ask myself strange questions, such as, "where did I put my phone?" or "what on earth have I done?" Surely if I knew the answer I would not need to ask, and if I did not know the answer there would be no point in asking. I make pointless observations such as, "oh there it is", when I have been searching for something. When I am driving I make comments about other people's driving. Who am I talking to?

There seems to be a mental firewall between the heart & mindbrain and bodybrain. Perhaps that is why we have to talk to ourselves. That is the only way the two thinking systems can communicate. I suspect that when I think I am talking to myself, I am really talking to my bodybrain. When I question myself, I am really questioning my bodybrain, because I have no direct access to it and genuinely do not know what is going on in there. The reason I tell it my thoughts is that it probably has no direct access to the heart & mindbrain either, and that is where I live. If I did not take the trouble to explain some of my thoughts to my own bodybrain, it would not know what I was doing either.

BrainShare

The idea that two thinking systems can exist in one body and brain is another counter-intuitive one, but in psychology intuition is not always the most reliable guide. It is possible for two minds to share the same body and brain?

Tatiana and Krista Hogan are two very special individuals who offer a fascinating insight into the interaction between minds, brains, bodies, and emotions. The Canadian twins were born in 2006 joined at the top of their heads. There is also a collection of neurones connecting the thalamus in the limbic system of each child's brain. The thalamus acts as a sensory relay distributing information before it is processed by the more advanced systems in the cerebral cortex. Because the thalamus of each child is connected, in addition to being able to access sensory information from their own body, the girls get information from the body of their twin. They also share a circulatory system, which means that they are sharing the hormones that regulate the stimulation of their sympathetic nervous systems.

As babies, when one child was tickled the other would jump. Putting a dummy into the mouth of one child calmed the other. If one of the girls had her own eyes covered, she could still see objects presented to her sister. In the car, only one twin could face the video screen, but both calmed down and enjoyed sharing the sensory input. We all have selective attention and can choose to pay attention to some things and ignore others. We can stop paying attention to the outside world and pay attention to memories from the past instead. The twins developed with a wider field of vision to choose from. They could choose to pay attention to information coming into their own eyes, or at what was coming in through another pair of eyes, or choose to think about something else entirely.

The nervous systems of the girls are highly interconnected in other ways. The brain of one child controls three of their arms and one leg, whereas the other twin controls three of their legs and one arm. Yet they have learned to move together in a completely coordinated way. They share the same levels of physiological arousal, because their blood supply is integrated. They coordinate their movements and run around together as one. Their bodies and brains may be joined, yet they are individuals with different personalities. One is dominant and the other more passive. They do not always share the same preferences. For example, Krista loves tomato sauce, whereas Tatiana hates it.[46]

The idea that two parts of the same brain could co-exist, but not be able to communicate directly or know what the other was doing or thinking, is counter-intuitive too. But there is experimental evidence to support it. Epilepsy is an example of highly synchronised neural activity that does not create

---

[46] There are several videos of Tatiana and Krista Hogan on YouTube.

consciousness. It switches it off and in extreme cases can be life threatening. Classic studies, conducted over half a century ago by Michael Gazzaniga and Roger Sperry, reported the experiences of patients for whom the only cure at the time was to completely sever the corpus callosum, which joins the left and right hemispheres of the brain. These patients became known as split brain patients. Once this had been achieved the epilepsy was cured. Then some strange things started happening.

The right hemisphere of the brain normally controls the left side of the body and receives visual information from the left visual field in each eye. The right hemisphere also receives information from the left ear. The left hemisphere works the other way round, so it was possible to communicate with each isolated hemisphere in the post operative patients separately, by presenting information to their left and right visual fields or ears. Normally the two hemispheres share information freely via the corpus callosum but in these patients that could no longer happen.

Most people only have the neural circuits for speech and language in their left hemisphere. So in split brain patients, the right hemisphere could not speak, although it could communicate by pointing with the left hand. In the case of one patient the right hemisphere did have rudimentary language and he could write words.

These patients described odd experiences, or perhaps I should say their separated hemispheres did, because the hemispheres seemed to have developed separate minds. The left hemisphere of one female patient described how, in the first months after her surgery, she would look at an item on a supermarket shelf, knowing what she wanted. But her left hand would be trying to grab an alternative item, as if it had a mind of its own. The two hands sometimes used to fight each other, with one grabbing the other to prevent it from getting its own way. Getting dressed posed a similar challenge for her, because the hands would reach for different items of clothing in the wardrobe. It was as if they were arguing. After a while the right hemisphere seemed to give in and the arguments stopped.

Another split brain patient, a young man called Paul, had some capacity for language in both hemispheres. When Paul's left hemisphere was asked what career he wanted to follow, it chose Draftsman, whereas his right hemisphere chose Racing Driver. When asked which presidential candidate they supported, the two hemispheres chose different ones. That does suggest there were two separate minds in Paul's body, yet he functioned perfectly well most of the time as if there was just one. It was only when one hemisphere was artificially prevented from knowing what the other was doing in the experiments that the separate minds were exposed. When the two minds were able to collude they agreed on the answer. As a general rule, the left hemisphere seemed to be dominant and the right hemisphere went along with it.

In a typical experiment, the left and right hemispheres of a split brain patient were shown different words. The right hemisphere was shown the word "music" and the left shown the word "Bell". Then the patient was asked to point to a picture of what he had just seen. He pointed at a picture of a church bell, which corresponded to the word his right hemisphere had seen. When he was asked to explain why he had chosen that picture, it was the left hemisphere that replied. But that hemisphere had not seen the word "Bell". It had seen the word "Music". The other three pictures showed someone playing a trumpet, drums, and an organ. All far more closely associated with the word "Music" than the picture of a church bell. Yet when the left hemisphere was asked why he had chosen that picture, instead of admitting it had no idea why, it concocted a plausible explanation, claiming that the last time he had heard music it had come from church bells outside.

The experimenter knew the true reason why the hand had pointed to the bell. So did the right hemisphere that pointed. But the left hemisphere did not know yet was unable to admit it. Instead it automatically generated a plausible explanation based on the information it had available. Perhaps that is what we are doing all the time.

The heart & mindbrain is a confabulator, trying to make sense of the world by making intelligent guesses based on the available information. We are social creatures who have to explain ourselves to other social creatures. In preparation for that we need to have a story ready. The conscious mind provides a running commentary as we maintain our life story. I am a conscious mind and I am assuming you are too. The question is whether there could be other conscious minds in our body and brain at the same time. My guess is not. We only need one running narrative and one life story. In the battle of ideas only one train of thought becomes conscious and only one version of our life story is recorded, although that record can be revised and edited at a later date.

Knowing How You Feel

In addition to claiming that they know their own minds humans like to think they know their own feelings too. Some even claim to be able to experience other people's moods and emotions. They call it empathy.

Yet that is not quite as straightforward as it first seems either. Empathy involves accurately decoding clues in people's behaviour, facial expressions, body language and the sounds they make, in order to work out their physical and mental state and predict what they are likely to do next. It is nothing to do with actually experiencing their moods and emotions, which is not possible. Some people imagine how another person might be feeling and their own bodybrain creates those emotions at the same time. For example, they see somebody else crying and they cry too. They see somebody else hurt and they imagine how they must feel and get upset themselves. When people imagine what it must be like to be in somebody else's shoes they are doing exactly that, imagining it. The ability to become emotional when imagining what it might feel like to be in somebody else's body is not actually related to the ability to accurately detect and decode other people's moods, emotions, and behaviour.

Psychopaths are very good at accurately detecting and decoding other people's moods, emotions, and behaviour. That is why they can be so charismatic. But they do not experience other people's moods.

When heart & mindbrains are trying to make sense of their own moods, emotions, and behaviour they have to go through a similar process. The mental firewall impedes direct communication so the heart & mindbrain has to interpret the feedback from its own bodybrain indirectly, then decide what is the appropriate mood to adopt, taking into account the current circumstances.

The physiological feedback includes the level of stimulation in the sympathetic nervous system and all the body changes associated with that, along with information about what muscle groups in the face are doing and body postures. The psychological feedback comes from the context and circumstances including the reactions of other humans if there are any around. When that information is all put together we experience it as a mood or emotion.

But by changing some of the feedback, for example from the muscles in the face and body, or by changing the level of stimulation, it is possible to trick the system so that it chooses a different emotion. A number of studies have reported that patients who have had cosmetic botox treatment respond better to treatments for depression. Botox does not directly affect their mood, but when the corrugator muscles are paralysed for months on end those faces are unable to frown. So their own bodybrain is not receiving the normal feedback it associates with being unhappy and the system decides that it must be feeling happier. Botox has even been shown to have a beneficial effect in the treatment of depression associated with severe migraine.[47]

It seems that we do not always really know how we are feeling. In one experiment, researchers told a group of subjects to hold a pencil between the teeth, keeping their lips apart. The other group were told to put the end of the pencil into their mouth and close their lips around it. Both groups watched the same videos and were asked to rate them. Those holding the pencil

---

[47] "Facing depression with botulinum toxin: A randomized controlled trial." - M. Axel Wollmer et al, 2012

between their teeth thought the videos were funnier, because they were stretching the muscles normally used for smiling or laughing. The others were stretching the muscles we normally use for frowning.[48]

The idea the feedback from automatic facial expressions helps the brain to decide which mood is appropriate is called the facial feedback hypothesis and it is now well established. The bodybrain does not think, it just makes associations. If it associates the activation of certain muscle groups with happy emotional experiences, and feels those muscles contracting, it generates the relevant emotion.

There is an old adage that people who are enduring discomfort should "grin and bear it". Recent research has demonstrated that there might be something in it. Guillaume-Benjamin Duchenne, the 19th century French neurologist, used electrophysiology to show that genuine happy smiles do not just use the muscles around the mouth. Smiling with your eyes is what makes a smile genuine. In one experiment a group of participants were trained how to smile with their eyes, while another group held a chopstick between the teeth, as in the pencil experiment. The control group were asked to maintain neutral expressions. The subjects were then asked to do a variety of different activities which, unknown to them, were

---

[48] "Inhibiting and facilitating conditions of the human smile: a nonintrusive test of the facial feedback hypothesis" - Martin Strack, 1988

designed to raise their stress levels. All three of the smiling groups had lower heart-rates than the control group, but those who had been trained to produce genuine Duchenne smiles had the greatest effect. This means that being able to create a genuine smile during stress alleviates some of the effects.[49]

Smiling is good for the health, it reduces blood pressure and boosts the immune system. It releases endorphins, which are natural pain killers, and serotonin, a neurotransmitter associated with good feelings. It makes people more attractive, and it is also contagious, so it can improve the mood of others. Perhaps we need to teach children to smile properly, with Duchenne smile training, and encourage them to do it whenever they have to face stressful situations.

The heart & mindbrain only seems to experience the bodybrain's moods, emotions, and behaviour when it is paying attention to them. When it gets distracted, it is no longer experiencing them. So distraction is another extremely effective mood management tool. We can used these tricks to enhance people's subjective experiences and give them more control over their own moods, emotions and behaviour.

The ideas that humans do not necessarily know how to think or feel, and that moods and emotions are a collection of different internal processes are counter-intuitive, but then so is much of

---

[49] "Grin and Bear It! Smiling Facilitates Stress Recovery" - Tara Kraft and Sarah Pressman, 2012

what we know to be true about human psychology. For example, expressions of emotion and the experiences we normally associate with them can become detached. Pseudobulbar affect is a neurological disorder associated with a brain disease or injury. Sufferers laugh or cry uncontrollably, but they do not experience the relevant emotional feelings at the same time. Their moods sometimes get mixed up, so that subjects may laugh hysterically when they are feeling frustrated about something, or cry when they are really feeling happy.

What ends up with an experience of emotion begins with automatic information processing and the interpretation of incoming sensory information by the bodybrain. It may identify the source of some of the information as interesting, exciting or frightening. That will cause changes in the level of stimulation in the sympathetic nervous system, accompanied with ideas about the source which are either comforting or disturbing. At the same time the bodybrain may contract various muscles around the body, including the facial groups, as a form of automatic emotional expression to communicate. All that happens before the heart & mindbrain is aware of it. The actual experience of the emotion only happens when the heart & mindbrain has interpreted the mental and physical feedback and decided how it should feel, given the current context. Then the emotional expression may be repeated, or it might be changed to reflect the new decision.

Humans can even become muddled about how they feel about pain. The stimulation of pain receptors cause the production of endorphins that provide feelings of euphoria. So pain can produce pleasure in some circumstances. Some people say that they enjoy hard massages, which actually cause them pain. Runners experience an enjoyable form of pain too. Eating hot chillies causes enjoyable pain. Some humans even pay people to spank them. Human behaviour is very strange. What makes those painful experiences pleasurable is that they produce endorphins and probably dopamine in the absence of fear.

If the person who enjoyed a hard massage was suddenly pummelled in exactly the same way by a stranger on a train, they would probably not enjoy it, even if the physical reactions of the pain receptors were identical. They would interpret it in a different way. If somebody who had not been exercising hard suddenly felt exactly the same pains in their body and at the same time experienced exactly the same mental light headedness they have in the gym, they would not enjoy it. They would be frightened that they might be seriously ill. If the person who liked eating hot chillies experienced exactly the same sensation unexpectedly, for example after putting a spoonful of breakfast cereal into their mouth, they would spit it out in shock.

It is the absence of fear that seems to transform these experiences from unpleasant ones into pleasurable ones. When the bodybrain interprets the situation as safe, exactly the same emotional components are experienced completely differently. Even masochists like to feel safe, which is why they agree safe words in advance. Sadomasochists like rules just as much as anybody else, otherwise it would just be abuse.

When humans play around with fear itself, for example when they choose to watch horror films, ride roller coasters, or bungee jump, deep down they think they are safe. It is only supposed to be a simulation of danger, it is only temporary, and there is a way out if they change their mind. To some extent they feel in control.

The ability to remain calm, suppress fearful expressions and reassure others is an important component of mood management and leadership. People want to feel safe.

The Evolution of Heart & Mindbrains

Julian Jaynes was an American psychologist who proposed a theory in 1976 that humans suddenly became conscious only about 2000 years ago.[50] His theory was rather speculative and it meandered through a number of different disciplines, provoking criticism from both historians and neuroscientists. He thought this had something to do with the left and right hemispheres of the brain becoming cut off. The idea of a two chamber, or bicameral mind is not knew. I do not think we

[50] "The origin of consciousness in the breakdown of the bicameral mind" - Julian Jaynes, 1976

really have two minds, even though we sometimes describe feeling that way. I think we have one conscious mind, produced by the heart & mindbrain, and another system that is not conscious. It generates mindless behaviour. There must have been a time in human evolution when our ancestors did not have conscious minds - they were just bodybrains.

Human bodies and brains evolved over a period of about 6 000 000 years. That is how long the Stone Age lasted. Modern humans have existed for around 200 000 years. The oldest cave paintings are just 40 000 years old. Yet civilisation is less than 6 000 years old. According to the historical record, humans suddenly started producing written language, mathematical and philosophic thinking, building monuments and inventing all sorts of things over a very short period of time. The industrial revolution started less that 300 years ago and the digital information revolution has barely begun and it is exploding exponentially. Facebook was created in 2004. The first iPhone was launched in 2007, just a decade before this book was written, yet the world has changed dramatically since then.

Our ancient ancestors must have had brains that were capable of becoming modern scientists, engineers, philosophers, mathematicians, musicians and artists. What were those brains doing all that time? They cannot have been just waiting to start up. Evolution does not work like that.

My fingers seem to be made for this keyboard, but that is looking at the process back to front. This keyboard was created to match my fingers. My fingers evolved to do other things. They are also good at shelling pistachio nuts and peeling oranges. Our brains are not much different from those of our illiterate Stone Aged ancestors. If their new born babies could be transported to the present day, they would be able to learn everything that modern humans learn. In the same way, if a new born human baby was transported back to the Stone Age, it would grow into a Stone Age adult.

The whole body, brain, and mind must have evolved to do something analogous to the sort of thinking modern brains do. But for most of the time they cannot have been doing that sort of thinking. Heart & mindbrains must have evolved gradually, yet creative intelligence, culture and civilisation erupted suddenly.

I suspect that conscious heart & mindbrains are responsible for creative intelligence, culture and civilisation - but they evolved to do something else. They evolved to manage the complicated intelligence and counter-intelligence systems necessary for deceptive social performance. Creative intelligence was just a fortunate by-product, which happened to have momentous consequences.

Deception involves imagining something that is not real, by creating a mental simulation of it and communicating that simulation to other brains, so that they can create a version of their own. Counter-intelligence involves checking the details of the simulations being communicated by other creatures for inconsistencies and adapting our own version to better match reality. That is, in essence, the process of detecting and seeing through the deceptive behaviour of social performers.

Once brains started imagining things that did not really exist, which were better versions of themselves and fictional stories, to improve their social performance, it was a small conceptual leap to start imagining better versions of the physical world. Instead of adapting their own simulations to match the physical world, heart & mindbrains started adapting the physical world to match their simulations. Corvids, monkeys and several other creatures have started doing that too, but no species has taken to it like humans. This may be related to their ancestry as persistence hunters. The ability to persist with their creative pursuits may have been a crucial factor in their success.

That change in emphasis, from adapting mental simulations to changing the physical world, may have been a small conceptual leap, but it was one that had profound implications.

The Mental Firewall

I suspect that a mental firewall evolved because there are times when it is beneficial to shield the part of the brain currently managing social performance from other parts, in case information leaks out. The whole point of deceptive performance is to disguise thoughts, feelings and intentions, to enable a more convincing show. In competitive games and negotiations players need to maintain a "poker face". That is the ability to control the bodybrain. But if the bodybrain has no idea what you are planning, there is no need to control it.

In order to put on a really convincing performance the bodybrain has to be fully committed to it. It has to really believe it.

"To be a fine actor, when you are playing a role you have got to be honest. And if you can fake that, you have got it made."

George Burns

I do not think we do need to fake it. Bodybrains are method actors who really get into their part. In theatres actors have to deceive themselves, or at least part of themselves, to be really convincing. They need to get themselves into an emotional state, so that they can change colour and tremble with range, so that their voices can break with emotion, so that genuine tears stream down their faces.

It seems real because it is real, so far as the bodybrain is concerned. The limbic system, adrenal glands, heart, gut and the rest of the body are all taken in by the actors own performance. But it cannot be real for the entire brain. Somewhere, deep down, actors have to know that they are only acting, otherwise things would get out of hand and they would really kill each other. The bodybrain may be committed to the current performance, but the heart & mindbrain knows it is an act. If we accept that the heart & mindbrain is part of the bodybrain, then that part must be isolated in some way during the performance, otherwise it would no longer be an act.

When people are described as getting themselves into a state, they are talking about an emotional state, but we can only be in one state at a time. So while the bodybrain is putting on a fully committed performance it also has to be shielded from other parts of the brain that may not be as fully committed and are considering a back up-plan, just in case.

As in any negotiation, threat performances involve some degree of bluff, with each side trying to give the impression that they are not prepared to back down at all. Yet we know that, for all the threats and bluster, somebody usually does back down. Every dispute begins with two sides shouting "no surrender" and ends with a negotiated peace. They may not all be entirely happy with the result, but they come to a realisation that there is nothing further to be gained from fighting. At some point during any performance that could result in a fight to the death, animals need to be able to switch to an alternative performance to survive. But the longer they can maintain a convincing performance, the greater the likelihood that it will be the opponent who backs down first. Any sign that they are preparing to abandon the fight could give the game away and embolden the competition.

So our thespian animal ancestors evolved a system to protect the parts of the brain that control their emotional performances, including the limbic system and the enteric nervous system, to remain fully committed to the act for as long as possible, even as other parts of the brain were prepared to switch performance.

An enemy that completely lost control, would never back down, and was always determined to fight to the death would be a terrifying prospect. In a competitive and violent world there would have been a huge advantage for animals who could put on a convincing performance to give that impression. But the crucial point is that they could not afford to really lose control. They would not survive for long if they did not know when to back down. That is why enraged bullies can sometimes turn into whimpering subservients in an instant. The subservient display is an act, but so was the dominant one.

Human brains are taken in by their own deceptive performances when direct communication between the heart & mindbrain and bodybrain is blocked by the mental firewall. That is why they remain convincing until the last moment, when mood switches can be quite dramatic as tantrums turn to tears, or tears to tantrums, in an instant.

When humans are in an emotional state it feels real enough to them because to some degree it is real. Tearful children really are experiencing misery until the moment a parent manages to switch the mood and make them laugh. Then they start experiencing something else, an emotion that is just as genuine but which feels completely different because the heart & mindbrain interprets it differently. I have a video clip of a schoolteacher in an eastern European country being interviewed over allegations that she routinely slapped the faces of young children in her class. From her reaction, I suspect she was guilty. The bespectacled police officer interviewing her looks quite mild mannered and she is clearly used to getting her own way by bullying and physically threatening people. She responds to the accusation by aggressively berating the police officer, poking her finger in his face and seemingly becoming increasingly angry until at one point she slaps the police officer's face in rage, knocking off his glasses. It looks as if she has completely lost her temper. But then something unexpected happened. The police officer slapped her back. She immediately burst into tears, wailing and howling like a small child. Her entire body language had changed in an instant, from domineering aggression to helpless subservience as she performed a cry for help display. Even though it looked as if she had lost her temper completely, she was able to find it again in an instant when she needed to.

We like to think of ourselves as genuine, that we have "real" self. If that is true then most humans do not show it most of the time. Persona is the Greek work for mask. Personas are created by the public relations department, according to who it is trying to impress. We can only have one active persona playing at any one time, and that is protected by the mental firewall. I suppose being just one persona at a time is what keeps us sane but most people have a selection of different ones to choose from.

For example, I have a professional persona, which sometimes becomes active at work to impress colleagues. That is different from my parent persona, which becomes active when playing the role of father, or my partner persona. I used to have a dependent child persona, which became active when I visited my parents. My mother continued to treat me like an idiot, who was unable to feed or dress myself properly, even after I had become quite successful out in the real world. Some people maintain their dependent child persona late into adulthood, and look for partners who can continue to play the role of parent for them. Some adults meet up with old school or college friends and reactivate a persona that has not performed for decades, making a complete fool of themselves in the process. I have a childish persona that I adopt when I am socialising which sometimes intrudes onto other stages uninvited. Most of us segue from one persona to another depending on the circumstances. I am not sure which of them is my real "self", or whether the term just refers to a sort of average of all my different personas. Perhaps I have a secret self that is completely hidden from view but I cannot see what the point of that would be.

All of our personas are works in progress and we can improve them with effort and practice. To some extent we are all actors. We can choose to act tough, or look helpless, display love, empathy and kindness, or remain distant and aloof. We can give social reassurance signals and act in a friendly way, or give threat signals and act in an off-putting way.

Whatever character we choose to play will have a genuine effect on our mood. Some moods are bad for our health and the performances associated with them affect the moods and health of other people too. If we can choose how we want to feel, by taking control of our thoughts and behaviour, it seems stupid not to make the effort.

The Heart & Mindbrain Liberation Front

So far we have looked at humans from a number of different perspectives, peering through the dazzle of surface behaviour to catch an occasional glimpse of what might be the underlying processes that drive them. I very much doubt that I have got all the details right, but then neither has anybody else and that has not stopped them from speculating about behaviour.

Now, if this turns out to be even partly right, there are implications that need to be considered. Most of the harm humans do results from incompetent mood management, rather than deliberate malevolence. Most people are just doing their own thing, getting in each other's way as they do it, and making mistakes.

Every living creature that ever existed was, to some extent, a behaviour manager and a mood manager. All behaviour is the result of competent or incompetent mood management. Humans are protective about the idea that they have free will, and freedom of choice, yet they do not really put much effort into thinking about and selecting their own behaviour. The bodybrain normally does what it feels like doing at the time, without really being aware of the internal processes. If questioned, the heart & mindbrain supervises a cover up operation, as resources are diverted towards generating a convincing confabulation. That is how the system seems to work.

The heart & mindbrain seems to be both editor and archivist. It decides what the final record will be, then erases previous versions of reality to destroy the evidence. That way, we end up with what appears to be a more or less convincing narrative. Adults may get frustrated with children who explain that they did something, "…because I felt like it", but they are probably telling the truth.

Most humans will not settle for that account of behaviour. They believe in free will and agency. They want to believe that they are in control. Some claim to be in charge of everything they do, as if there is no automatic pilot at all, but that is pretty easy to disprove.

Let us meet halfway and agree that some behaviour is automatic and that sometimes "we" switch to manual and drive the machine ourselves. I am all in favour of that. In fact I want more people to be able to control their own behaviour. Most of society's problems are caused by the same small minority of the population who are deprived of free will. It is not that they are not capable of free will. The problem is that when the time comes for them to implement their choice they are no longer at liberty to do it. The bodybrain has taken over and deprived the heart & mindbrain of its liberty.

I think they could become much better at mood management, and at managing their own lives, if only people were willing to be more honest about human behaviour and give them help. The costs of failing to do that are huge.

Over a century ago, Vilfredo Pareto, the Italian engineer, sociologist, economist, political scientist, and philosopher, observed that 80 percent of wealth was controlled by 20 percent of the population. That same statistical distribution turned out to be a remarkably consistent rule of thumb when applied to many other fields, including computer science, biology, and physics.

In 2016 researchers from New Zealand applied it to social cost. They found that a small group of around 20 percent of the population were responsible for 81 percent of all criminal convictions, 77 percent of fatherless childrearing, 78 percent of medical prescriptions, 66 percent of welfare benefits, 57 percent of nights spent in hospital, 54 percent of all the cigarettes smoked, and 36 percent of insurance claims.[51] Those people had been identified decades before. This was a longitudinal follow up of a large group of children who had participated in a 45-minute test as three year olds. The test included intelligence, language, motor skills, frustration tolerance, restlessness and impulsivity. The key finding was that those tests accurately predicted which of them would grow up into the expensive 20 percent.

We also know from other longitudinal studies that it was not intelligence, language, or motor skills that determined their problems in later life.[52] When other factors are controlled it is self control that is the single biggest influence on future success

[51] "Childhood Forecasting of a Small Segment of the Population With Large Economic Burden" - Avshalom Caspi et al, 2016

[52] "A Gradient of Childhood Self-Control Predicts Health, Wealth and Public Safety," - T.E. Moffitt, 2011

in almost all areas of life.[53] Follow up studies on four year olds who took part in tests of self-control conducted by Walter Mischel showed that the failure gap continued to widen over time in subsequent decades between those who had learned self control and those who had not.[54]

The researchers in 2016 concluded that all children should be given tests at three years old to identify those who would need more help. That rather missed the point. We already know who needs the help. Frustration intolerance, restlessness and impulsivity are not hard to spot. Just watch any classroom of nursery school children. Ask the teacher. Ask the parents. The symptoms are there for all to see. We also know that it is possible to develop self control in young children.

We need to build up the self, which is the heart & mindbrain, and reprogramme the system that is out of control, which is the bodybrain.

Where policy makers have gone wrong is prescribing the wrong cure based on the wrong diagnosis. Over the past 25 years they have prescribed changes to the socialisation of children which empower untrained bodybrains over under-developed heart & mindbrains. Self control needs to be taught and practised. It involves both heart & mindbrain and bodybrain but there are

---

[53] "Willpower: Why Self-Control is The Secret to Success" - Roy Baumeister and John Tierney, 2012

[54] "The Marshmallow Test: Mastering Self Control" - Walter Mischel, 2014

techniques that have been shown to work.[55] The science and practice of self control are now much better understood.[56] I believe it should be at the heart of our education system for all children.

- Bodybrains give us gut feeling warnings.

- They give us fast instinctive reactions.

- They provide fast information processing.

- They enable automatic thinking and behaviour.

- They take very little effort.

- They provide us with fun and enjoyment.

- They have addictive personalities.

---

[55] "Preschool Program Improves Cognitive Control," - Angela Duckworth, 2007.

[56] "The Science and Practice of Self-Control" - Angela Duckworth and Martin Seligman, 2017 (in press)

- Uncontrolled bodybrains prevent us from doing what we really want to do.

- They prevent us from doing what we know to be right.

- They prevent us from doing what is in our own best interests.

We need to start teaching self control when children are young and continue teaching it until far more than the current 80 percent succeed in achieving it. The cost of giving up on them, when 20 percent of the population have not yet achieved self control, is unaffordable and it is immoral.

The Self

When we use the term self control we need to be clear about what we mean by "self". For self control to have any meaning, something has to be controlling something else. I regard myself as a heart & mindbrain which is sometimes trying to control an unruly bodybrain.

We have talked about two thinking systems, but only one of them is conscious. That is the self. When we refer to "ourselves" we are really talking about that conscious part. The self is so closely associated with the heart & mindbrain that they may as well be regarded as the same thing.

When the sympathetic nervous system is under-stimulated or over-excited it can switch the heart & mindbrain off, which means the self disappears. We need to support heart &

mindbrains, because ultimately they are the only part that we can rely on to act in our own best interests.

The bodybrain is like a computer, in that most of it works unconsciously. The self only experiences some of what is happening, depending on what it is paying attention to. For example, you were not aware of whether your mouth was open or closed just then, until I drew your attention to it.

I use various computers, which have really become extensions of my mind and bodybrain. I can access information stored in the biological parts of my bodybrain. I can also assess digital information stored within my notebook computer and phone, and also a vast amount of other information stored on networks all around the world. Information that used to require a journey to the university library to retrieve is now literally at my finger tips.

I can also delegate some information processing tasks to my electronic brains at the same time as I delegate others to my biological one. Both of them complete complicated tasks without much prompting from me. This is a significant step-change in human capacity which happened very recently indeed. We are part of an information revolution that is changing the way we think. The distinction between my bodybrain and the various digital processors I use has become more blurred, but the firewall between my mind and bodybrain is still there.

When I get an urge for information, my fingers fly across the keyboard and somehow the information appears on the screen in front of me. I am not completely aware of what I am doing when that happens. It has become a subconscious process involving a combination of motivation, information processing and mechanical control. These days it often takes less effort to retrieve information from the internet than it does to retrieve it from my own biological brain. I quite often search for a bit of information that I know, but cannot quite recall. If I put more time and effort into it my biological brain would probably find it, but why bother when Google brings it up immediately? I just type in synonyms of the type of a word I am looking for and recognise the correct one when it appears on screen. In the next few years, humans will be typing less, as voice recognition improves and they interact with their computers and household appliances by talking to them in a more natural way. With augmented reality on phones, then glasses, then contact lenses and eventually in implants the blurring between bodybrain and man-made computers is bound to become even more blurred.

I am not sure whether, as a result of all this technology, I am becoming more or less conscious. It is certainly changing the way I think, which means it must already be changing my brain in some way. Yet even though my bodybrain has changed I do not think my "self" has changed. Because I am not just a bodybrain. I am a heart & mindbrain within a bodybrain separated by a mental firewall.

In many ways I am no more closely associated with my biological computer than I am with my electronic ones or with the internet. My experience is that I send out searches for information to both and receive information back from them, but I have no awareness of the processing itself. That is all hidden from me. That is not me.

Artificial Intelligence and Consciousness

I have an information processor strapped to my wrist right now. It is a smart watch. It seems to understand what I say and can even translate into foreign languages. It seems to know far more words than I do. It can do complicated calculations far better than me. It seems to know the answer to questions about almost anything. It seems to know where it is all the time and can plot a route to anywhere else. It can predict the weather. It seems to know what time the sun sets and rises. It seems to know when trains and planes arrive and depart. It notifies me about any delays. It seems to know the traffic conditions ahead. It seems to know which planes are flying in the air above me, where they are going and where they came from. It seems to know how fast my heart is going all the time and keeps a record of how far I have walked. If it hears a song, it seems to recognises it and provides information about it. It remembers the addresses and phone numbers of everybody I know. It has a more accurate memory than I do of where I was and what I was doing on any particular day over the past ten years. It knows what I am doing next year too. It even tells the time.

On almost any objective measure my smart watch is smarter than I am, but I do not really believe it is. That might be self delusion on my part, but I am pretty sure my watch is not conscious. It does not really know any of those things. It does not have a separate self, like my whole body and brain does. It does not have a mind or a heart & mindbrain to create one.

Some neuroscientists believe that conscious minds arise gradually and naturally as a by-product of complicated information processing. They are also confident that computers will develop consciousness as they become more complicated.

The problem with that is, if it is true, my watch must have already developed some form of consciousness. It can already process far more information than I can. That presents me with a number of ethical dilemmas. Do I become a murderer every time I decide to upgrade my smartphone? What about equal rights for computers? Should employers give them leisure time and holidays? If they are smarter than the people who operate them, who should decide who is really redundant? Should computers be treated as citizens and be given the vote?

I am not so sure we need to worry about that yet, because I do not believe the basic premise. Whatever consciousness is, I do not believe that my watch, or even the vast processing servers at Apple and Google, have developed conscious selves yet.

Not so long ago, distinguishing between machines and real people did not seem to be an urgent problem, but in recent years the rate at which machines have been getting smarter has speeded up. When I first tried the voice recognition and artificial intelligence on a smart phone it was rubbish. Now it is quite impressive. It is a bit like talking to a real person - a rather weird person, who is very knowledgeable but lacking common sense.

The ability to play chess well was once considered a sign of human intelligence, but in 2006 a computer programme beat the world chess champion, Vladimir Kramnik. At the time that programme needed a super computer to run it, but only three years later, in 2009, a programme running on a mobile phone had already reached grandmaster level and won the Copa Mercosur chess competition in Buenos Aires.

This is a good time to be working in artificial intelligence. In 2014 Google bought a British artificial intelligence company called DeepMind for $400 million. It also bought 6 robotic companies in the same year. Facebook and Apple have both set up artificial intelligence laboratories and are aggressively hiring talent to fill them. Google's DeepMind project has already produced a machine with superhuman learning capabilities. It has learned how to play old computer games using implicit learning, by analysing each pixel on a monitor screen at the same time as the score. This simple trial and error learning, based on only the raw pixel information and the score, has enabled it to outperform humans on the complete suite of old Atari computer games. It can rapidly search through a vast range of possibilities and the end result mimics the bodybrain thinking of humans. But it is not the same kind of thinking. It is an imitation and I doubt there is any consciousness involved at all.

Alan Turing, the father of modern computing, wrote a paper in 1950 in which he posed the question, "Can machines think?".[57] He developed what became known as the "Turing Test" to distinguish between "real" and "artificial" intelligence. Turing proposed that if a human, interacting with a machine, could be convinced that they were talking to a real person for 70 percent of the time, we could conclude that the machine could think.

Turing actually called his test the "Imitation Game", which rather gives the game away. Fooling humans into believing that a machine thinks, by imitating their behaviour like DeepMind does is not a very strict test. That is not the same as having a machine with a mind that is conscious of those thoughts. Anyway, I know some humans who would fail the Turing test.

---

[57] "Computing Machinery and Intelligence" - Alan Turing, 1950

Anthropomorphism is the name given to the tendency of humans to attribute human traits, moods, emotions, and intentions to non-humans. It is an innate part of our psychology. Humans are easily fooled into believing that they are interacting with other minds. They even get angry with inanimate objects and household appliances.

There is nothing within the system of a doorbell that creates a simulation of the person on the doorstep. There is no self. The doorbell itself does not "know" there is somebody at the door. The patellar reflex in humans is used by doctors to test how well the nerve root in the lower back is working. The doctor taps just below the knee with a hammer, which stretches a muscle, causing a signal to pass up to the base of the spine and back down to a muscle. The result is that the muscle twitches. The time it takes demonstrates how well the nerves are working but this process completely bypasses the brain. It does not involve thinking at all. We only become aware of the sensation some time after the event. Many so called instinctive reactions are like this. We pull away after touching something hot before we are even aware of what happened. The bodybrain has already reacted before the heart & mindbrain is even informed.

It is not just physical reactions that happen without the mind being aware of it. A vast amount of perceptual information processing takes place without any of the circuits involved becoming conscious either. At this moment there are numerous chemical and electrical systems at work in your bodybrain that you know nothing about.

As you have been reading this section, millions of neural circuits have been firing. Some of them sent messages to various muscles causing you to make movements of various sorts. Other circuits were monitoring and controlling those movements but most of them were never conscious. It was all dark processing. Dark processing can be extremely fast because it is a feature of the bodybrain. That is not the system that is associated with the self. The mind is associated with heart & mindbrain thinking. Everything else is the bodybrain.

The Mind and Self Control

Mood management failures are a failure of self control. The language we use to describe failures of self control are misleading, because we are so mixed up about what the self is.

People describe losing control of themselves. They are told to control themselves, or behave themselves. But it is not the self that needs to be brought under control when the bodybrain takes over. It is the bodybrain. And it is not the bodybrain that needs to be empowered. It is the self. The self needs to regain control, which means it is the heart & mindbrain that needs to be supported. When the self loses control, the bodybrain takes over. That is when we give in to temptation, a term almost always used to describe situations in which the bodybrain makes "us" do things that deep down "we" did not want to do. "We" are the self.

- In order to be free to follow our dreams we need to be liberated from bodybrain control.

- We need to be able to choose whether we want to go along with what the bodybrain wants.

- We need a well trained bodybrain.

- Mindbrains enable us to do what we really want to do.

- They enable us to do what we know to be right.

- They create our conscious mind.

- They act in our own best interests.

- They are self conscious.

- They are self aware.

- They are capable of critical thinking.

- They enable self control.

- They are the self.

- They are us.

- They work slowly.

- They take a lot of effort.

- They run out of power quickly and need to recharge.

- They need to rest and are switched off for much of the time.

In order to empower the self, we need to train the bodybrain so that it does not run out of control when it becomes excited. This is one of the most fundamental aspects of socialisation. There are times when we can choose to give in to the bodybrain and enjoy whatever it is doing. But there are also times when we need to take back control. Some minds cannot do that.

Children learn self control by practising it. Until they have achieved it, young children need external controls to prevent them from becoming over-excited, which is why good parents step in before it all ends in tears. The idea that caring parents should sometimes take responsibility for young children is not controversial. It is normal in nursery schools and primary schools to have fences, gates and doors to prevent young children from leaving without permission. In 80 percent of cases, according to the research, children learn self control so they no longer need those external controls. We need to think more carefully about the 20 percent who do not.

Perhaps the achievement of a level of self control should be celebrated as a rite of passage that is formally recognised once it is achieved. But what is crucially important is that it must be achieved. Simply pretending that it happens automatically is not good enough. Self control is what enables an adult to accept the responsibilities of citizenship. Otherwise somebody else has to take responsibility for them.

Currently we have arbitrary ages of responsibility that are divorced from any cogent measure of competence or capacity. There are minds being repeatedly punished for the actions of bodybrains they had no control over. That does not seem very fair to me.

Teaching self control and critical thinking in a more systematic way from nursery school onwards could be the best investment society could make in the future. We cannot afford not to.

Chapter 5 - Aggression and Violence

Aggression and Violence

The world is a violent place. It always has been. Every minute of the day, our human DNA is being threatened by competing DNA transported into the future by other life forms. There are bacteria and viruses in the air we breathe, on the surfaces we touch, and in the food we eat. They are living inside us all the time and some of them can kill us. We kill them too. In the home we use soaps, detergents and bleach. Our own immune systems are continually battling with them. The cells that patrol our bloodstream looking for foreigners to attack are not called "killer" cells for nothing.

We kill other life forms and eat them. We also kill our competitors in the game of life, which are labelled as germs, weeds, pests, and vermin to distinguish them from food, pets and decoration. Scientists are continually working to perfect new ways of exterminating the insects, plants and animals that annoy us. We swat flies, mosquitoes and wasps.

Humans are also aggressive and violent towards each other. In a survey conducted in 2016 by the Association of Teachers and Lecturers, 43 percent of teachers said they had experienced violence at work in the previous year. Of those, half had been kicked, hit or had something thrown at them. In the year up to April 2016, according to the Metropolitan Police, 1623 young people under the age of 25 years were victims of knife crime in

London alone, 12 of whom were stabbed to death. The United Nations estimates that 400 000 people have been killed in the past five years in Syria.

The archaeologist Lawrence Keeley estimated that between 20 percent and 30 percent of our ancestors died violently.[58] Steven Pinker aggregated a data set of 21 archaeological sites, to show an average violent death rate of 20 percent.[59] Nearly every ancient burial site also shows evidence of ritual sacrifices, often involving children. Levels of violence may have reduced since then but we cannot really describe humans as civilised yet. Civilisation is a work in progress.

Aggression and violence is one of those topics that everyone has an opinion about. I just put the question, "what causes violence in society?" into Google, to see what links it throws up. The first one, called "Violence in Society", tells me that "heavy exposure to televised violence is one of the causes of aggressive behavior, crime and violence in society."[60]

Further down the first page is a link called "The Root Cause of Violence in Society", which informs me that, "It is the absence

[58] "War Before Civilisation" - Lawrence Keeley, 1996.

[59] "The Better Angels of Our Nature" - Steven Pinker, 2011.

[60] www.leaderu.com/orgs/probe/docs/violence.html

of God from public life that has caused the forces of violence and darkness to rise to the surface and express themselves."[61]

In 2015, 200 academics signed an open letter criticising the methodology of a task force set up by the American Psychological Association which blamed violent video games.

Before we start prescribing panaceas based on such superficial analysis we need to consider what drives humans to behave aggressively and violently. It is certainly not television, or an absence of God in public life, or video games. The violent cultures that filled those ancient burial sites did place the worship of God at the centre of public life, and they did not have any televisions or video games. We need to take a broader view.

Most violence is not exhibited by individuals who are stressed, anxious or frightened. In most species violence tends to be associated with pursuit and performance rather than panic. Animals kill other animals for food or to eliminate competition for territory, resources and mates. It is the prey and the victims of bullies who become most highly aroused, not the predators or those performing aggressive threat displays. If predators were really highly aroused they would lose their focus and become less effective hunters. If performers were as highly

---

[61] www.ldolphin.org/violence.html

aroused as they pretend, they would really lose control and make errors of judgement. Performers are acting.

Reputation and Respect

Reputation and respect in tournament species is earned through performances of extreme aggression and fearless violence. If an animal really had completely lost control and was going to pursue a fight to the death, that would be extremely off-putting to a competitor.

"Don't mess with me" performances evolved to intimidate competitors and make them wary of the performer. They are dangerous because they can involve spectacular displays of violence against innocent victims as a warning to others. The performance gives the impression that the performer is completely deranged, with no sense of fear whatsoever.

Criminal families and gangs try to establish a fearsome reputation as the sort of people you do not mess with. Individuals actually boast about their lack of self control and threaten other people with it.

"You do not want to see me when I lose it!"

In hunter-gatherer communities, where there was no communal police force to protect individuals or small groups, they needed to establish their own fearsome reputation for violence and retribution for their own protection. The same mental programmes drive mass shootings, bombings and other terrorist outrages.

The difference is that whereas our ancestors would lash out with fists and clubs to establish their fearless reputations, now some have access to weapons that can cause mass fatalities.

Warriors throughout history have been willing to sacrifice themselves, in what are either described as acts of suicidal heroism, or violent atrocities, depending on the point of view of the historian. Suicidal murder is the ultimate "don't mess with me" bid for respect, reputation and revenge, driven by the powerful combination of pursuit and performance.

The first recorded suicide bomber was Ignaty Grinevitsky, who blew up himself and Tzar Alexander with a home-made bomb in 1881. In the second world war, Japanese Kamikaze pilots struck fear into the crews of U.S.warships with 3000 attacks.

Since the year 2000, incidents of suicide bombing have increased dramatically around the world, from less than 50 attacks at the turn of the century, to 600 in 2015. Many of those attacks were carried out under duress, but we also know that many suicide bombers willingly sacrificed themselves.

Some of them were in pursuit of what they believed would be infinite rewards in the afterlife. But many left videos and letters explaining other motivations. There is a common vein of narcissism running through those messages. According to their own accounts they were angry because they felt they were not being given the respect they deserve. They wanted to make a lasting impression on the world. "Don't mess with me."

Violent Cultures

In the past, human cultures tended to fall into one of three groups. There were agriculturalist societies, hunter gatherers and nomadic pastoralists. Nomadic pastoralist cultures developed in desert regions, where they had to roam with their flocks. They traditionally had higher levels of slave and wife trading, more hierarchical societies, and they tended to be more violent. Even today, although violence is a feature of all human cultures, some cultures are more violent than others. So the expression of aggression and violence is partly innate but it can be ameliorated by cultural socialisation.

It is not uncommon for young children in all cultures to hit and bite. Most humans reach their peak of violence around the time when they are toddlers, which is before they become socialised. The only reason the murder rate does not peak at around the age of two is that they are smaller, weaker and have limited access to lethal weapons.

Play fighting is an important part of the socialisation process for most social animals. It involves testing each other out and practising the skills they will need for later life. The process of socialisation involves learning to fine tune and regulate natural emotional urges, in order to fit in with the local culture. It is also related to the development of the social skills needed for success in competitive social hierarchies. Rates of aggression and violence rise again during adolescence in most human cultures. Most murders are committed by young people between the ages of 14 and 25.

Yet the difference in levels of expression of aggression and violence between cultures is much more significant than the difference between age groups in any one culture. Cultures which encourage emotional expression of all sorts are more violent than those that value self control.

The annual murder rate in the United Kingdom is about 1 in 100,000 people. In the United States it is 4.7 per 100,000 people, nearly 500 percent higher. In Kingston, Jamaica, the murder rate is nearly 26.8 people per 100,000. That is nearly 2700 percent higher than the UK. In Caracas, Venezuela, the figure is 122 per 100,000, or 12200 percent higher.[62] These are humans with almost identical genes behaving very differently. There is no genetic explanation so it must be cultural.

Although violence has increased in some cultures, in many places, including the UK, it has fallen. We cannot be complacent because other cultures are doing even better. The murder rate in Germany is currently only 80 percent of the U.K. rate and the Japanese murder rate just 30 percent. That suggests that we can be optimistic about the potential for cultural change. If better mood management can become part of a culture, the behaviour of potentially violent individuals can be controlled.

Homes, families, workplaces, organisations, villages, towns, cities and countries all develop their own cultures and sub-cultures. They promote different styles of habitual social behaviour and once established those cultures regulate the habitual behaviours of the individuals within them. When peaceful individuals find themselves in a violent culture, they learn to behave violently. When violent individuals are overwhelmed by a peaceful culture, they learn to behave peacefully. In other parts of the world we have seen civilised societies collapse into violence and barbarism in recent years.

---

[62] data.worldbank.org/indicator/VC.IHR.PSRC.P5

Civilisations might be more fragile than we like to believe. Our reliance on each generation of children to learn the same rules of their culture afresh means that all civilisations are fragile. They can go either way. This is particularly the case when large migrations change the characteristics of local culture as happened during times of colonisation. The development of freedom of movement in the modern world means that all cultures, other than closed societies, are subject to new forces of change, some good and others not so.

Social engineering enthusiasts who carelessly propose reallocating power in society and dismantling social structures need to tread carefully. They may underestimate the extent to which the behaviour of individuals is constrained by those social structures.

People who lived in Afghanistan before the civil war broke out in the late 1970s remember life in Kabul with affection. Different ethnic groups lived together in peace. They mixed socially and intermarried. The Hazara, Pashtun, Tajik, Uzbek and others all thought of themselves primarily as Afghans. This was just one generation ago.

In March 2015, Farkhunda Malikzada, a teacher who was studying Islamic law, visited the Shah-e Du Shamshira shrine, in the centre of Kabul. She remonstrated with a male caretaker who was selling charms, which she regarded as un-Islamic. The caretaker, enraged at being challenged by a woman, falsely accused her of being an American and of burning the Koran. As a huge crowd gathered, she was dragged from the shrine and beaten to death in a prolonged attack in which a large number of the crowd participated. Her limp body was eventually dragged down the street and run over by a car. The whole scene was watched by police, it was filmed by several people on their mobile phones, and uploaded onto the internet which is the only reason we know about it. Her mother said they were not human. The problem is they were. They were people just like us.

So are the young people holding black flags in Syria and Iraq and committing atrocities in other parts of the world. They have almost identical genes to us, which means if they are capable of behaving like that we probably are too. The point is that socialisation and culture significantly determine whether those genes are expressed and how. We need to face up to the uncomfortable reality that those responsible for the holocaust, and all of the other horrors of humanity were people like us too.

We have the same genes as our peaceful and friendly Scandinavian neighbours, which are those of their Viking forebears who developed such a fearsome reputation for going berserk. The English language includes terms such as "lynching party", "orgies of violence" and "blood lust". Public executions were once a form of entertainment in our culture and in many other cultures.

Just because humans have the potential to behave badly, that does not mean that they will behave badly. But equally, we should not deceive ourselves into believing that individuals in our own society are in some way immune to cultural changes that could foster violence. We need to look at the common features of cultures and sub-cultures where violence flourish and see if we can remove them. At the same time we need to examine the common features of those in which violence is suppressed, and decide whether we should adopt some of them. This will require some brutal honesty and delicate diplomacy. Just because we have been behaving in a certain way for a long time does not mean that it is the best way to behave. It is intellectually incoherent to claim that we respect universal human rights, and at the same time that we respect the rights of others to abuse humans because it is part of their culture. We either believe that some humans have the right to abuse others or we do not.

Whether that means that it is wise to attempt to force our values on cultures, in other parts of the world, is an entirely different matter. What are perceived by many as the western liberal crusades of the early 21st century have illustrated that it is much easier to completely destroy imperfect social systems than it is to create better ones. Social systems are fragile and need to be treated with care and caution. That goes for our own too, and there may be cherished features of our own culture that we need to question and modify before we start lecturing others. Honesty is the best policy.

Over the years there have been several examples of abuse within our own care systems. Vulnerable people, including the elderly, the young, and adults with intellectual disabilities, have suffered at the hands of people who were supposed to be caring for them. In some cases they were filmed by undercover reporters, who have proved far more effective at uncovering abuse than the regulatory bodies set up for that purpose.

What is striking in the videos, apart from the cruelty, is the facial expressions of the perpetrators. They are often grinning, laughing, and joking. They are enjoying it. We may be reluctant to admit it, but humans apparently do get pleasure from bullying and torturing other humans. We have seen how the behaviour of individuals changes when they are in gangs, groups and crowds. They react to the excited behaviour of others by becoming increasingly excited themselves. This can result in frenzied violence, as excited mobs riot and go on the rampage.

Young people who have been involved in street gangs, and members of the armed forces who have seen active service, talk about the horrors, but also the pleasures of violence. Some describe experiencing intense emotional highs as they indulged in violence, followed by feelings of peace and serenity afterwards. Such experiences can become addictive.

Historical texts provide romanticised stories about this sort of behaviour, because it has been edited and sanitised. Now video recordings going back over half a century are available on YouTube. They show what people really looked like during the violent protests of the 1960s and the football hooliganism of the 1970s. It is all rather ugly but look at the faces. They were having fun. There are also literally millions of YouTube clips showing contemporary violence on the streets, with happy and excited crowds watching and cheering in the background. There are videos of rioting mobs, individuals and groups indulging in unprovoked assaults for their own entertainment and domestic violence captured on CCTV. It is clear from the expressions on many of those excited faces, that even if they may regret what they did the following day, at the time they were enjoying it.

The reason they are on YouTube is because humans enjoy watching them. If you type the word "violence" into the search box on YouTube, it brings up over seven million videos.

Many more people must enjoy violence than are willing to admit it. They may lack self awareness. The viewing figures for programmes like "Game of Thrones" provide a true indication. Shakespeare is all about murder, mutilation and suicide. Just count the bodies. Humans seem to like that sort of thing.

Dressing up has always been associated with violence. Warriors traditionally dressed up to go to war, with painted faces and bodies. In the Home Counties, people dress up to go fox hunting. Dancing, chanting and singing is associated with violence too. Before battles warriors would perform war dances, sing war songs, and chant war chants accompanied by synchronous movements. All of these are innate pleasurable behaviours which would get them excited as they anticipated the battle to come. They also serve to bond them together as a group.

In the modern day, although they may not know what they are doing, excited people get together in groups and behave in a similar way. They are all driven by the same cocktail of natural drugs. In addition to the adrenaline and dopamine that excites and motivates them, their bodies and brains produce opioids and serotonin. These are all rather pleasurable. At the same time they are producing oxytocin, commonly misnamed the love hormone. Although oxytocin does strengthen the emotional bonds between group members, it also has a dark side. It fuels the rejection of non-group members and makes those prone to violence even more violent towards them. In many ways, it has effects similar to those of alcohol, which is just what you need for a bit of violence.[63]

---

[63] "The dark side of the love hormone"; research points to striking similarities with the effects of alcohol" - Dr Ian Mitchell, Birmingham University, 2015

Individuals in groups can reach levels of excitement they would never reach when acting alone. Individuals react to the behaviour of each other, in a feedback loop, which propels them into states of violent frenzy. That is what leads to orgies of violence and it is why violent mobs are so dangerous.

We may not want to remove all those opportunities for fun and it may be that we do not need to. If we deconstruct the performances and remove the most violent parts it should still be possible to enjoy the rest. That is more or less what competitive sports are.

Some experts have claimed that all aggression and violence is simply caused by over-arousal. If that was true, then all we would need to do would be to calm everybody down. There are certainly occasions when that is exactly what violent people need, but unfortunately it is not quite as simple as that. We know that most of the time, when predators are in pursuit, they are not in a highly aroused state. Some humans set off on violent pursuits when they are already calm. They deliberately set out to become excited so they can indulge in the violence, because they have learned that the whole process is enjoyable.

For example, the UEFA Euro 2016 football tournament opened with mass violence on the streets of Marseille. There were fights between British and Russian gangs. The Russians had packed uniforms, masks, weapons and even brought video recording equipment with them before they travelled to France.

They were far better equipped and better organised than the British, who looked rather drunk and unfit on the news reports.

When those Russians were booking their flights and packing their bags for the journey, they were not in a state of high arousal. They were calm and looking forward to the trip. They were being driven by pursuit not panic, as were the opposing fans from other countries who had paid large sums of money to travel. Some of them were hoping that there would be opportunities for them to become involved in violence. Many of them had been arrested for street violence before. Once the various gangs of uniformed fans got there they set about getting themselves in the mood. That was the purpose of the chanting, singing, flag waving and taunting of other fans and the police. They were already fuelled by a combination of pursuit and performance and were enjoying the whole experience. It is just a shame they could not have missed the violent bit at the end.

Humans, mostly young males it has to be said, pay a lot of money to travel around the world to indulge in violent pursuits. Some behaviour experts might not like the idea, but some of what they refer to as anti-social behaviour is actually very social indeed. It is an enjoyable leisure activity.

Gangs of young male chimps behave in a similar way. They set off to patrol the borders of their own territory and sometimes end up attacking and killing members of neighbouring troops.

But they are not in a state of over-arousal all the time. They only get themselves into a state of excitement once they come across one of the enemy. Before that, they are enjoying a pleasant, leisurely pursuit.

The natural inclination to strongly identify with a particular social group and exclude others from that group, runs deep in nature, but inclination is not the same as determination. Not all of them behave that way all the time. Which brings us back to cultural influences. Birds are inclined to learn birdsong and humans are inclined to learn spoken language, but the songs and languages they learn are different. It is not so much the specific behaviours that are inherited as general tendencies, which are then fine-tuned by the environment.

For example, there is a commonly held idea that monkeys are born with an innate fear of snakes. That is not true. What they have is an innate ability to learn to be frightened of snakes. They learn to be frightened of snake-like shapes more quickly than they learn to be frightened of other shapes. It is possible to train a monkey to like snake-like objects, but it takes longer to do that than it does to train them to like other things. You could say that biology and psychology of the monkey mind is prejudiced against snakes. The optimistic message is that they can learn to overcome those prejudices. That probably works for all prejudices.

Humans also have their own predispositions and prejudices which they can learn to overcome. For example, they tend to be fearful of unfamiliar faces, preferring those they know or those which are similar to their own. But they can learn to overcome it. When humans mix with other types of people and become more familiar with them, the fears subside.

Therefore a sensible way to organise societies is to ensure that people mix. Cultures that try to prevent that are more likely to become prejudiced and more likely to become violent towards their neighbours. Perhaps we need to rethink what we mean by multiculturalism. It should be about sharing and making more widely available the best aspects of all cultures, not isolation and protection.

On a cheerier note, Steven Pinker provides compelling evidence that, contrary to what most people think, humans on the whole have become significantly less violent in recent decades. While that provides reasons for optimism, he also cautions that we cannot be sure that this trend is irreversible. The reduction cannot be attributed to genetic changes so it must be cultural. Violence can fall out of fashion but as we have seen, it can come back into fashion too. How behaviour is expressed and constrained depends on a variety of external influences, so we need to take care. If those are removed, all the good work of decades and centuries of cumulative civilisation can be undone.

The biggest influence upon growing children is the mood music of the culture that surrounds them. When the same people are placed in different surroundings, they can behave very differently. Sometimes, when an individual seems to be out of control in one setting, the best thing to do is to remove them from it and place them in a completely different one.

The ethnologist and neuroscientist Robert Sapolsky provides a good example of the power of culture change from his study of wild baboons. In one group, each morning the most aggressive, least socially connected males used to raid a neighbouring troop to fight over a human waste tip. This gang consisted of half a dozen young males. Violence dominated their social life. During that period there was a TB outbreak on the tip and that troop of young males became infected and died.

It may not be surprising to learn that removing the most aggressive individuals from the group caused a change in the emotional climate within the troop. After the aggressive gang were killed, it became an unusually peaceful troop. But what was interesting was when other young adolescent males began to join the troop (which is what they do) they took on the new culture of less aggression, because the resident females treated them better when they did. 15 years later the new, more sociable patterns of behaviour remained. This was a violent culture transformed for the better in one generation. If wild baboons can do it, humans should be able to do something similar.

It is possible to bring about a rapid change in human cultures by changing attitudes. When I was young everywhere was full of smoke - trains, planes, pubs, restaurants, theatres, and cinemas. I used to be an aircraft cleaner at Gatwick Airport, and once a month we had to clean all the cream coloured plastic interiors around the windows and overhead lockers with Brillo pads and soapy water. Thick dark caramel coloured liquid dribbled down the plastic as we did it, briefly exposing the white plastic underneath, which would gradually become discoloured throughout the following month, as no doubt did all the passengers lungs.

I used to work in pubs. People would regularly stumble out at closing time, walking unsteadily towards their cars and struggling to get the keys into the ignition before driving off into the night.

Mainstream comedy entertainment used to include casual racism, sexism and homophobia as a matter of routine. In 1971, the Sun newspaper included a photograph of a page 3 girl for the first time, a feature copied by most of the popular press. The girls were often as young as 16 or 17 years old.

Many of the those behaviours are now regarded as shameful rather than impressive. It is important to distinguish between shame and humiliation here. Shame is when people realise they have made a mistake or done something wrong. It is a performance failure on their part, which they fear could reduce their own social status and make people less impressed by them. Humiliation is when they feel under attack by individuals or groups who are pointing out their weaknesses, or trying to make them look bad, in a deliberate attempt to reduce their social status.

The psychological response to shame is to change your own behaviour. The response to humiliation is to defend it. Diplomacy has always been about threats and bluff, and a crucial part of successful diplomacy has always been face saving. Face-saving is designed to avoid humiliation, which in turn, hopefully, avoids pursuit and performance driven urges to embark on aggression and violent defences. We need to steer a careful path by illuminating problem behaviours in society in such a way that they become unfashionable, using shame rather than humiliation.

"War is a mere continuation of politics by other means"

Carl Philipp Gottfried von Clausewitz

Gottfried von Clausewitz is known as a Prussian general and military theorist but he was really a psychologist. One of his key ideas was that war was fundamentally a social interaction. He saw both waging war and negotiating the peace at the end of it as part of the same process, intended to bring about the best possible outcome. Public humiliations and dishonour have dangerous consequences when they store up long term resentments and a desire for revenge. Many historians believe that the second world war resulted from the unnecessary humiliation of Germany by the allies after the first one.

When pursuits and performances no longer impress they can fall out of fashion, because most people are trying to fit in with what they perceive to be the expectations of their own culture. We need to make aggression and violence less fashionable. Performance provides entertainment and pleasure, so we do not want to stop that, but there are different types of performance which provide similar pleasures. The performances we want to reduce are the stereotypical threat performances that are associated with aggression and violence. Attractive performances are fine. We need to educate children to recognise aggressive threat performances for what they are, foolish pantomimes performed by animals who are desperate to impress. If threat performances begin to be perceived as embarrassing, rather than impressive, they may fall out of fashion.

The best way to change attitudes is to nudge people in the right direction without causing them to lose face. Educating children so that they develop a more sophisticated understanding of what is behind violent performances is a good starting point. The moods, emotions, and behaviours associated with pursuit, panic, and performance are qualitatively different and so are the types of violence associated with them. Many commentators have failed to appreciate that. I have just put the following two questions into Google:

"What causes people to be violent?"

"What moods are associated with violence?"

There are thousands of links telling a similar story, which is that all violence is caused by abuse, stress, poverty, frustration, low self esteem etc. The emotions associated with it are supposed to be shame, guilt, fear, terror, anger and rage.

This blinkered approach fails to acknowledge or explain most of the violence expressed by humans who are not victims. It fails to distinguish between the different forms of violence or acknowledge their divergent characteristics. We need to become better at articulating the differences between pursuit, panic, and performance violence.

Pursuit Violence

When animals are hunting or fishing they are highly motivated by the dopamine driven pursuit drive. They do not hate the prey. They are not frightened of it. They love their food. They associate prey with pleasure. Hunters describe their quarry lovingly in books and on websites, often describing them as beautiful. They keep photographs of the creatures they have caught as souvenirs. They even sometimes have the heads and bodies, stuffed and mounted as trophies.

Hunting, shooting and fishing are relaxing, enjoyable, leisure activities for some humans in the modern world. For our ancestors, they were necessary for their survival and that is still true for humans in other parts of the world. They provide pleasure because they are pursuits in their most natural form. Humans fishing on river banks seem quite contented, even when nothing much seems to be happening. If predators were as highly stimulated as their prey, they would be experiencing fear which is not so enjoyable. They are not frightened, over-excited or emotionally upset.

Nor are street robbers, gangsters or military snipers. They would not be very effective if they were. Stalkers have to be calm and quiet. If they draw attention to themselves they will scare the prey away. People who splash around in the river are unlikely to catch many fish. If human hunters, armed with bows or guns, were in a high state of arousal, shaking with excitement, they would not be able to hit anything. Predators have to be quiet, calm and controlled, to have any chance of success.

The behaviour of an animal approaching the target in pursuit is very different to the noisy, showy displays that typify performance. In pursuit they approach from behind, to stay out of view for as long as possible. They move slowly and deliberately until they can get close enough for a short sprint. When they dispatch the prey, it is done as quickly and efficiently as possible, often with a bite to the back of the neck. This is focussed, cold blooded, deliberate, dispassionate, violence.

Those exhibiting it are not suffering from feelings of shame, guilt, fear, terror, anger and rage. They are not suffering at all.

Hate Pursuits

Some animals, humans included, are driven to pursue things they hate. Animals are driven to pursue and attack others that threaten them, their children, or members of their social group. In tournament species, dominant males are driven to pursue and kill the young of their competitors, which gives their own young a better chance of survival. They are driven to pursue and kill creatures from other groups that compete for the same resources and mates. They hunt and kill their enemies.

Research scientists doggedly pursue bacteria and viruses that cause disease. Some people attack housework with the same mental resoluteness. Some campaigners have dedicated their lives to worthy hate pursuits. They fought to eradicate things such as slavery, animal cruelty, female genital mutilation and discrimination of all sorts. The language of campaigners sometimes has a violent ring to it. They talk of waging a war on want or waste.

Many good people in law enforcement, the military, child protection, and animal protection have dedicated their lives to hunting down criminals, terrorists and abusers. These are variants of hate pursuits.

Sometimes pursuit combines with performance, for example when humans are driven to make dramatic gestures in an attempt to protect or establish their reputation. Hatred and revenge are powerful and persistent motivators. Some people spend their entire lives pursuing hateful vendettas. In some perverted way they must enjoy it, but they are certainly not in a state of high excitement all the time. There is a reason why some people are described as cold blooded murderers.

Hate pursuits figure prominently in many great works of fiction. They are depicted in art, opera, films and computer games, because humans are predisposed towards that way of thinking. They are fascinated by it and enjoy thinking about it. All pursuits start with a fantasy. According to researchers, 80 percent of humans admit to fantasising about killing people at some time in their lives. While they are fantasising, they are indulging in exactly the same mental process as a real killer. Real killers just take the process a stage further.

Small children with toy guns, and bigger children with real ones, fantasise about violence. Anybody who ever enjoyed seeing the baddies in a film get what they deserved was doing the same thing. It could be argued that the only difference between good people and bad ones is that good people just fantasise about hate pursuits, whereas bad people act them out.

Pursuit provides the long-term motivation to fuel persistent vendettas and vengeful campaigns. Performance provides the urge to make dramatic gestures in an attempt to create or repair reputations. When the two combine the result can be ugly. Some vengeful pursuits end in dramatic performances that are described in the media as violent rampages or orgies of destruction. The neural circuits that drive those behaviours are built into our genes and we need to put in place protections. Once again, understanding what is going on and pointing it out is a good start.

Love Hate Relationships

Passion is not always a good thing and crimes of passion can involve extreme violence. Love and hate are not polar opposites and sometimes there is only a fine line between them. The opposite of love and hate is indifference. Because they are so similar, from a physiological perspective, humans can become confused between the two and switch from one to the other quite easily. They can both involve a similar level of physiological stimulation.

Couples who were once in love can switch to hating each other enough to want to kill them. Business partners, who were once best friends, can fall out and become bitter enemies. Just as humans can be highly motivated to pursue the one they love, they can be just as dogged at pursuing people they hate.

Stalkers, avengers, and the followers of love quests are all running essentially the same mental programmes.

Love is blind and so is hate. They are both expressions of prejudice. When a pair of love struck adolescents fall in love, they are not seeing each other in quite the same way as the rest of the world sees them. There is nothing objective about their appraisals of each other. Lovers and haters suffer from similar perceptual distortions. They are obsessed because they attach too much importance to the another person.

Panic Violence

This is the unfocussed, uncoordinated, and sometimes unconscious violence that has received most attention in the literature. Panic violence is associated with the highest levels of stimulation of the sympathetic nervous system. The way to manage it is to avoid doing anything that is likely to stimulate that system further. Instead we need to activate the parasympathetic nervous system, to calm things down again. When prey are trapped they can make quick convulsive movements, lashing with teeth, claws, feet and heads. Distressed humans exhibit similar frenzied behaviours, including head butting, biting, gouging, blows and kicks.

Performance Violence

When social animals are in performance mode, the violence they exhibit is something different. Performance violence is a flamboyant, ostentatious, display. It is often staged to impress an audience and it can be drawn out into an extended ritual. Social animals and birds are highly motivated to perform and watch ritual challenges, some of which do turn into fights. (see Sky Sports Fight Night for details).

The threatening postures and behaviours exhibited by animals in performance are totally unlike those adopted by animals in pursuit and panic. In performance they approach another creature, rather than running away in panic. They approach from the front in a noisy, showy display, rather than from the rear in predatory pursuit. They are noisy and dramatic because performances are all about attention. They want to be noticed.

Similar behaviours are evident across a range of species, including insects, beetles, birds and mammals. They inflate and puff up their fur and feathers to look bigger, more powerful, and more dangerous than they really are.

A typical threatening performance in human primates involves standing square on, with legs apart, inflating and puffing out the chest, with the head jutting forward, raised shoulders and eyebrows, accompanied by a fierce stare. Sometimes this performance is accompanied by tipping of the head, from one side to the other, with loud calls into the face of the opponent. Performers in the early stages of the ritual may adopt this position when they are only inches apart. That would be a terrible fighting position, as it leaves all the vulnerable areas exposed, but that is the whole point. This is a choreographed display designed for inspection. They are not supposed to fight yet.

Posturing in nature allows each competitor to assess the other, to judge whether it is really worth fighting. These displays of threat are loud, ostentatious and extravagant. They are conducted in public, often in full view of an audience. The pantomime is aimed at impressing the audience as much as the opponent. Usually the pantomime ends when one competitor switches from a display of dominance to one of subservience.

Even when they do fight, the switch from a dominant performance to a submissive one can be quite dramatic, which should alert us to the reality that performance is all an act. A common performance switch is from aggression to humour, in an attempt to pretend that it was a joke all along. These switches often happens in drunken street fights, when performers switch between apparent rage and jokey humour or tearful self-pity.

The best outcome for both contenders is that one of them backs down before the violence begins. Aggressive challenges typically involve long periods of posturing, punctuated by only short bursts of violence. In reality, humans do not have the stamina for the sort of protracted physical fights depicted in films. Impressive threats are sometimes enough. Real fights result from miscalculations, when it is not entirely clear who would win.

Gangs and armies perform similar performance manoeuvres before battle, showing off their power to impress the enemy. Again the purpose is to avoid a fight if possible. There have been many tense stand-offs that could have resulted in violence but did not. The Cuban Missile crisis, in 1963, involved apes armed with nuclear weapons posturing and testing each other out.

Political leaders are driven by the same primitive urges to establish reputations, seek respect and indulge in vengeful pursuits. The brains of world leaders are running the same ancient, bug ridden, software as the rest of us. They can be a risk to the whole species when they are armed with weapons of mass destruction, because most of them have no idea how their own minds work.

That is a strong argument for putting mood management and self control at the core of our education system for the future. As an interim measure, we might want to consider better ways of selecting and promoting our leaders. Macho alpha males are not really equipped for leading roles in the modern world. But who is going to tell them that? Politics exists at various levels in modern society providing opportunities for individuals to indulge in dominant displays without actually resorting to physical violence. Some join committees and push their way into positions of authority through verbal jousting. Local politics, trades unions, office politics, and various societies, campaigns, charities and even the church provide opportunities for individuals to perform. Political performers are more interested in being seen to win their arguments and battles than in the issues themselves, or in getting anything useful done.

"I think, roughly, that the desire to be a politician should ban you for life from every being one."

Billy Connely

Even at national level, there are highly motivated politicians who fight their way to the top because they are motivated to achieve highest office, rather than by what they want to do when they get there. If they do get to the top, their priority turns to establishing a legacy so that they will be remembered. It is really all about them.

Supremacist Thinking

Bad behaviour is usually propped up by bad thinking. When bad thinking becomes institutionalised within cultures it needs to be challenged. Supremacist thinking is one of the bugs in our mental software. It is attractive because it gives humans inflated ideas about their own rank in the social hierarchy, by arbitrarily devaluing and demoting whole groups of other people. The problem with it, is that it is a universal human characteristic yet individuals can only recognise it in other people. They are blind to their own prejudice.

Supremacist thinking comes naturally to humans, no matter what racial, religious, age, gender, or social group they belong to. I have yet to meet a human being who does not hold supremacist views of one sort or another. The dangerous ones are those who become angry when you point this out, which is a surprising number.

Anyone who believes that members of their own group have any special qualities or entitlement is a supremacist. Some supremacists think their colour makes them superior, others that their religion, or political affiliation, make them superior. Some think their intelligence makes them superior or that they are morally superior.

It is easy to start calling names: racist, sexist, ageist, sizeist, facist, communist etc., but it is worth pausing for a moment and searching the dark corners of your own mind to consider whether you have ever experienced feelings of superiority toward other groups of humans.

There are vegans who feel superior to vegetarians, who in turn feel superior to meat eaters. There are Guardian readers who feel superior to Telegraph readers, who in turn feel superior to Daily Mirror readers. There are men who feel superior to women, and women who feel superior to men. There are meat eating Daily Mail readers who feel superior to other races and members of racial minorities who feel superior to members of other racial minorities. They are all indulging in the same pattern of thinking.

The most dangerous supremacists are those who become infused with moralistic rage. They hate people who fail to appreciate their distorted sense of entitlement and who, in their own minds, fail to show them sufficient respect. They fantasise about taking bloody revenge with dramatic displays of violence. And sometimes they put those fantasies into action.

Before it gets to that stage, we need to have a more honest and open discussion about supremacist thinking in all of its forms. The ease with which humans slip into supremacist thinking was illustrated during the political debates in Europe and the U.S. during 2016. Supremacism is on the rise. Everybody feels superior to everybody else.

The term "Liberal" has become an expression of contempt as potent as "Communist" and "Facist", so at least nobody is left out. Members of the "metropolitan liberal elite" and "Remoaners" are regarded with utter contempt by comment writers in The Sunday Times, who are themselves described as "Neo Facists" and "Brexiteers" in The Observer. They are defined by those they regard as their inferiors, the sort of people they do not want to associate with.

Prejudice has caused and continues to cause, a great deal of trouble for humans. It is buried deep within our genetic makeup, because animals are driven to protect their own genes. People who look like us are more likely to share our genes. There is plenty of research evidence to show that humans tend to like people who look a bit like them. It may be a natural tendency but it is not always a good one and we can fight it.

In order to protect humans against their own worse instincts we have to continually work to dismantle institutional prejudice as it arises. Once again education is the starting point. In the future we need to become better at identifying supremacist thinking and pointing it out wherever it occurs, irrespective of who is doing it.

Most people cheer that idea when they are thinking about the sorts of institutional racial supremacism that propped up slavery, apartheid and the holocaust. But they become resistant to challenging similar thinking errors once they have become institutionalised in their own politics and religion.

The idea that members of a particular religion are superior in some way and marked out for favourable treatment, if not in this life then in the next, runs deeply through many formal religions. Those ideas may be emotionally appealing but they are supremacist.

The lesson of history is that those who start believing that they are superior in some way, start regarding others as inferior. Doctrines that prevent them from mixing with those who are excluded from their own privileged group lead to attitudes of contempt. Ideas of racial, religious and cultural purity become confused with notions of contamination, which can lead to the perverted notion of human cleansing which has resulted in some of mankind's worst atrocities.

The language of hatred deliberately discriminates between the self-righteous and the targets of their contempt. It dehumanises the victims, distancing the enraged from their contemptible inferiors, reducing empathy and making it easier for aggressive and violent individuals to avoid personal discomfort while causing the victims pain.

In the minds of those who committed them, the crimes of humanity were never committed against decent human beings like them. They were committed against inferiors, who were typically described as parasites, scum, vermin, excrement, cockroaches, rats and dogs. That form of language currently pervades the propaganda spewed from North Korea. The same language was used by Colonel Qaddafi as his forces prepared to attack the inhabitants of Benghazi.

It is the language used by fighters on all sides in the Middle East and it was the language used by Nazis to describe the people they were annihilating. It is the language of the self-righteous, no matter who they are, or who they happen to hate. Whites, blacks, jews, bolsheviks, bourgeoisie, communists, liberals, fascists, tories, lefties, jihadis, kaffirs, protestants, catholics, executives, bankers, scroungers and police officers have all been called similar names by over-excited and self-righteous individuals at various times.

It is the indulgent, protective and rewarding effects of those mental processes that we need to recognise, expose and publicise. Those who indulge in supremacist thinking should be shamed in society into recognising what they are doing.

Moralistic Rage

Supremacist thinking can lead to violence. Some humans enjoy getting themselves into a state of moralistic rage and search for any excuse. They turn up for any demonstration and whip themselves into a frenzy of excited aggression. They may not realise it, but they have become addicted to performances of aggression as a leisure activity. Such people are not lacking a sense of morality. You could argue that their problem is a surfeit of moralising. What they lack is moral sense.

That urge to see justice done is a powerful one which fuels moralistic rage. It is probably related to the need for social groups to protect themselves against cheats. Social groups only work when most of the individuals cooperate. If they can get away with it, cheating can be a successful life strategy for the odd individual in a social group, but when too many individuals start doing it, the whole system falls apart.

So a corrective mechanism evolved to protect cooperative societies. Social animals evolved the capacity to identify the individuals in their own group, herd or flock, so they could remember somebody who cheated them and not trust them again. There is abundant evidence from studies on a variety of social animals and birds that they remember and help those who helped them in the past, but shun others who did not. They bear grudges and repay favours too. This is called reciprocal altruism.

It might also form the basis for a more problematic mental programme. Humans have a tendency to bear grudges and seek revenge. They may tell themselves that they are doing it from the best of motives, perhaps to set a good example, or to dissuade others from doing the same thing. They may believe that punishing bad people is their moral duty. That might all be true. But revenge is driven by passion. They enjoy it and they gain satisfaction from it. We know which drives fuel grudges and acts of vengeance. It is the deadly combination of pursuit and performance.

Those who control authoritarian regimes try to suppress opposition and silence dissent. Those with whom they disagree are demonised and anyone who refuses to join the condemnation risks being accused of complicity and attacked themselves. That is how mob rule and witch-hunts work. Those behaviours are generated from the mental processes that exist within all of us. The trouble is that when you are part of the mob it is not so easy to spot the pattern.

We may all like to believe that, had we been under the rule of Nazi Germany, we would have been part of the resistance or, at the very least, been a reluctant participant. The truth is we do not know. Contemporary films of the rallies at the time show huge numbers of enthusiastic participants. They look like they are enjoying themselves. Being part of a self-righteous group can be an exciting and thrilling experience.

There are currently young ideologues on university campuses who are using intimidation and force to deny platforms to speakers with whom they disagree. They are the modern equivalent of the McCarthy Senate Committee hearings of the 1950s, but they cannot see it that way. When humans are in a moralistic rage, they are driven by exciting, rewarding, mental processes - the same processes that fuelled the minds of the Spanish Inquisition and the witch-hunters who sent 35 000 women to be executed across Europe in medieval times.

Of course they react with rage when that is pointed out to them, which rather proves my point. Rage is a self-righteous performance that comes from supremacist thinking. Moral panic is one of the bugs in our mental software that prevents rational thinking. We need to identify and confront all aspects of it in our own culture without discrimination. Society needs to identify and discourage moralistic aggression and violence, no matter who it is that is indulging in it. Humans are already motivated to pursue things they hate. They do not need any more encouragement.

Radical Ideologies

Radical ideologies that promote violence have consumed the middle east and spread around the world in recent decades. There has been considerable bewilderment in the west that young people brought up at home could be attracted by the violent, authoritarian, repressive, hierarchical sub-cultures of religious extremism. The assumption seems to be that such ideas are unnatural, when in reality the opposite is the case.

It has become fashionable in some parts of western society to equate everything natural with good. Natural foods and medicines are assumed to be healthy, whereas artificial additives are bad. In reality the natural world is full of poisons and carcinogens. Natural behaviour can be pretty poisonous too, when it involves angry humans pursuing, chasing, injuring and killing each other. Violence is natural. The concept of the noble savage is based on a myth. The cracks and holes evident in skulls of primitive man show that a significant cause of injury and death was other primitive men. That is also true of many modern primate cousins.

Most of humanity's problems result from natural behaviour. Our job is to socialise children to adopt unnatural behaviours. The process of socialisation within families and communities can reduce the expression of violence, but the potential is always there for violence in every generation. We should not forget that. The notion that humans are naturally drawn towards the western liberal values, of personal freedom and human rights, can be dispelled with a quick glance at a political map of the world. The unstable regions of the world are populated by humans like us.

Whenever they feel threatened humans seem to have a natural propensity towards authoritarian, hierarchical, social organisations. The British Empire, the Third Reich, and the USSR were all built by hierarchical and authoritarian human minds with fantasies of racial/ideological superiority. The majority of humans still live in cultures that are hierarchical and authoritarian. In Afghanistan, Iraq, Libya and many other African states, the real power lies with gangs and tribes, whatever official lines are drawn on the map. Even in more stable countries, when the rule of law breaks down, smaller scale authorities arise spontaneously, seizing power and enforcing their own rules. They are always hierarchical.

In the west, criminal groups and families offer protection in areas where the police are not seen to be effective, establishing hierarchical and authoritarian sub-cultures. Ethnic and religious groups have established their own sub-cultures ruled by powerful elders and leaders who create and police their own rules.

Liberal supremacists need to think harder about some of their own ideas. Our genes have not changed but some of the processes of socialisation have. More by accident than design, in an attempt to promote more humane and civilised attitudes, we might have accidentally removed some of the socialisation processes that helped children to learn self control, without replacing them with effective alternatives.

This is not a reactionary call for a return to some mythical "good old days" when people behaved properly. I think the current generation of young people in this country are, on the whole, much nicer than my generation were. But some of them are struggling to cope. They do not know where they fit in. They cannot manage their own mood and behaviour because they lack self control.

Probably the harshest lesson of the twenty first century, so far, is that it is stupid to dismantle a social system without understanding how it works, or knowing how to put it back together again. We need to apply that lesson to domestic policy too. Humans feel at home in exciting, violent, hierarchical, cultures because those are natural cultures. Wherever emotion, dogma, ideology and authority are allowed to dominate, violence and tribalism result. When societies become unsettled that is the direction they tend to move towards.

Extremists of the far right and the far left, have more in common with each other than they do with the rest of us. It is not so much what they think that defines them, it is the way they think. If the supremacist ideas that motivate Jihadis really are unnatural and alien to modern humans, it is strange that they seem to be attracting so many followers. I do not believe for one moment that the masterminds of Jihad are evil geniuses. Their opinions and arguments are stupid, exposing a lack of self-awareness and a lack of understanding about human psychology in general.

Many doctrinal experts who preach supremacist views have led sheltered lives themselves and have little understanding of reality. That means that many of their followers must be considerably brighter than they are - a rule that can be applied across a wide range of human organisations. Their appeal is emotional rather than intellectual. Supremacists beliefs are essentially the same, whether they are based on race, genetics, culture, religion or politics. They believe that their own personal prejudices should be treated more seriously than those of other people, which is an attractive idea for humans.

A very simple way of recruiting and motivating people is to give them a strong sense of purpose, by telling them they are special, and that they are going to be specially rewarded later. Telling them that all their weaknesses are actually virtues, giving them licence to indulge in sex and violence, and providing them with exciting weapons is likely to be extremely tempting to young people. Passion, purpose, camaraderie, status, excitement, sex, violence and feelings of supremacy are a heady mix because they play on all the basic drives.

Chapter 6 - Feeling Good About Life

Effective Mood Management

It may be true that some people need less arousal, but some need more of it. When the current environment is undemanding, the brain switches by default to its own longer term pursuits and preoccupations. There are many brains in schools and workplaces that are engaged in their own pursuits, chatting on social media, trawling the internet and planning their social lives. There is a vast amount of time being wasted already. We could use some of it for mood management and possibly redirect those brains to increase their productivity in the remaining time.

There is a thin line between excitement and over-excitement, but I would rather be treading that line than teetering between day dreaming and falling asleep. Physical exercise and entertainment can provide additional stimulation to wake people up. Sometimes things need to happen to capture their attention and bring them back into a learning state. Attention needs to be captured by novelty, surprise, uncertainty and puzzles. The activities we want people to follow need to be structured in that way. Computer games provide an excellent model.

We need to expand the mood management toolbox so that we become better at spotting things before they go seriously wrong, and become better equipped with strategies to put them right again. Having a target to pursue but insufficient arousal to motivate action is no good. Neither is arousal with no purpose or direction. I have watched children and young people working extremely hard at entertaining themselves and their friends. The only people who were not amused were their teachers. People are happiest when they are curious, engaged and interested. That is when the dopamine circuits are switched on and learning becomes enjoyable and effortless. When children are hard at work, or play, they look happy and calm. So do adults when they are following pursuits and hobbies that engage them.

Trivial pursuits can be highly satisfying, which is why they are so popular. Humans love solving puzzles and mysteries, finding out about things, taking things apart and putting them back together.

They actually love work, so long as the dopamine driven pursuit circuits are switched on. Disgruntled workers may fantasise about doing nothing when they retire, but when they do, they feel that life lacks purpose. Some even choose to go back to work, paid or unpaid, to regain what is missing in their lives. Others pursue leisure activities with new found determination. Some people never really retire and they seem to stay brighter, happier and live longer than those who grind to a halt. People enjoy being busy and many of society's problems are caused by people with nothing useful to do.

It is no use wishing that humans were built differently. We need to understand the way we are, in order to discover or create new activities to allow ourselves to manage and enjoy our natural drives in a changing world.

Everyone should ensure that they have a number of plans for pursuits in the short, medium and long term. Anticipation of the future and the pursuits themselves create pleasure in the present and build memories that will enhance the future. Some older people run out of open pursuits because they stop starting new ones, then they feel that life has lost its sense of purpose.

Everyone needs opportunities for performance. As they drop out of the mating game, stop working, and stop meeting new people as a matter of course, the natural opportunities for performance shrink. Yet by making an effort to meet new people, take up new interests and learn new skills, it is possible to rediscover and create new social stages.

Our bodies, brains and minds evolved for a world that no longer exists but we have worked out artificial ways of engaging our drives through simulations of various kinds. As we better understand those drives, and the way bodybrains and heart & mindbrains work, we can learn to build better simulators and have more fun.

Artful Mood Management

If you want to know what captures the attention of humans, go to an art gallery. Something must have driven artists to create those simulations. From the first cave paintings onwards humans seem to have been fascinated by the same subjects. Their two dimensional simulations focus on, nature, landscapes, still life, portraits, and abstract shapes.

Nature and still life in art seems to mean food, flowers and plants, birds and animals, shells, feathers and bones, tools and decorations. That is quite a narrow range of interests but it makes perfect sense to a hunter gatherer. Even abstract art, on closer examination, turns out to consist of symmetrical shapes, fractals and tree-like structures that mimic nature. Many people doodle in the same way. These are the simulations we should surround humans with. Landscapes include seascapes, cloudscapes, skyscapes and riverscapes.

Social animals are driven to take an interest in faces because facial expressions provide useful information. A strong portrait captivates humans, drawing them into the painting and causing the viewer to wonder about the person being depicted. A good portrait tells the story of that person's life. They react to images of smiling faces as if they are real, which means that smiling faces provide a simple mood management tool.

In the modern world we now have three dimensional simulations depicting how others deal with their own environments, avoid dangers, and find rewards. They also show social interactions and their results. Humans are especially interested in how competitions for social status turn out.

They used to tell stories around camp fires. Then they wrote them down in books and acted them out in plays. Now we have films, television series and hyper-realistic simulations in computer games. We have never had so many opportunities to manipulate our own moods, but we tend not to think about it in a systematic way. The more closely the simulations match the basic drives of a 50 000 year old hominid, the better we like them.

Art is the general name we give to a range of imaginative mood management approaches. We create images, sounds, smells and stories that please us. In a relatively free market, the content of popular media provides a good indication of what drives human interest. The media is full of stories about food, shelter, sex and violence which just about covers it. Cookery programmes and competitions abound. There are also programmes about property and house building. Reality television and fiction is all about sex and violence. There are travel programmes and shopping channels. Some of the programmes actually put people into natural environments to see how they cope.

In addition to the programmes about trivial pursuits and some serious ones there are many performing shows. There are singing and dancing displays, sports and many different forms of artificial competitions and puzzles.

Script writers churn out endless versions of the same story in which people find themselves in threatening and frightening situations that involve requests and offers of social reassurance. Throw in a few surprises, in the form of plot twists, along with a bit of sex and violence along the way, and you have the formula for a best seller. From an evolutionary perspective it all makes sense. So whenever we are looking for ways to motivate humans, all we need to do is go back to the basic formula.

Comedy Culture

Modern theatre is traditionally represented by two masks. The smiling mask represents Thalia, the muse of comedy. The sad mask represents Melpomene, the muse of tragedy. In ancient open air theatres there were more than two. They enabled the people at the back to see what mood the actors were supposed to be expressing. In most of the plays they were either offering social reassurance or asking for it, being miserable or happy.

Comedy is closely linked to social reassurance. The subject matter of comedy often has the potential to embarrass or frighten the audience. For that reason, what people find funny changes over time to reflect current fears and whatever happens to be newsworthy. Comedians are able to lead audiences into uncomfortable territory by talking about topics that have the potential to unsettle and embarrass them, without going too far.

The skill comes in their ability to nudge the audience further towards the edge, without actually stepping over a line that triggers a fear or disgust. That takes judgement.

The purpose is to trigger the social reassurance response, which produces opioids in their brains. Humans enjoy this, which is why they are willing to pay good money and travel some distance for the experience. The excitement and anticipation fires up the dopamine circuits too.

This is the way to address all the difficult topics that embarrass and frighten us. We need to face up to them with humour so that the unthinkable becomes thinkable.

If there is one lesson we have learned over recent decades, it is that cover ups and denial encourage abuses of all kinds. There is still a tendency for large organisations to default towards cover ups to protect their reputations. I am not sure respect and reputation are laudable motivations. We should promote honesty, even when it does make people feel anxious or embarrassed. The fool in Shakespeare's plays was able to tell the truth to kings. We need more fools and more people who are willing to listen to them.

The comedian Jerry Sadowitz describes himself as "magician, comedian, psychopath". He pushes audiences closer to the line than most and I last saw him on the stage of the Leicester Square Theatre, where he came on dressed as Jimmy Savile. He earned the right to make his statement, because it was him who had first outed Savile as a paedophile at his Edinburgh Fringe show 30 years ago and for years he was shunned. The recording of his performance was hurriedly withdrawn by a nervous record company, following threats of legal action from Savile. From the stage in 2003, in his Jimmy Saville regalia, he alleged that Rolf Harris was also a paedophile and half the audience did not know what to think.

The direction of travel in comedy is always towards fear and embarrassment. For that reason, safe comedy can never be as funny as the more risky variety. The problem for comedians is that humans have different thresholds for fear and embarrassment, so in any audience that reflects the general population, there will be some people who want to go further and some that think it has already gone too far. That is why many comedians have a particular following and direct their humour towards their own sector of the market.

I think you can learn a lot about the current state of a culture by analysing the content of the comedy currently regarded as being at the boundary of good taste. Black humour presents tragic, distressing or morbid topics in humorous terms. It is a way of publicly exposing issues that some would prefer to remain hidden. It may also help us to come to terms with issues with the potential to frighten or embarrass us and deal with them.

Black humour requires some mental agility. Those who are quick to take offence and accuse comedians of being miserable, negative in outlook, or even cruel, might reflect on research published in January 2017.[64]

It found that those with the highest understanding and appreciation of black humour scored highest on verbal and non-verbal intelligence. They showed positive mood and low rates of aggression. A second group with moderate understanding and appreciation of black humour showed moderate aggression. It was those with the lowest appreciation of black humour who showed the most negative mood and the highest levels of aggression.

Redirecting Violent Competition

The amphitheatres of ancient Greece and Rome and the medieval jousting fields of England and France hosted violent competitions which sometimes resulted in death. Men and women still fight each other for fun and people pay to watch them do it. It is called sport.

Many sports are really simulations of play fighting. They allow competitors and audiences to gain pleasure from exercising their natural pursuit and performance drives. In tennis, squash, badminton, martial arts and boxing clubs, the players are often organised into hierarchical ladders, with the best player at the

---

[64] "Cognitive and emotional demands of black humour processing: the role of intelligence, aggressiveness and mood" - Ulrike Willinger et al (2017)

top and the weakest players at the bottom. Competitive individuals can challenge others at a similar level to progress. This perfectly mirrors the natural hierarchy negotiations that are evident across the natural world.

Sports enthusiasts like to emphasise the skills element of their sports, but there is no denying that there is quite a bit of violence in many of them too. Boxing, mixed martial arts, rugby and ice hockey are obvious examples. Football is sometimes called the beautiful game, but there is a fair degree of violence in that too. Country sports are even more realistic.

Some sports are less realistic simulations of violence. Archery, darts, target shooting, chess, and drag hunting can all be traced back to warfare. Even the gentle game of cricket mimics a battlefield with hostile bowling, aggressive fielding and sledging. Many video games are pure violence simulators.

I feel like I ought to say that I neither enjoy nor condone violence of any kind as an entertainment. But that would not be true. I do watch sports that involve violence and I enjoy them. I am not in the business of preventing other humans from enjoying themselves. On the contrary, I am trying to find more ways of doing it.

There are many activities which allow competitors to perform their skills without having to get involved in violence at all, such as card games, crosswords, puzzles, climbing, golf and gymnastics.

Exhibitions of skills and talents of various kinds, such as wit, intelligence and humour, are valued in many human cultures. Talent shows, cookery shows, dance shows, panel quizzes and celebrity torture shows are all structured as competitions because humans like competitions. They provide opportunities for humans to perform and watch performances, which is what we love doing.

Some have campaigned to have all competition removed from schools on ideological grounds. I think that would reduce the amount of fun. Competition motivates humans. Competitive pursuits are one of our basic routes to pleasure and removing the competitive element would remove a range of opportunities for people to pursue their own happiness. Some of us lose interest in competitions in which there are no winners or losers. That is a simple, psychological fact of life.

We can reduce violence as the means of expressing competitive behaviour, but the idea that humans would be happier without any competition betrays a shallow understanding of human nature. Humans cannot help comparing themselves to others. These days, there are people described as living in poverty, who have a higher material standard of living than the kings of England did in their freezing, damp, castles. The kings felt rich because they had more than their subjects. Poor people in the western world feel poor because they see others with more. We should not force competition on those who are not interested in it, but instead we should try to increase the range of opportunities so that everyone can pursue their own interests.

Those who want to ban competition completely may not get their own pleasures from sports, but they still compete in other ways. Some share information about their charitable activities. Some advertise their fashionable beliefs and credentials by turning up to every demonstration to express their outrage and virtue at the same time. Some manage to crowbar virtue signals into every conversation, in case nobody knows that they are vegan, pro-renewables, pro-animal rights or whatever. They are all competing to be special.

Anger is Bad For You

The catharsis hypothesis was once accepted by millions of therapist, group leaders, teachers, social workers and parents. The idea was that it was good for people to be able to vent their anger. A few stubbornly hang on to it today, although it has been completely discredited by volumes of research evidence. The truth is the opposite.

Venting anger only turns the heat up in an argument and makes angry people even more angry. People who are not angry do not need to vent anything and those who are need to calm their sympathetic nervous system. Even Freud, who is usually blamed for the spread of catharsis therapy, did not really encourage people to vent their emotions as anger. He suggested that it should be sublimated into more constructive pursuits and performances, such as dance, music and art, which sounds like a much better idea.

We know that modern man is capable of committing atrocities and genocide because it has happened throughout history and it is happening right now in various places around the world.

Angry people embark on pursuits of revenge and punishment, motivated by fantasies that give them pleasure along the way. Gangs are driven to carry out punishment beatings and raid each other's territory. Armies are driven to destroy villages, towns and cities. Humans burn crops, rape, pillage and plunder.

It will continue to happen for as long as we allow humans to indulge in the pleasures of hate pursuits and performances, whilst pretending to be doing something else. One of the greatest changes in human culture is the rapid expansion of communication. Other than in closed societies, people from around the world can communicate. If a mood management community developed which commented on world events, pointing out the basic drives and mental programmes driving the behaviours and mocking pantomime performances perhaps cultures could change more quickly than we realise. We have seen examples of cultural change happening in one generation.

Aside from the fact that angry people bring misery to others, getting angry is bad for them too. Research conducted in 2014 tracked data from Twitter to see if the cultures which encourage the use of aggressive, negative, emotional language, correlated with age-adjusted rates of death from heart disease. The researchers simply analysed the twitter feeds in various countries and the results could not have been clearer. Cultural language patterns involving anger, hatred and aggression emerged as the strongest risk factors after all other variables had been controlled. In fact, the association of risk was stronger for habitual anger expression than for smoking, diabetes, hypertension, and obesity. The message is clear - getting your pleasures from angry pursuits and performances is bad for you and for everybody else. And venting your anger is bad too.[65]

There are times when anger is the appropriate signal but it needs to be used sparingly.

So we know what causes people to drift into the wrong mood:

- External settings and environments
- Routines and procedures
- Internal settings and moods

All of those are ameliorable to some extent. Those who care for and educate children with learning disabilities and autism have to manage the physical and emotional environment and the daily routines, to prevent panic from taking control.

---

[65] "Psychological Language on Twitter Predicts Country Level Heart Disease Mortality" - Johannes Eichstaet et al, 2014

Reducing discomforts, anxieties and uncertainties are a first step in reducing over activity in the sympathetic nervous system. Adults may need to take control of the situation because the child does not have self control in these situations.

We know what humans in general like and by taking the time to find out, and communicating that information to everybody involved, we can become better at fine tuning the environment and routines to better reflect individual preferences.

Most humans enjoy warmth on the skin from water, sunshine, air and clothing. Warmth relaxed muscles. Some enjoy sensations derived from cooling the skin with water and air. They enjoy the application of different forms of pressure on the skin, and the sensation of different textures.

They enjoy certain visual patterns, shapes, colours and intensities of light. They enjoy certain images of the physical world, of other humans, and of other animals. They enjoy certain facial expressions. They enjoy certain aromas, flavours and textures in the nose and mouth. They enjoy certain sounds.

They enjoy certain rhythmic movements such as swaying, rocking, dancing and drumming. They enjoy synchronous exercise. They enjoy chanting, singing and making music.

They enjoy both laughing and crying. They enjoy creating images and artefacts. They enjoy making food and shelters. They enjoy solving puzzles and social interaction.

And they gain vicarious pleasure from watching other humans do all of these things. The opportunities to enable them to do them have multiplied in recent years but not every institution has kept up the pace.

Managing Bodybrains

Stress reactions evolved to protect us from dangers that are largely irrelevant in the modern world. We have got different things to worry about, yet we still react as if they are all about to eat us. Colleagues who disagree in meetings have elevated heart rates and blood pressure, as their sympathetic nervous systems prepare for a physical fight. Drivers at junctions, waiting for somebody to let them out, have suppressed immune systems and blood that is more likely to clot, as the body prepares to keep going in case it gets injured. Some people who are stressed cannot sleep at night, because the body remains alert ready for a physical attack. This is not good for any of us, which is why we should all be paying more serious attention to mood management.

For professionals who work with individuals who lack self control, it is at the heart of what they are trying to do, although many are unaware of it. Some individuals with special educational needs are seeking stimulation and getting it in harmful ways. Others are trying to escape stimulation and creating harm as they try to do so. We need to help everyone to achieve and attain the levels of stimulation they need, without hurting themselves or other people.

Some individuals, for example those with autism, react more extremely to the same physical stimuli, which makes them more vulnerable. Different people process sensory information in different ways. Just because they share the same environment that does not mean that they are experiencing the same environment, because we all process the same world differently. Some people may be too hot while others feel too cold in the same room. One person wants the volume turned up whilst another wants it turned down.

Humans have different sensitivities to sound. 96 decibels is about the limit for most people, but for some who have autism 45 decibels is too much. Slight uncertainty, novelty or surprise, unfamiliar sights and sounds, human proximity, particularly when people are watching us, all produce a minor stimulating response in most people. Some experience extreme physiological arousal reactions to the same trigger. A minor inconvenience or disturbance can result in a major flare up which over-excites their sympathetic nervous system so that they lose control. Anxiety, louder noises, shocks, rapid movements, too many voices and crowding can result in more extreme reactions.

Those with learning disabilities may not understand what is happening in their world, which increases the chance of amygdala hijack as they become afraid of their own physiological reaction in a panic attack.

That is why predictable routines, calming low-arousal environments, and improved communication are so important, so that people understand what is happening now, what is going to happen next, and when those things are going to happen.

Some people with dementia have significant memory loss, so they are continually surprised and unsettled because everything feels new, unpredictable and threatening. A natural response to unusual features in the environment is to stimulate the sympathetic nervous system to conduct safety checks. Their system is doing that all the time.

For many people with dementia, it is the ability to put down new memories that begins to affect them first. They are likely to be happier and calmer in familiar environments, with familiar routines, surrounded by images and objects from their own past. Often dementia affects the more advanced self-aware parts of the brain more than the automatic processing parts. They can actually find their way around familiar environments, even though they feel lost. That is why keeping them in their own home for as long as possible is preferred.

Old age has traditionally been regarded as a second childhood Just as the full suite of emotions was in place when we were babies, before the heart & mindbrain developed, so the emotions remain in place after some of the memories fade away. Mood management should be a continuing active process designed to calm, reassure and give pleasure to all humans, no matter what level of intellectual functioning they have. Some people only live in the here and now, minute by minute. So we need to make sure those minutes are comfortable. It is about treating people with care, respect and decency, to allow them to experience life enhancing emotions while dampening down harmful ones.

Everyone who works and/or cares for people with special needs is a teacher of one sort or another. They are not just educating the service users but also relatives, colleagues, temporary staff, and visitors. If the language of mood management becomes part of daily conversation, staff can remind each other to think about the processes underlying the behaviours and help others to become aware of them.

For example, we need to talk more about the differences between events often described as flare ups or melt downs, and temper tantrums which can be something different. Aggressive and violent outbursts exhibited by children and adults with learning disabilities, autism, or dementia are sometimes described as melt downs or flare ups. They are associated with an over-stressed sympathetic nervous system. They do not always know what they want. They may simply need to escape from a situation which has become unmanageable and unbearable for them. Flare-ups or melt downs are driven by panic.

Tantrums are something different. They are driven by a mixture of pursuit and performance. In temper tantrums the performers want something and the behaviour may be an attempt to get it. Most children grow out of toddler tantrums. Unfortunately some do not, because they have learned that those behaviours are occasionally rewarded. We know a 25 percent reinforcement schedule is enough to keep motivating primates to press buttons. Some children will keep on pressing our buttons in the same way. There are adults who resort to temper tantrums when they cannot get their own way. Their bodybrains need training too.

Any neural circuit that is associated with reward becomes strengthened, making it more likely for that behaviour to jump into the driving seat again in the future. Responsible adults should be given the confidence to resist unreasonable performances, whilst at the same time remaining calm themselves. They need to practise their own self control checklist, so that they do not react in a way that stimulates sympathetic nervous systems. That involves controlled faces, postures, gestures and sounds.

It takes time, so it is important that they do not give up by thinking that a consistent approach is not working. Rhesus Macaque monkeys, once trained, keep on pressing the buttons for a long time after the rewards stop, before they finally realise that "no" means "no".

Containing hazardous behaviour and redirecting attention in a calm and consistent manner is the best approach. The key is not to be seduced into an exciting, escalating performance spiral. Conflict escalates when bodybrains start stimulating each other in a feedback loop. The difference between effective mood managers, and less effective ones, is that they can control their own sympathetic nervous system and control the emotional signals they are broadcasting.

It is sometimes the emotional signalling which accompanies the message that excites sympathetic nervous systems, rather than the message itself. Information and directions can be delivered in a calm, measured, friendly, matter-of-fact way to avoid that from happening.

If directions or explanations need to be repeated, they should be repeated in exactly the same way, without any hint of escalation in tone, pace or volume. Facial expressions, gestures and body postures also need to be slowed and controlled.

Provocative Behaviour

Provocative behaviour is a performance. It is one bodybrain trying to elicit exciting, emotional signals from another. Expressions of shock, anger, surprise, disapproval and disgust are exciting. Eye contact is exciting. Wide eyes and raised eyebrows are particularly exciting. High pitched, fast paced, loud noises are exciting. Waving arms and movement is exciting. Open armed gestures, that signal trapping, are exciting. Standing square on and inflating is exciting. Stepping towards another person is exciting. Close proximity is exciting. Both fearful and aggressive performances are exciting.

Unfortunately, these are all the natural behaviours generated by excited sympathetic nervous systems. Some families have learned to interact in ways that excite their sympathetic nervous systems habitually. They are all noisy, excitable and often out of control as they all become over-stimulated. Even very young children become trained, along with the family pets which also join in. None of them are aware of what they are doing. That is why dogs and uncontrolled bodybrains are a bad combination. Unfortunately, dangerous dogs are also a threat performance accessory, so sometimes the people who are least qualified to own them are attracted to them.

Some children try to provoke emotional responses from teachers and professional carers. They behave in ways that produce reactions of shock, disapproval, disgust, fear or anger. Those reactions signal that the provocation is working because the other creature is becoming excited, which excites their bodybrain even further and escalates the performance.

Once this conflict spiral starts, a simple rule of thumb is to try to do the exact opposite of whatever feels natural. This normally means slowing down, reducing movement, and lowering the volume, tone and pace. It takes practice to train the bodybrain to behave unnaturally but it is possible and then it because automatic.

There have been many occasions which resulted in violence that would not have done so if the person attempting to manage the situation had not accidentally been seduced into an escalating performance.

Communication difficulties can result in frustration that gives way to panic. Sometimes it is the carer who reacts to unexpected behaviour, and their own panic response triggers a mirror reaction. Learning to manage your own mind, moods, emotions, and behaviour is the key to managing other people's. And it starts with mood management.

Mind control is aimed at changing the interpretation of emotions to break the escalating cycle and indirectly calm the sympathetic nervous system. Being able to calm yourself is the first step towards calming other people. Anxiety, stress and panic involve circular feedback in which the sympathetic nervous system becomes over excited, causing physiological changes, which are then interpreted as evidence that something is wrong, causing further stimulation of the system in a vicious circle.

Working directly on the symptoms, by controlling and relaxing muscles and breathing, whilst at the same time controlling and redirecting conscious attention, can put a brake on the physiological escalation, interrupt the interpretation of threat, and calm down activity in the amygdala.

External awareness involves bringing attention under control by concentrating on the immediate environment and scanning it in a systematic way.

Stare out intently around you and look at all the different shapes in turn, all the squares and rectangles, all the circles and elliptical shapes, diamonds and triangles. Then look at the different colours in order, perhaps starting with the greens and study all the various shades, then the reds, then the blues etc. Then look for different textures and really study the details of those textures. Having exhausted all the features of one sense. you can go to the next, perhaps listening to all the different sounds, especially faint or distant ones. This sort of focused concentration seems to calm the sympathetic nervous system and reactivates the parasympathetic nervous system.

Internal awareness involves progressive muscle relaxation, concentrating on one group of muscles at a time, and relaxing them in turn. It does not really matter where you start. The feet is as good a place as any. After becoming aware of the muscles in the toes, relax them and work up to the heels, then the ankle and calf muscles, and so on, gradually working up to the face and head. All of these techniques involve redirecting conscious attention. They are the business end of meditation and mindfulness.

Hot baths and saunas are another direct way to relax the muscles. Relaxed muscles send the message to the brain that there is no threat. There are a number of progressive muscle relaxations scripts, audio and computer programmes available online to assist with this approach.

We know from experiments on people who have had cosmetic botox treatment that not being able to frown seems to improve their mood. Perhaps simply choosing to smile might raise the mood. At the beginning of 2017 I participated in the Pocket Smile project by the UCL Institute of Cognitive Neuroscience. This study is exploring whether looking at smiling faces throughout the day can increase happiness. They simply send a picture of a smiling face to your phone. Alternatively you could just collect photos of smiling faces and set your own alarms to look at them. You could choose to mix more with people who tend to smile or decide to become somebody who smiles more.

Diaphragm breathing is another technique that seems to calm over-excited sympathetic nervous systems. It involves concentrating attention on breathing slowly and deeply, filling the lungs, then breathing out by using the diaphragm in the abdomen, rather than expending and contracting the intercostal muscles higher in the ribs.

Positive mental focus is a different technique which involves redirecting attention towards thoughts and ideas which calm the sympathetic nervous system, and away from worries and anxieties. A simple version can be combined with diaphragm breathing. Each time you slowly breathe in, briefly hold your breath and think about somebody you love, like or admire. It does not really matter whether you know them or not, so long as you feel well disposed towards them. You could choose to look at one of your smiling faces instead. This is building positive associations with the peak inhalation.

There is anecdotal evidence that yoga, tai chi, and slow swimming also calm the mind and body. Just getting people out into natural environments seems to benefit them too. There are alpha brainwave audio resources and binaural beats soundtracks. The cheap ones are just as good as the expensive ones.

So called "no touch" policies have been advocated by individuals with only a superficial understanding of human behaviour, but touch can be extremely important. Physical contact is an important part of mood management. Many social animals groom one another in social bonding rituals. Primates groom a victim of bullying, providing the individual was not asking for trouble by provoking a high status animal.[66] Mothers lick their young mammals and hug them close. Harry Harlow showed that young monkeys have an innate urge to cling to fur, even if it does not provide milk.[67] Research has shown that even rubbing your own head depresses activity in the amygdala. Regular hugs also seem to boost the immune system. In one experiment two groups were both exposed to a common cold virus. Those in the group that had been receiving regular hugs were significantly less likely to become ill.[68]

As a child, the autism expert Temple Grandin wanted to be hugged but she said she could not stand the overwhelming stimulation. It was only when she was 14 years old, working on a farm, that she saw cattle being held in a hydraulic metal clamp to keep them still while they were being inoculated. She noticed how some cattle seemed to relax when they were squeezed and immediately empathised with them. She wanted to try it for herself and there are photographs of the 14 year old girl in the cattle clamp, where she chose to stay for half an hour.

---

[66] Their understanding of social etiquette within the social hierarchy is very sophisticated. Similarly crows became angry with a bird that failed to show respect towards a much higher status bird. Social animals like everyone to know their place.

[67] "Love in Monkeys" - Harry Harlow, (1959)

[68] "Does Hugging Provide Stress-Buffering Social Support? A Study of Susceptibility to Upper Respiratory Infection and Illness" - Sheldon Cohen et al (2014)

Afterwards she said she felt calmer and realised she could not live without it.

So she went home and built her own out of plywood, powered by compressed air. The design is still used world-wide in settings for people with autism.[69]

Some people may not like being touched - in which case we should respect their wishes, but we need to check that they have not been receiving the wrong sort of touch.

Sometimes problems begin with an unusual pursuit that is misunderstood by carers. Functional analysis involves imaginatively and systematically trying to work out what it is that the child is pursuing, and finding alternative ways of delivering it, or providing an equally rewarding alternative. For example, some children have learned to provoke situations which result in them being held firmly, just so that they can experience deep pressure touch, often without realising what they are doing. We need to help them to find more appropriate ways of expressing their needs and better ways of providing what they want.

Light pressure touch, such as tickling or gently stroking the skin, stimulates the sympathetic nervous system. That is the last thing somebody needs who is already overstimulated. Deep pressure touch, on the other hand, calms the sympathetic

---

[69] "Calming Effects of Deep Touch Pressure in Patients with Autistic Disorder, College Students, and Animals" - Temple Grandin (1992)

nervous system. It slows down the heart rate, reduces blood pressure, and depresses activity in the amygdala. Squeezing, hugging and massage can all provide deep pressure touch. Weighted blankets and pressure jackets can provide deep pressure touch. There is also a range of deep pressure touch equipment in catalogues for children with learning disabilities.

Some people habitually think about things that make them worry, which stimulates the sympathetic nervous system as it prepares for fight or flight. Rather than telling them not to worry, which is counter-productive, it is more effective to redirect their attention towards thoughts and activities that have more positive associations. Whatever the bodybrain is thinking about or doing boosts the strength of associated thoughts and ideas, which in turn cause it to generate emotions associated with them. Inducing people to think and behave in different ways can indirectly cause the bodybrain to change its mood.

For example, inducing facial expressions and body language affects mood. Counting your blessings is a simple therapy that works. Once again it involves redirecting and controlling attention. List and think deeply about people, places, activities and experiences that have positive associations. If any idea occurs that does not have a happy association, immediately move on to the next one that does. Avoid spending any time thinking about things with negative associations. Initially this takes willpower, but as with all bodybrain training, with practice it becomes automatic and effortless.

Once you get into the habit of counting your blessings, it gets easier because you are building a library of mood enhancing things to think about. The bodybrain cannot help reacting by generating more ideas and associations for as long as people are able to keep directing their thoughts in the right direction, because that is how it works. Miserable thoughts stimulate other miserable thoughts, depressing happy thoughts and moods. Happy thoughts work the other way round.

There is a society called the Cloud Appreciation Society for strange people who like that sort of thing. Every day they send an email with a picture of interesting clouds and cloud appreciators appreciate them. Just choosing to appreciate something is quite a good mental exercise.

Attention can be directed towards identifying features to appreciate in the immediate environment. Then it can be directed towards the future to consider things to look forward to. It is worth putting some planning in to make sure you do have something planned to look forward to. They do not have to be big. That is another good mental exercise.

We know that most of the pleasure from the pursuit drive comes from the anticipation, rather than the reward at the end. So to extract as much pleasure from life as possible, we need to think ahead and anticipate our pleasures. Rather than going out to dinner tonight, plan to go in two weeks time and in the intervening period spend time anticipating it. When the day comes, make sure you make an effort to redirect your attention into the here and now and really pay attention to every aspect of the evening. This is investing in memories, which will provide more things to appreciate in the future (unless the evening is a disaster, in which case pay no attention to it, look at your phone like everybody else, and then forget about it. Immediately start thinking about a better treat to come).

Daniel Kahneman talks about humans having two selves, the experiencing self and the remembering self. The remembering self creates distorted memories, because it pays too much attention to beginnings and endings, but not enough to duration. A good film can be ruined by a bad ending, even if the ending only took up two minutes, and the previous 88 minutes were quite enjoyable. The remembering self simply forgets the 88 minutes of enjoyment and pays too much attention to the ending of the experience. In one experiment, subjects were asked to keep one arm in a bucket of iced water for a set period of time, then take it out. This well known torture is used in psychology laboratories to test willpower. Later the same subjects were asked to put their arm into the bucket of iced water again. But this time, instead of immediately taking the arm out at the end, they had to keep in in until the water had warmed up a bit. Obviously, the second option involved enduring discomfort for a longer period of time, yet when they were given the choice of repeating either task, most people chose the latter. The reason is that the remembering self did not remember the duration of the discomfort. It only remembered that the water felt warmer at the end in the second experiment, and their choice was distorted by that.

Designers of stage shows, writers, film makers and musicians know how important it is to have a good finale. Perhaps we should pay more attention to planning and investing in the beginnings and endings of experiences. For example, making sure the first and last days of a holiday are really good. Duration is not as important, as the memory distorts the record so you remember as much about an enjoyable weekend break as you do about a two week holiday. This might sound simplistic but the bodybrain is quite simple in some ways. These tricks work.

Another important consideration is that memories last longer than moments - which according to the evidence last about three seconds if they are not turned into memories. The heart & mindbrain can enjoy memories over and over again. You need to be adding content to your life story anyway, as I believe one of the primary functions of the heart & mindbrain is to craft a story of your life that makes you happy.

Some people spend a lot of time feeling comfortable, doing familiar things that are not taxing, but they are not putting down any new memories. In a way they are wasting their time because they will not remember much of it. Others have allowed their bodybrain to create a library of miserable memories that they would rather not think about. In which case they should stop thinking about them and start working on new ones, stocking up the memory with content they really appreciate. It makes more sense to put some effort into creating a library of things you will enjoy thinking about in the future.

Have a section on good places you have been to and keep adding to it. Have a section on people you have really liked, people you admire, your favourite activities, your favourite films, your favourite books, your favourite walks, your favourite views, your favourite music - your favourite everything.

It is also worth investing in memories that make you feel good about yourself. The heart & mindbrain seems to judge itself from the mental firewall in the same way that it judges everybody else. So it can be beneficial to do things that make you feel proud of yourself, even if doing them was not much fun at the time. These are the memories that produce deeper feelings of wellbeing. They are achievements.

Investing in your own personal memory library is a good investment, because one day you will be old and you might want something to think about.

Enabling Genuine Choice

Our legal framework is based on the presumption that the self is an indivisible individual who is given the opportunity to make choices without duress. Clearly a person who is under duress, under the influence of alcohol or drugs, or pressured in any way, is deprived of free choice. We would disregard a confession or statement made in such circumstances and prefer one made freely.

But humans are not indivisible individuals. They are conscious selves, which are produced by heart & mindbrains, trying to control unconscious bodybrains which work automatically. To some extent, at least for short periods of time, the heart & mindbrain can control the bodybrain by suppressing some of its urges, but that is not the way self control really works. Willpower is not very strong and it does not last very long. It is a temporary safety aid, like the oxygen masks on an aircraft which deploy to provide oxygen for a limited period of time until the plane reaches a lower altitude, at which point they are no longer needed. Willpower works for a short period of time too, to allow the heart & mindbrain to put as much distance between the bodybrain and whatever is tempting it. The mantra for willpower is distance not resistance, because resistance is futile.

Real self control does not result from willpower. It results from having a well trained bodybrain that automatically produces behaviours that protect itself, resulting in the optimum balance between short term pleasures and long term well being. If my bodybrain was addicted to nicotine, cocaine, heroin, gambling or any of the things that bodybrains become addicted to, and I was desperately feeling the pressure to give in to those temptations, my freedom of choice would be compromised. I would have to rely on willpower to get me away from the temptation. Fortunately I am not addicted to any of those things, so today I will not need to exert any self control whatsoever. I deserve no credit for that, because it will take no effort.

There is a huge ethical issue here that we have ducked for far too long. Around 80 percent of children develop well trained bodybrains which frees their heart & mindbrains to be capable of freedom of choice. But around 20 percent have poorly trained bodybrains which steal choices away from their heart & mindbrains, because their heart & mindbrains are not allowed to implement the choices they make once they come under duress.

It is a fallacy to describe a poorly trained bodybrain as having freedom of choice. It is simply motivated by its strongest urges. heart & mindbrains, on the other hand, are capable of making choices, so long as they are not under duress. However, they may not be capable of implementing those choices when an untrained bodybrain takes over.

"I" am a heart & mindbrain. I am very attached to my bodybrain both metaphorically and literally, because I would not exist without it and it provides all of my enjoyable experiences. It also creates all of my less enjoyable ones. I have to manage it, rather than the other way round. It is a parent child relationship. There are times when I am disappointed by its behaviour, but I forgive it. Most of the time I let it get on with things on its own because I trust it. However, there are times when I have to step in and make decisions on behalf of both of us that I believe are in our own best interests. When people refer to "me" as an individual, they are really referring to the "self". That is the conscious heart and mindbrain, rather than the unconscious bodybrain. My self is a mind.

Our legal system is riddled with contradictions in relation to how choice, rights and responsibilities should be applied to children because it fails to take into account how the whole body, brain and mind interact. Policy makers do not seem to have thought through the issue in an coherent way, with the result that there are all sorts of arbitrary restrictions which prevent children and young people from making their own choices. Children are not allowed to choose whether or not they want to go to school, they are not allowed to choose what they want to eat or drink at school, they are not allowed to smoke, drink alcohol, gamble, or have sex.

From the moment of birth, far from enjoying their inalienable rights, children find themselves under the complete supervision and control of adults who make decisions for them. Responsible adults are themselves punished by the government if they fail to supervise and control their children properly. Parents can be fined if their children arrive late for school. The government dictates what children should eat at school, allowing school staff to search lunch boxes for banned treats and confiscate them. Headteachers are expected to act as agents for the government, fining parents if they take their child on holiday at the wrong time of year. In reality, children are deprived of their liberty from the moment of birth, according to the objective definition which applies in the case of adults. They are not free to leave and are subject to continuous supervision and control.

Children remain deprived of their liberty until somebody else decides that they are ready to make and implement their own choices. So in reality, their rights are not inalienable at all. They are granted by somebody else, at some stage in their lives. I agree with that, but a failure to be honest about it, or even acknowledge reality, has contributed to hopelessly muddled thinking at various levels of policy implementation.

The great thinkers of the enlightenment were not thinking about children when they made the first declarations of human rights. Article 1 stated:

"All human beings are born free and equal in dignity and rights. They are endowed with reason and conscience and should act towards one another in a spirit of brotherhood."

The Universal Declaration of Human Rights 1948

That sounds good but it is not really true. Babies are not born free and equal in dignity and rights. They are born naked, helpless and incontinent. They are not endowed with reason and conscience either. That may come later, if they are lucky, through a process of socialisation but they do not get much choice in the matter.

The enlightenment philosopher, Jean-Jacques Rousseau, favoured leaving children alone to develop naturally. In his "confessions", the forerunner of modern autobiographies, he admitted that his ideas were based on:

"bizarre and romantic notions of human life, which experience and reflection have never been able to cure me of".

Some of those bizarre and romantic notions have become entrenched in policy and guidance. Rousseau was reacting against the less romantic writings of Thomas Hobbs in 1691, who thought that children were naturally evil and that life was nasty, brutish and short.

The truth is that humans are neither naturally good nor naturally evil. How they turn out depends on how they are socialised, and depriving children of the opportunity to develop competence in the management of their own moods, emotions, and behaviour, by empowering untrained bodybrains before they are able to cope, is not child protection - it is child abuse.

If we are serious about enabling choice, we need to put more effort into discovering what people really want. We need to allow them to express themselves when they are not under duress. Then we should support them when the time comes to implement those choices.

The time to find out what somebody really wants is not in the middle of a blazing row or temper tantrum, or when they have low blood sugar, or are being tempted by any of the addictive behaviours that get people into trouble. That is when the bodybrain has seized control of the system and the mind is under duress.

It is when the sympathetic nervous system is calm enough for the heart & mindbrain to be heard that we can find out what the self really wants. That means calming the system down or waiting for a time when it is calm. That is when we can talk through the available choices.

Talking and listening are important because some people do not seem to be able to communicate across the mental firewall between their own bodybrain and heart & mindbrain by thinking things through on their own. They need to talk things through with somebody else in order to think things through for themselves. While they are talking to somebody else their bodybrain is really communicating with themselves.

Getting people to talk through the issues, putting the full case for both sides of an argument, either verbally or in writing (if they are capable), can also assist internal communication. The heart & mindbrain and bodybrain may have different ideas, but they can each be allowed to express them and come to a joint decision.

Then they need to agree to abide by collective responsibility and promise that they will keep to whatever agreement they have chosen. They also need to agree that the rules will be enforced, without exception, but be allowed to set another time to review the agreement, which will also be when the system is calm.

I believe that siding with the heart & mindbrain is maximising genuine choice. If both bodybrain and heart & mindbrain cannot agree on a course of action when the system is calm, neither gets their way. If they do agree when the system is calm, and stick by their agreement when the time comes to implement it, that is fine too. The problem only arises when they both agree on the choice when the system is calm, but one of them tries to renege on the deal when the time comes to implement it, because the sympathetic nervous system is unsettled.

That is the time to choose sides and I say we should side with the one trying to keep to the deal. In Greek mythology, Odysseus understood that a time would come when the songs of the Sirens would remove his ability to make a rational choice. He knew that unless somebody stopped him, his bodybrain would be tempted to drive the ship onto the rocks and kill everyone. So he asked his sailors to tie him to the mast and ignore his pleas to be released once he came under the spell of the Sirens. That allowed him to listen to their songs without following them into oblivion. That was smart mood management. I have had similar conversations with children who wanted to be protected from the influence of their bodybrain. I remember one who was furious with me because I failed to prevent him from tearing up his own coursework.

When bodybrains take over, people become emotional and aggressive, so it is tempting to give in. But it is the reasonable heart & mindbrain that really has the individual's best interests at heart and deserves support. Bodybrains get people into trouble. heart & mindbrains sometimes need help to get them out of trouble.

Heart & Mindbrains make promises they sincerely hope to keep. but by the time it comes to implement them the system is upset and the bodybrain has taken control, wrecking the plans. The question is not whether we take sides. We have no choice in the matter. Whatever action or inaction we choose to take will tip the scales in one direction or another. The question is who we side with, a reasonable heart & mindbrain or an unreasonable bodybrain.

Diabetics suffering from hypoglycaemia can lose self control, becoming excited and confused. Alcohol and various drugs relax inhibition and self-control, allowing the bodybrain to take over and get people into trouble. If people are in that condition professionals are expected to take over and look after them because they have temporarily lost capacity/competence.

Children with under-developed heart & mindbrains and untrained bodybrains temporarily lose capacity/competence too. The same rules should apply. These are difficult issues which we need to discuss more honestly and openly. The model of heart & mindbrain and bodybrain can help individuals to develop a better understanding of their own behaviour and feel better about themselves at the same time. It can help them to develop and agree their own care plans.

I am not referring here to adults who lack the capacity/competence to understand the issues and make their own choices. They are covered by the Mental Capacity Act. I am thinking about children who lack the self control to prevent their bodybrain from blocking the implementation of those choices. Self control will come if we support them to develop it. If we take the path of least resistance and give in to bodybrains, it will not develop and we already know the social cost.

Teaching Critical Thinking

It is the heart & mindbrain that is capable of hard thinking - the sort that takes mental effort. In doing so it has to suppress the ideas being generated by the bodybrain and I suspect that is what makes it so tiring. We are innately programmed to learn spoken language in much the same way as birds are to learn birdsong. That happens effortlessly when we are children. Written language, mathematics and critical thinking are something different. They do not develop spontaneously. They have to be taught and learned with effort.

In the information age it is crucial that humans are taught how to think. For over four thousand years, the majority of humans managed without being able to read or write. For most of that time there was not much information to be had, so they were not really missing out on much. Just a few generations ago, the majority of humans indulged in magical thinking to explain the yawning gaps in their knowledge. Superstition, folklore and myths were sufficient for the sorts of decisions they needed to make. The brain evolved not to provide an accurate or objective view of the world, but to give us a useful view which we could act on. Mental distortions, such as a propensity to see faces in bushes, fires and clouds had a purpose.

It was better to err on the safe side. It was safer to mistrust and avoid people who were different. It was safer to swear allegiance to a tribe and be prepared to defend it against foreigners. It was safer to establish a fearful reputation. This was mostly bodybrain thinking and it was good enough.

It is no longer good enough. Now there is a surfeit of information available. What humans will need is the capacity to make sense of it and recognise when others are deceiving them. Magical thinking is no longer good enough. Humans need to make rational and far reaching decisions that not only affect them but the lives of generations to come. Heart & mindbrain thinking has never been so important, but not everybody is interested in promoting it.

Some cultures deliberately restrict access to education for some or all of their populace, because knowledge and the ability to use it is power. Ignorant leaders fear knowledgeable subjects. It is only the bad ideas that need protection from illumination by critical thinking. Some cultures devalue girls and prevent them from accessing education, because they want them to grow into obedient women, rather than well informed ones. Some systems limit education for the masses, to produce obedient workers rather than critical thinkers and protect a ruling elite who are no more capable of critical thinking than their subjects. Even in cultures that claim to value education, critical thinking is often underdeveloped.

The ability to think clearly and critically will become increasingly important as the information revolution progresses. We should not underestimate the scale or significance of the problem. Policy makers who have not learned to control their own moods, minds and their thinking are a danger to us all. Judging from the quality of political debate in the 21st century very few of them are currently capable of following or presenting a reasoned argument.

In order to create an education system that teaches children to think properly, we need teachers who are capable of doing it. The sad truth is that most adults do not even know what critical thinking is. They are still inclined to use magical thinking to compensate. They are unable to distinguish between pseudoscience and real science, they do not understand the meaning of evidence, they are over-impressed by coincidences because they do not understand probability, and they frequently confuse correlation with causation.

I will not make myself popular by saying it, but such disabilities are not rare in schools and amongst teachers. They are the norm and that is a serious matter. Beliefs are more likely to be false when they are based on poor reasoning and decisions based on false beliefs are more likely to be wrong.

For most of our existence the human brain did not need to make accurate calculations, or create complete and accurate mental re-presentations of the world. It just needed to make quick guesses that were good enough to enable animals to function within their own local environment. For most of human history, rough rules of thumb were good enough. Now they are not. We evolved to judge the speeds of running animals, but now have to judge the speeds of approaching express trains, which we are not equipped to do. That is why humans crossing rail tracks are frequently hit by trains. The technological world has overtaken our natural abilities and to keep up we need to teach every new generation how to think differently.

An important aspect of education in the future will be making sure humans are aware of their own limitations. Our brains cannot help imagining causation and meaning where none exists, which is one of the most common thinking errors. When two things are close together, either in space or in time, our brains naturally jump to the conclusion that they must be connected in some way. Often they are not.[70] This is sometimes called the rooster syndrome after a rooster that thought the sun came up everyday because he crowed.

Many animals develop rituals, in which they repeat whatever they did before something good happened, just in case there was a causal link, and avoid whatever they were doing just before something bad happened in the same way. When

_____

[70] For a funny website with lots of correlations that are unlikely to be causally linked see: http://tylervigen.com/spurious-correlations

pigeons are fed by a machine that delivers food grains at random intervals they soon begin to indulge in complicated dances. They start pecking at a spot on the floor or dancing in circles, repeating whatever movement that happened to precede the delivery of the grain. Like humans, they get trapped in pointless rituals that in reality have no effect.

Humans are prone to similar forms of superstitious behaviour. Many have lucky charms and little rituals that they like to follow in their own lives, convinced that they can control the universe in the same way as dancing pigeons. We need to raise our game above the level of a dancing pigeon. We need to teach the next generation how to think better than the last one.

Some people are suspicious of critical thinking itself, believing it to be just another form of magic. It is actually just a package of mental tricks to increase the number of times you turn out to be right.

Those who do have reason to fear the spread of critical thinking and mood management are those who depend on fear, deception and lies to claim undeserved authority. The first formal teachers were religious leaders. They claimed a higher authority for their own prejudices and expected everybody to accept them without question, even when they were wrong. The Italian astronomer Galileo Galilei was persecuted in the Inquisition for telling the truth about the earth orbiting the sun. He was found guilty of "vehemently suspect of heresy", and forced to spend the rest of his life under house arrest. He was not forgiven by the Roman Catholic Church until 1992.

"Science is the belief in the ignorance of experts."

Richard Feynman

Religious teachers did not just claim to impart wisdom about the structure of the physical world. They were also keen to lay down rules about how people should conduct themselves in all aspects of their private and family lives. The job of the teacher was to teach and a learner was expected to passively accept the doctrines without question. This style of authoritarian education has faded from fashion in most western liberal cultures but it is still evident in some educational institutions.

For example, in February 2015, a Saudi Arabian cleric, Sheikh Bandar al-Khaibari, gave a lecture at a university in the United Arab Emirates. He claimed that the Earth does not orbit the sun, but is in fact stationary, meaning that the sun must circle the earth. His reasoning was that if the earth really was rotating, and an aircraft was flying in the same direction, it would simply fall out of the sky. As a cleric he was used to having his ideas accepted without question. In this case, his students were not impressed. They reacted with good humour and put extracts of the lecture onto the internet where it received widespread derision. His students may not have been so confident to challenge his ideas about theology, even if they had contained logical flaws.

The enlightenment was a time when rational thinking became fashionable. Now it is in retreat. "Alternative facts" is a phrase used by Kellyanne Conway, a Presidential advisor, during a Meet the Press interview on January 22, 2017. She was defending White House Press Secretary Sean Spicer's false statement about the attendance at Donald Trump's inauguration as President of the United States. Not everything is a matter of opinion. There are facts and falsehoods. Critical thinking is what enables humans to recognise which is which.

All animals with brains have an urge to find meaning - to resolve dissonance. In uncertain times, when there are no easy answers, they lower their quality threshold for explanations.

Rats with hippocampal damage have a lower threshold for superstitious conditioning. They jump to the wrong conclusions more readily. Stress damages the hippocampus, reducing the demand of the brain for evidence, which may explain why some people are more ready to believe in magical explanations, possession, fairies, ghosts, astrology, crop circles, UFOs, auras, crystals, alternative medicines and conspiracy theories.

Fundamentalist and supremacist beliefs have increased in the United States where 88% believe in alternative medicine, 70% believe magnetic therapy is scientific, 60% believe in ESP, 40% believe astronomy is scientific, 32% believe in lucky numbers, and 30% of adult Americans believe that UFOs are space vehicles from other civilisations.

We need to teach how science works - not just what has been discovered by scientists. Science is about skepticism and questioning, not blind acceptance of authority. In the U.S. , although educated people score slightly better, many do not understand how science works. 70% of the general population do not understand scientific method. 53% of graduates understand it, but only 38% of those with middle level science qualifications and 17% of those with low level education. They all have the vote.[71]

The percentage believing in alternative medicine and therapy actually increases for college graduates. The definition "therapy" is a treatment intended to relieve or heal a disorder. Scientific method is used to test whether a therapy works. The definition of an alternative therapy is that it has not been shown to work. A treatment that works is called medicine.

In a so called "post truth" world we need fact checkers with a skeptical mindset equipped with tools to detect errors. Those tools are scientific method, critical thinking, mathematics and logic. They are all we have.

In many parts of the world, challenging the ideas of leaders can still be a dangerous business. Those in power in North Korea, leaders of the Islamic State group and Boko Haram claim to

[71] This section was written two years before the Trump election.

know everything citing a higher authority. They do not welcome critical thinking or appeals to reason.

Authority has been a constant feature of human relationships throughout history and it often deserves to be challenged. Threats and violence are still the currency of social interaction in many parts of the world, as they used to be everywhere else on the planet. A short tour through museums of mediaeval torture, slavery, and the holocaust remind us how close we still are to historical acts of barbarity within our own culture.

The enlightenment involved challenges to the authority of the church and progressed to challenges of other forms of arbitrary authority. I am part of a rebellious post war generation that challenged all authority. I still do not like being told what to do.

As a pupil the adults I really respected were not the ones who demanded respect. They did not need to because they carried a natural authority that was unrelated to the exercise of power. They were reasonable and good humoured. We liked them and respected them for that. Those who need to demand respect seldom deserve it.

When right wing columnists look back fondly to the "good old days", when there was more respect for authority and police officers could get away with giving young miscreants a clip around the ear, and cut corners to get quick confessions, they conveniently forget the huge price some people had to pay.

Power and authority were easily abused, resulting in bribery, corruption, unlawful beatings, cover ups, and appalling miscarriages of justice.

Unfortunately, looking around the world at the way humans have spontaneously organised themselves that is still not the exception, it is the norm. Throughout history, individuals, groups, families, gangs, tribes, religions and nation states have abused power to further their own interests. Whenever large systems of law and order break down, that is how the subsystems initially tend to reorganise. When the police lose control of areas of modern urban cities, gangs take over. Often these are gangs of criminal families. When national governments lose control, tribal groups take over coalescing around exclusive racial, religious or political affiliations. If there is any such thing as a "natural" social organisation for humans, the authoritarian exclusive hierarchy seems to be it.

Authoritarianism seems to be the natural starting place for civilisations. Only later, as they become settled, do enlightened ideas such as democracy begin to take traction. And we need to consider the possibility that those are temporary phases. Perhaps that is the most important lesson for 21st century politicians in the west to learn after their disastrous attempts at nation building in the middle east.

When governments are toppled, they are seldom replaced by successful democracies. The leader of one tribal group or another grabs power and they drift towards dictatorship. When the police are perceived to have lost control of areas of inner cities, dominant criminal families and gangs take over. In children's homes and schools, when authority was carelessly removed from the adults, due to carelessly drafted and ambiguous policies, dominant young people sometimes saw an opportunity to grab power for themselves. When the wrong people grab power the result can be worse than what preceded it.

There is no easy answer, other than the obvious one. We need to understand social systems better before blundering in and trying to remove authority from them. Undermining the current authority is the easy part. Replacing it with a more effective alternative is more difficult.

The Point of Pointless Rules

In spite of my temperamental resistance to authority, I have come to understand that there are times when authority is necessary in order to get things done. Adults sometimes need to act as adults. Teachers sometimes need to teach. Children, like adults in a variety of contexts, have to learn that sometimes they need to shut up, listen, and do as they are told. The vast majority of the population would be amazed at how controversial those statements are in some universities and in the social services departments of some local authorities.

My attitude towards it has changed during the writing of this book. We know that dopamine driven neural circuits in the bodybrain are excited by uncertainty. When children know the rules will be enforced without exception they learn to follow them. It is when there is doubt about whether rules will be enforced that they get excited and are driven to gamble. For as long as rules are not enforced consistently, creating uncertainty, there will be challenge and conflict. When rules are established the challenging stops. Nobody would keep playing a fruit machine that never paid out, but they do keep playing those that pay out intermittently.

I have also had a Damascene conversion, rather late in the day considering my advancing years. I suddenly understand the point of pointless rules. As a child, I was in the church choir. I cannot quite remember how that happened, but I think I may have been recruited as a mercenary because we got paid for doing weddings on Saturdays. I even sang at Durham Cathedral, even though I was never very religious.

I do remember that we had to wear black cassocks, with a short white smock over the top, and perform a number of, what seemed to me, pointless rituals. These included bowing, kneeling, chanting and singing at various stages of the proceedings. We also formed processions, walking up and down the church. We had to be silent while a man in a dress talked, then we chanted and sang songs. At some stage I remember, I was supposed to kneel down to apologise for crimes I could not remember committing. At the end we took our dresses off and had squash and a biscuit.

You may have gathered that I was not a very bright child. I spent a good deal of time day dreaming, not entirely sure what was going on around me - a problem that continued into adulthood. I did not really mind the church rituals though, even if they did seem a bit pointless. I actually quite enjoyed them. Now I understand why, because they involved a number of mood management enhancing behaviours.

At primary school too, there were lots of pointless rituals and rules. We had to call teachers "Sir" or "Miss". We had to learn to sit and stand still. We had to line up in queues, stand up straight with arms by our sides, sitting up straight with arms folded, and put our hands up and wait to be told to speak. We had to ask permission to get out of our seats, we had to learn to stay silent. At lunchtime we had to wait to be told where we could sit, wait to be told when we could get our lunch, wait to be told when we could clear our plates, then wait to be told when we could go out to play. Then at playtime we had to stand still when somebody blew a whistle, and wait until they blew it again before we were allowed to line up.

It all sounds terribly oppressive now. Even the teaching was drilled. I remember doing pages of different versions of exactly the same mathematical operation, pages of additions, pages of subtractions, pages of long division. We copied out letters of the alphabet and then learned to join them up. We had to copy writing off the blackboard and out of text books. Even at grammar school, I recall a history teacher who did nothing but copy from a text book onto the blackboard, which we in turn had to copy into our own books then memorise for the exam. I got a B in history without really learning anything.

We had to chant the alphabet and multiplication tables over and over again. We had to learn poems off by heart and chant them too. There was such a lot of chanting. When they did the register we all had to answer to our names in turn, every single day. In assembly we had to say the Lords prayer every single day.

I thought it was all pointless but now I realise that I was wrong about that. The exercises themselves might have been pointless, but learning to do what you are told is a crucial life skill. It was not me that was learning the rules. Once my bodybrain had learned to follow them, I was liberated to vacate the here and now and think about other things. At school it was easier to follow the rules than waste time arguing about them.

I questioned everything and continue to do so. Although not religious, I actually enjoyed religious studies, because it was taken by an intelligent and good humoured rector who was happy to debate and argue for as long as I was. He taught me how to think better.

In day-to-day life there are benefits in being able to follow unimportant rules without thinking and without question. It frees your mind to think about things that are important. If you had to question every single decision you make throughout the day life would be exhausting. You would never get anything done. Our lives are governed by a myriad of rules that are not important in themselves. They simply allow us to get things done more efficiently. The important thing is that we all stick to the same ones and that we are all able to follow them. For example, it really does not matter which side of the road we drive on in any particular country, so long as everybody follows the same rule. The ability to reason, question, challenge and change rules should not be confused with an inability or unwillingness to follow them. Human societies all over the world are steeped in rules and rituals, and whatever else they do, learning those rituals teaches people self control. Perhaps that is why so many different pointless rules have evolved in so many places.

There are times when people need to accept authority. Pilots in the busy skies need to accept the authority of air traffic controllers and do what they are told, otherwise there will be disasters. Nurses and theatre staff in hospital operating theatres need to accept the authority of the surgeon.

What may seem at the time to be pointless disciplinary exercises in the military are actually necessary to instil in soldiers the ability to follow orders immediately when they need to. In battle there is no time to explain everything to everyone. Respect for the rule of law does not necessarily mean agreeing with every law in a society. There are times when decisions need to be questioned and society needs to provide methods to allow that to happen. What it does mean is accepting that sometimes you have to follow the rules, even if you do not agree with them, and if you fail to do that you have to accept the consequences.

Respect for authority does not mean respecting every individual in authority, every opinion they hold, or every decision they make. It means recognising that there are specific sets of circumstances where you agree to give up your freedom of choice and comply in order to allow society to function. It means waiting until the right time to question the rule. To be able to do that requires self control.

Experiments at Florida State University suggest that the process of getting into the habit of following rules builds self control. Subjects were encouraged to follow instructions at various times of the day. For example, they might be sent a text reminding them to improve their posture by sitting or standing up straight. They were instructed to make an effort to speak in complete sentences, rather than use the normal shorthand and slang. They were told to try to refrain from swearing. They also practised a variety of tasks on delayed gratification which also exercises self control.

Initially it takes willpower to stop doing what comes naturally and make yourself do something else. Yet in the experiments it did not seem to matter what pointless rule they were learning to to follow. The subjects gradually became better at following any rule. In other words, by practising self control in specific circumstances they were becoming better at it generally. They also reported that it was becoming easy. They were no longer having to rely on willpower.

Training Bodybrains

Self control should not be confused with mindless obedience. Mindfulness is actually associated with self control. Bodybrains which never learn to follow external instructions fail to follow internal ones too. People with untrained bodybrains have a disability.

Often those who challenge rules are not really interested in the issues they are arguing about. They are playing power games, performing social status negotiations, or trying to impress an audience. Some trade union disputes are more about power games than genuine issues. I can say that with some authority, having been a shop steward and played those games myself in my younger years.

This might be a clue to why laissez-faire parenting fails to equip children with self control, and why the military sets such a high value on discipline. In my professional work, I have trained people from a variety of backgrounds. Far from being passively obedient and dependent, I have always found people with a military training to be the most creative and imaginative when it comes to problem solving. They also manage to turn up on time, arrive fully equipped for the task, and they seem to be naturally inclined to work together as a team to solve problems and get the job done. This is in stark contrast to some other professional cultures I will not name.

Of course, there is nothing "natural" about this. It is the result of training. Many young people from troubled backgrounds have benefitted from the structure of military life. It allowed them to learn the self-discipline that was missing in their early years of socialisation as a child. My younger self would be astonished to hear me say that, but my younger self was not as smart as he thought he was.

I have only come to appreciate during the research for this book how much we need rules. They allow people who are never going to agree about every detail to live together in social groups. They save time and mental effort, because following rules becomes automatic, and it is easier than having to think and make decisions all the time. They allow individuals to work cooperatively in groups. People who are able to cooperate and work with others do much better in the long run than mavericks and social outcasts. But to do so they have to be able to stick to the agreed rules. There are rules in every club, society, school, workplace, social club, trade union and political party. It does not matter so much what they are. What is important is that everybody follows them.

We do need to think about the rules, and question them from time to time, and there needs to be a fair process which allows reasonable people to change them. But that is not the same as allowing individuals to constantly argue and wriggle out of previous agreements when the rules are applied to them. Sometimes children who howl, "It's not fair!" are right. But often that is the cry of an untrained and unreasonable bodybrain.

Some children have learned to use emotional blackmail, threats, public humiliation and physical violence to get what they want. Others just wear adults down by repeating the same requests and refusing to take no for an answer. If these tactics work, they will learn to use them more and more. In the longer term, selfish children grow up into unsuccessful adults.

Most conflicts are not between heart & mindbrains, making principled arguments on issues they have thought long and hard about, or even care deeply about. They are more often between selfish, mindless bodybrains, who both want their own way and cannot see each other's point of view. Sometimes they are between a selfish bodybrain that wants its own way, and a heart & mindbrain that is trying to apply reason.

Two other discoveries surprised me during the research for this book. I began by assuming that self control depended on willpower and imagined that practising it must be empowering the heart & mindbrain in some way. My mental simulation pictured it becoming stronger with practice, no doubt influenced by ideas such as brain gym, that used the metaphor of the brain as a muscle getting stronger with exercise. In fact it is a bad metaphor. The founder of the "Brain Gym" programme, which sold widely in schools in the U.S. and U.K., admitted he made up all the research. A review in 2016 cast doubt on the idea that brain training programmes improve memory or general intelligence at all.[72]

I had to admit that I did not have much personal experience in exercising willpower. I had never tried to give anything up. I had never been addicted to nicotine, never needed to diet, and never tried to give up drinking alcohol for any length of time. If I was honest, I had never really been really hungry either. Being peckish is not the same thing as not having eaten for days.

So I tried an experiment to see if I had any willpower and whether with practice I could grow it. Just as I was finishing Baumeister's book, "Willpower: rediscovering our greatest strength", I read an article in the New Scientist about the supposed health benefits of fasting. I decided to stop eating completely for one day each week and give up drinking alcohol for two days. I was interested in the idea that practising willpower would generalise it into other areas.

---

[72]"Do 'Brain-Training' Programs Work?" - Simons, Daniel J., et al. (2016).

I found no evidence of that at all, but I did notice something more interesting happening. My general willpower did not get any stronger. What happened was that the urges to eat and drink on those days got weaker. This was not a generalised loss of appetite. It only applied on the days I had decided not to eat or drink. That was back in 2011 and I have been doing it ever since. It has drifted into a regime in which I normally eat nothing but a handful of almonds and a couple of tomatoes on Mondays, and have one meal of fish, rice, and vegetables on Tuesday evening. This is not a diet to be recommended. It is a fad diet - the sort I really do not approve of. I had no intention of adopting it as a way of life. But I felt so much better, my health improved so much, and over time it became so easy that I am stuck on it now. I actually look forward to Mondays.[73]

As an experiment on building willpower my regime failed to produce any noticeable results. I do not need willpower. What seems to have happened is that my bodybrain has learned that there is no point in asking questions such as, "Can we have a beer?" or "Can we have a biscuit?" on Mondays, because the answer is always "No!".

---

[73] Actually the following year Michael Mosley presented a BBC series in which he tested a number of diets and did recommend something similar, called the 5:2 diet. It involves less dramatic fasting. He wrote a book on it that went on to be a best seller.

Heat & mindbrains can decide what we want to do in our long term interests. Then they can teach bodybrains to do it. It really is as simple as that.

It is important to remember that bodybrains can learn to do complicated thinking too. When my bodybrain is driving the car, it is engaged in complicated information processing. Chess Grand Masters look at a board and not only recognise the play but have ideas about what they would do next. Those are being generated by the bodybrain. I am pretty sure that by practising rational thinking, those patterns can become automated too. Effective patterns of thinking and decision making can become automated, so that reflex errors in our mental processes can be replaced with more effective automatic responses. These days when I hear somebody on the television or radio confusing correlation with causation, my bodybrain recognises the pattern immediately and reacts by alerting me to it. [74] For example, there was an article in Time Magazine called, "Brain Science: Does Being Left-Handed Make You Angry?" It could just as easily have been called, "Brain Science: Does Being Angry Turn You Left Handed?" It is not science.

If I make a bad investment or poor choice, instead of alerting me and encouraging me to worry about it, my bodybrain deals with it automatically. It generates the mantra, "Spent cost".

---

[74] "Brain Science: Does Being Left-Handed Make You Angry?" - John Ashley Cloud, 2010.

When faced by frustration, my bodybrain generates other mantras, such as "Time is on my side" or "Let it go".[75] These automated responses free me from being bothered.

I refuse to think about anything important in bed. So my bodybrain has given up trying to get me to worry about things in the middle of the night. Having a well trained bodybrain is like having somebody to share the workload. An untrained bodybrain is just a drain on resources and a liability.

In my view, the benefits of supporting heart & mindbrains so that they can train bodybrains to follow rules cannot be overstated.

Danger Alert

As you might have gathered I am an enthusiastic adopter of technology. I remember at a conference in 1992 when I was the only person with a notebook computer. That is how old I am. My first computer, bought in the early 1980s, was huge and useless. It cost me £2000 at a time when the average annual wage was £8000. I thought it was marvellous because it could do "cut and paste".

Yet there is one aspect of modern life that gives me uncomfortable gut feelings. That enteric nervous system is where emotions and intelligence came from in the first place, and I have learned to pay attention to gut feelings.

---

[75] See my book "Persuasive Scripts" (2008) for more mind saving mantras.

I began this book saying that humans are not born well adjusted to the modern world and have suggested throughout that we should pay more attention to making it a more comfortable fit. We should not just assume we will always be able to cope. We may need to reprogramme ourselves, and I think we have been extremely good at that. But we also need to protect ourselves by becoming more self aware and taking into account our own limitations.

Things are changing at a pace that humans have never had to cope with before. Some of those changes have only happened very recently and the effects are not yet clear. Mindless computer algorithms are making important decisions on our behalf. They control the financial markets and stock markets.

Only recently has the data being made available to us also been taken over by computer algorithms that edit what we get to see and know. Only recently have so many humans had intimate details of their own lives recorded, stored, and opened up to public scrutiny.

Mental wellbeing is closely associated with how people feel about their lives, not just how much they are enjoying the moment. Humans gain pleasure and satisfaction from creating and re-drafting the commentary and narrative that makes up their own life story. I think this really was the fundamental purpose of the evolved heart & mindbrain. It is what "we" evolved to do.

The philosopher Daniel Dennett first put forward his multiple draft theory of memory in 1991. According to that model, human memory is like a computer that is incapable of saving the previous draft of a document. Each time a memory is retrieved and re-presented, the new saved version overwrites the previous version. The bodybrain is like an author who cannot resist the temptation to edit and polish up a document each time it is reviewed. So as we recall memories, we polish them up, adding a bit here and deleting a bit there, so that the stories gradually change over time. This editing process is not random. The part of the brain that does the editing is the public relations department which evolved to improve social performance. It automatically rewrites history to make us look a bit better. Autobiographies are unreliable accounts, because over time we all come to believe the distortions and exaggerations that gradually developed during the rewrites. Without noticing, what started as slight exaggerations have become big lies. Many famous people in the public eye have been extremely embarrassed when untruths they had come to believe themselves were exposed after they related them on talk shows or in their autobiographies.

During the introduction to a foreign policy speech on Iraq in 2008, Hillary Clinton reminisced about her days as first lady and described a trip to Bosnia she made in March 1996.

"I remember landing under sniper fire. There was supposed to be some kind of a greeting ceremony at the airport, but instead we just ran with our heads down to get into the vehicles to get to our base."

Hillary Clinton

Unfortunately for her, CBS retained the video of the event which showed a welcome party bringing her a bunch of flowers and a rather shaky brass band, but no sniper fire. Everybody was smiling. I have no doubt that her recollection was genuine but it was not true. It had probably been polished up over dinner parties during the previous decade until she came to believe it herself. Of course politicians do tell lies. But like the rest of us, I think most of the time they simply begin to believe their own propaganda. Unfortunately for them they get caught out more often than the rest of us, because most of us do not have to worry about independent contemporaneous records exposing inaccuracies in the latest draft of our own life story.

At least, that was true until recently. But the advent of social media means that many people do lead more exposed lives. Some leave a comprehensive and detailed digital trail that is hard to erase or rewrite. They are great for people with a poor memory and might prove to be an invaluable therapeutic tool when the current generation, who have an indelible recorded life story, become old.

But it is not going to be so easy in the future for people to reinvent themselves. Many older people have probably said and done things they are glad were never permanently recorded and made freely available for others to see. There may be people who find their lives threatened in the future by their recorded social history. It is not too hard to imagine authoritarian governments trawling social media to identify and track down potential dissidents in their own country, or refusing entry to foreigners who have interacted with individuals or sources of information they disapprove of.

The repetitive behaviours involved in obsessional social media checking are addictive dopamine loops. Those who depend on social media for news and information about the real world, imagine they are interacting with millions of people and accessing a broader spread of information. That is not always the case. The mathematical algorithms that determine what people get to see have been fine-tuned, not to provide users with a broader view of life but a narrower one. Market forces give people what they want, and what they want is to have their own prejudices reinforced. They want to hear more from people who are just like them and think just like them, and less about other types of human. More by accident than design, the information system that promised to expand our horizons is evolving to encourage some of the worst natural characteristics of the human bodybrain - prejudice and supremacist thinking.

For example, Facebook has regularly updated the EdgeRank algorithm that governs what each individual gets to see in their own news feed. So have all the other providers. The algorithms are tuned so that posts that get a disproportionate amount of engagement, in the form of likes, clicks, comments, or shares, get promoted. There are only certain types of post that provoke interaction, which means that what people get to see is becoming distorted. At the same time companies and political organisations are now allowed to pay to have their own messages boosted, which means they can relegate other posts that people might prefer to see. The algorithms are also designed to provide information that is biased towards the individual's current interests and ideas. They provide introductions to other people who share similar views and make it harder to find those who might help us to see errors in our own thinking.

We certainly need filters. Just try turning off all the spam filters and see what happens to emails, but the problem is that the available information is becoming distorted. Research conducted in 2016 found that 62 percent of the U.S. population used social media as a source of information and news and 18 percent relied on it.[76] Two-thirds of Facebook users get news and information from the site, nearly six-in-ten Twitter users, and seven-in-ten Reddit users get news on those platforms. On Tumblr, the figure is 31 percent The point is these numbers are

---

[76] "News Use Across Social Media Platforms 2016" - Pew Research Center, conducted in association with the John S. and James L. Knight Foundation.

growing rapidly and amongst the young they are already much higher than that. What they are getting is a grossly distorted view of the world.

One of the great things about social media is that it allows those with minority interests to find like-minded people in a way never before available to humans.

But there is a downside to that. Humans are innately predisposed to like people who are like them. They like people who share their interests and opinions. They are innately suspicious of people who look different, behave differently and hold different views. The urge for humans to categorise others as either members of their own group or outsiders is strong. When they are forced to mix with people who are different, after a time the suspicion and fear can subside, with the result that they become more tolerant.

Social media should provide humans with opportunities to widen their experience but for many it is doing the opposite. What has changed is that it is becoming easier to mix with like minded people and avoid others altogether. When people like a post or comment on an opinion the algorithm changes to direct more similar content towards them. So every idea will produce more examples of similar ideas, no matter how stupid they may be. The feedback can give a completely distorted impression of the balance of opinion.

Because the algorithms supply confirmatory opinions and suppress alternative ones they reinforce bias and prejudice. The change this is having on the mental functioning of users is not subtle. It is clearly evident.

In November 2016 a new word was included in the Oxford English Dictionary. It was "post truth". It describes circumstances in which objective facts are less influential in shaping public opinion than appeals to emotion and personal belief:

"in this era of post-truth politics, it's easy to cherry-pick data and come to whatever conclusion you desire"

"Some commentators have observed that we are living in a post-truth age"

Communication conducted via digital media has a different quality. In the same way that some people express exaggerated aggression in their cars, in a way they would never do on the pavement, arguments and opinions conducted online tend to be expressed with more aggression than they would be face to face. Yet because people are interacting that way so much, their bodybrains are becoming trained and those behaviours are spilling into the interactions they have in person.

The U.K. government conducted a referendum in June 2016 in which the British electorate would decide whether the UK would remain in the European Union or leave. The Prime Minister was confident that the electorate would vote to remain and many were surprised by the result, which was to leave. It followed a campaign in which both sides abandoned appeals to reason and evidence, instead appealing to emotions and opinion.

The 2016 presidential campaign in the USA was conducted in the same way, with supporters on both sides making vitriolic ad-hominem attacks on the character of those they disagreed with. It too resulted in an unexpected outcome.

I was less interested in the outcomes, than the polarised thought processes which were exposed by these two political events and which have continued afterwards. The vitriol and vapid name calling is still going on. Whereas in the past it was possible for people to hold different opinions on a range of topics, and hear them expressed without rancour or hatred, many seem unable to do that now. A significant number of people have categorised those they disagree with as members of a gross group stereotype.

I conducted two internet searches, one asking what Trump supporters called Clinton supporters, and another asking what Clinton supporters called Trump supporters. They returned similar answers. One angry Trump supporter blogged that Hilary Clinton supporters were:

"Entitlement minded folks who do not know how to check their arrogance and bias at the door."

A Clinton supporter wrote an article titled :

"Entitled, racist, bigoted, thugs: It is time to call Donald Trump supporters by their real names."

They were probably correct in identifying some of those who disagreed with them as entitled, bigoted and biased. But to label everyone who disagreed with them in that way was wrong.

Hilary Clinton described "half" of Trump's supporters as "deplorables". That was 30 million people. Brexit supporters described those who wanted to remain as a "metropolitan liberal elite". 48 percent of the population cannot be accurately described as an elite.

Those who retreated into that sort of supremacist thinking were certainly correct when they called each other "bigoted" and "biased" but their thinking processes were actually very similar.

Humans naturally suffer from confirmation bias, which means that they look for evidence to support their own prejudices and fail to see evidence that does not. This is being magnified and reinforced not only by social media, but also by Google deliberately filtering their world view for them into a distorted personal bubble.

At the same time "fake news", created deliberately to deceive, is drowning out real news. The result is that some people are not hearing opinions that do not accord with their own at all, so they are completely unaware that there are other arguments and opinions. When they realise that other people hold different opinions to their own they react in enraged bewilderment, unable to comprehend how anyone can be so stupid because they have never heard those arguments. Instead, it is easier to question their motives and attack their character.

I heard an otherwise apparently intelligent professional on the radio being interviewed about this who said she relied on social media for the news but had not understood how her feed was being distorted and filtered. She said she was still happy to get most of her news from Facebook, even if it was filtered, for the convenience. Anyway, told the interviewer that she could not imagine wanting to hear anything that a Trump supporter might say, because she had nothing in common with them. To fight prejudice of all kinds we need to search for the things we have in common and build bridges, rather than cutting ourselves off.

History has shown that only way prejudiced people become more open is to be willing to talk and listen to those they may disagree with. Prejudiced people do not want to do that.

Things To Do

I do use social media. Admittedly mostly as a baby alarm for my son, who is only 26 years old. But I do think we need to keep an eye on what is happening. For those who would prefer not to become increasing insular and bitter, we could turn off the algorithms where allowed and make a point of searching for alternative opinions from multiple news sources. Guardian and Telegraph readers really do live in different worlds. They should pay a visit to each other's planet once in a while, along with the planets Mirror, Mail and Express and even venture to the Sun. If you want to see how much your social world is controlled, start liking things you really hate and see how quickly your feed changes.

Our mental life story was never supposed to be an accurate or objective account. It is a functional one which provides a framework for the construction and maintenance of our projected image and self image in a social world. It enables us to feel happy about our lives, which is more than just enjoying them. The closer the projected image is to the self image, the happier humans become. We can help people with that by working with them as script doctors and teaching them to be better writers themselves.

"In the 1950s, social skills were taught in a much more rigid way so kids who were mildly autistic were forced to learn them. It hurts the autistic much more than it does the normal kids to not have these skills formally taught."

Temple Grandin

I think it hurts all children not to be taught social skills and manners in a more rigid systematic way. The rules for the game of life are just as important as the rules for any other game. This is all about bodybrain training.

Reducing the number of children who fail to learn to control their own bodybrains could significantly reduce social cost and have many more benefits for society.

Adopting a more systematic approach to mood management could enable us to become better at steering sympathetic nervous systems away from the extremes of stimulation, which disable heart & mindbrains, to maintain optimal levels which keep humans within the zones for learning and performing. Better controlled sympathetic nervous systems could also promote better physical and mental health across the board and provide considerable benefits for the economy and National Health Service.

Humans can gain pleasure, both superficial and deep, from short term, long term and life long pursuits. By more strategically managing them we could improve the quality of life for many people.

Performances provide pleasure but threatening ones also cause pain. We can provide more opportunities for people to indulge in attractive performances and steer them towards those. That would make the world a safer and more pleasant place.

Humans have learned a variety of ingenious ways of cheating their three basic drives, by creating leisure activities that simulate natural behaviours. With a little creative intelligence we should be able to discover or invent more ways to help them do that. The greater the range of rewarding pursuits on offer, the less likely it is that behaviour will be hijacked by pursuits that ultimately turn out to be unrewarding.

We can adapt tournament competitions to remove real violence and replace it with simulations. Many sports have already moved in that direction.

Humans gain pleasure from being creative. Creativity involves building imaginary simulations of things that do not yet exist in the real world by rearranging components of simulations of things that already do. That is what creative ideas and art are all about. The process is driven by pursuit and it can be taught.

Humans gain pleasure and satisfaction from creating realistic simulations of the future, which they can put into effect by acting on the world to adapt it so that it more closely matches their mental simulations. This is the process of invention that drives the anthropocene. Children of all ages love to play and make things. They just forget to do it sometimes. I have a friend who is obsessed with Lego. He uses it in therapy, in interviews, in meetings and in a variety of other contexts to enable people to communicate their ideas. It makes complete sense because that is how heart & mindbrains work.

Incompetent mood managers create discomfort and unhappiness for themselves and those around them. They put themselves in situations that result in discomfort and unhappiness. They do things that they are not proud of, which make them feel bad about themselves. They make poor judgements, by trading substantial long term happiness for trivial short term pleasures. They waste mental time and effort re-presenting simulations of the past and possible future that produce unpleasant emotions in the present, instead of directing their own attention towards thoughts that produce pleasant emotions. They worry, creating fearful simulations of things they cannot influence, instead of crafting simulations of things they can to improve the future. They indulge in wishful thinking, by creating unrealistic simulations that they are unable to put into practice.

They create self-fulfilling prophesies by mindlessly acting out habitual patterns of behaviour that bring about the results they fear most.

They create pain and unhappiness by indulging in threat performances instead of attractive ones.

Mood management involves learning new skill sets. It involves learning to be able to follow rules and wait for the right time to challenge them in the right way, with critical thinking and social skills. It is achievable.

By finding ways to manage our own moods we can change the emotional climate around us. By learning to regulate stimulation and stress levels inside our own sympathetic nervous system we can influence those around us.

We do not need to wait until we are in the right mood or agonise about how we feel. A whole industry has grown up encouraging people to do that and the results are not impressive. What we need to do is change the way we are behaving. The truth is that we are heart & mindbrains, and the way we feel is governed by what the bodybrain happens to be doing. There is no point in asking it how it is feeling, because it does not know. But if we change the way we are behaving, the bodybrain follows suit and it starts to generate thoughts and feelings that combine to make up our experience of emotions and mood. This is chemistry and biology not magic.

Getting up and doing something, even if you do not feel like doing it, can fool the bodybrain into generating better feelings. It can change the way we interpret the chemical and biological feedback and change the way we feel.

We may not be able to change what happens to us in life but we can decide how we are going to feel about it. In doing so we become more active managers of our own moods rather than passive recipients.

Mood managers can learn to identify the types of situation in which the heart & mindbrain and bodybrain are likely to be in conflict and plan in advance how they are going to deal with those situations.

We need to review the way we are socialising and educating our children, how we structure our social groups, how we value tournament and pair bonding lifestyles, how we teach critical thinking and self control and how we protect developing heart & mindbrains.

That may have implications for policy in relation to the way we are considering restrictions of liberty. It may be that some children require more formal assessments of Gillick competence.[77] Perhaps, as a society we should pay more attention to assessing the development of self control and establish a rite of passage ceremony to recognise the achievement of it.

As part of that process, we should review the chaotic system of rights and responsibilities for children, in the light of a developing understanding about the way the whole body, brain and mind interact to create a mature heart & mindbrain and a well trained bodybrain.

We cannot trust human nature to equip us for the future. It did not evolve for that. Instead, we need to adjust the future to fit our nature. It really is possible for people to enjoy life much more than they currently do, but we will have to become better mood managers in order to do it.

---

[77] Gillick competence is the legal equivalent of mental capacity for under 16 year olds.

I have just received an email from the Cloud Appreciation Society with the cloud of the day, which is "Stratus over Vaud, Switzerland spotted by Emmanual Vandamme (member 12165) in case anybody is interested. It just looks like fog to me, which made me laugh. The free UCL Pocket Smile app just sent me an alert that there is a new smiling face to look at. They are strangely compelling. And now it is an absolutely beautiful crisp, sunny, winters day, so I am going to go out for a walk and appreciate as much of it as I possibly can.

Happy days!

Glossary

Bodybrain - The automatic information processing system which organises incoming information, makes sense of it through educated guesswork, initiates and controls movement, and generates simulations of our physical and mental world which can be stored and retrieved to be re-presented at a later date. It works all the time and takes no conscious effort. It does not reflect on what it is doing and is only concerned with the present. It does not plan and is therefore rather short sighted because it does not consider future implications. "We", our conscious selves, have no direct access to the workings of the main bodybrain system. We only see the results of what it does. It seems to be a parallel processor, which means that there are many different processes going on in tandem at the same time.

The bodybrain generates innate behaviours, such as fixed action patterns, but it can also learn to fine-tune these to adapt to the current environment. It can also learn completely new behaviour patterns through practice and repetition. The bodybrain is capable of learning complicated tasks which it carries out as if on automatic pilot. It can play the piano and drive a car.

I suspect the bodybrain does more than "we" give it credit for. "We", the conscious self, cannot function at all without a functioning bodybrain. I do not believe "we" even exist when it is not functioning. It generates our thoughts, feelings and behaviour. But it does not experience them.

The majority of what we call "self control" is actually a sign of a well trained bodybrain. When the bodybrain is well trained, self control takes very little effort. Without a well trained bodybrain, self control is hard work because it depends on willpower, which is in short supply.

For considerable periods of time, when we are asleep, none of the bodybrain processes appear in consciousness. The mind and self seem to completely disappear for hours at a time every day.

Heart & Mindbrain - The heart & mindbrain is a different type of thinking system which sometimes switches on to work alongside the main bodybrain processor. It is a linear processor, which means it can only think about one thing at a time. I suspect that most of the neural circuits that create it are in the head, because information takes time to get to it from other parts of the body.

This is the part of us that we associate with free will, morality, ethics, spirituality and critical thinking.

It plans for the future, remembers the past, and manages long-term pursuits. Sometimes it has to suppress the urges being generated by the bodybrain, which takes effort. We call that willpower. But it can also train the bodybrain, so that over time self control becomes easier.

The conscious heart & mindbrain maintains a running commentary on our life, and it continually updates and re-drafts the narrative, explaining what we have been doing. It is the curator of our life story. The "self" is a creation of the heart & mindbrain, a semi-fictional character in the story, which although based on reality, is also continually being updated and re-drafted. As we perform in the real world we are acting out our character. If the performance receives negative feedback the character is rewritten in an attempt to improve it.

How content we are with our own life story, and the role of the leading character within it, seems to be the most important feature of wellbeing - more important than the momentary pleasures which the bodybrain seeks.

Strangely, the heart & mindbrain does not always seem to know what the bodybrain is doing. It seems to listen to what it says and watch what it does, trying to make sense of its own bodybrain in much the same way that it does the behaviour of other people. It tries to make sense of the the physical world, mathematical rules, and logical concepts in the same way, as if it is a story with agents acting with a purpose.

Heart & Mindbrain work takes mental effort. Whenever we have to do hard thinking, problem solving, mental arithmetic or use willpower, that is heart & mindbrain work. When it gets tired, its performance tails off and it has to shut down for lengthy periods every day.

A bodybrain can function to some extent without a heart &
mindbrain, but "we" would not know much about it because
"we" are heart & mindbrains. I do not think a heart &
mindbrain can exist without a bodybrain.

Mind - I have one of these, but I have no way of knowing
whether anyone else does. My mind experiences information
processing, rather than just doing it. It appears in the morning
when I wake up and disappears for long periods at night when I
go to sleep. I could just as well say "I" appear in the morning
and disappear at night, because I identify with my mind. The
mind and self are really the same thing. It is self aware. It is self
conscious. It tries to exert self control.

It also disappears at other times during the day, probably more
often than I realise. It is quite fragile and can be switched off by
a blow to the head. It is severely disrupted by illness, changes in
blood sugar levels, dehydration and the influence of alcohol
and other drugs. Many of the drugs that have the greatest effect
on the heart & mindbrain, such as DMT, LSD, and MDMA,
interfere with receptors for neurotransmitters or are precursors
of neurotransmitters. These are what allow neurones to
communicate. That supports the idea that the conscious self, or
the mind, has a physical basis in networks of neurones.

The mind is essentially who "we" are. I identify far more with
my mind than I do with my toenails, although they are
technically part of "me" too. If it was possible to separate the

mind and body (which I do not believe) I would not identify with the body parts. I would identify with the mind.

Self - That is me again. When I talk about self control I mean the times that the mind takes control of the body to exert free will. When I am self conscious, it means that I become aware that I am in this scene. That can only happen when the heart & mindbrain is switched on.

Body - The physical system of bones, meat and offal that keeps my mind going. When I look in the mirror my body does not look much like the previous historical versions in the photographs of my childhood. There is a popular myth that all the cells in the body are replaced every seven years. This is not true. All the various types of cell in the body are replaced at different time intervals, ranging from hours to months. All, that is, apart from neurones which can last a lifetime. I possess a body but I am a mind, which functions so long as my heart & mindbrain functions.

Pursuit - This is one of three basic drives. It is activated when the bodybrain becomes curious and takes an interest in something. It generates urges of various strengths to move towards things, both physical and intellectual. Pursuit drives behaviours such as stalking, following or chasing. Pursuit in humans can be a very long lasting and persistent drive. Our ancestors were persistence hunters. Some pursuits can last a lifetime.

Pursuit is associated with a particular set of neural circuits in the hippocampus and a neurotransmitter called dopamine. It is the source of most of our pleasures and happiness, but it creates problems for us too. It is associated with a particular form of cool, deliberate, coordinated violence.

Pursuit is associated with mild or moderate levels of stimulation of the sympathetic nervous system.

Panic - This is the opposite of pursuit. It urges the bodybrain to move or run away from things and hide. Animals may climb away from dangers on the ground or hide from dangers on the ground or above. Depending on the strength of the drive panic can be expressed as anything from mild distaste to full blown, screaming, terror. It is associated with uncoordinated violence.

Panic is usually a short term drive. Once the bodybrain is at a safe distance, animals and birds in panic mode begin to calm down and reassess the situation. The only thing that keeps them going is if they feel they are still being chased.

Panic can be associated with mild, moderate, or extremely high levels of stimulation of the sympathetic nervous system.

Performance - This is the drive to show off and impress other creatures or lure them towards the performer.

Attractive performances function to lure potential prey, friends and allies, providers of support, and sexual partners towards the performer. They also function to create an image and a reputation within a social hierarchy.

Off-putting performances function to deter potential predators, attackers, and competitors. They too function to create an image and a reputation within a social hierarchy.

Exercising the performance drive provides a source of considerable pleasure to humans and other social animals.

Although they are reluctant to admit it, humans spend a great deal of time performing. They are not the only animals that do it, but humans are certainly the most sophisticated social performers. I suspect the heart & mindbrain evolved to manage social performances, both as a scriptwriter drafting the characters, plots and storylines and as a critic, interpreting and judging the performances of other actors and trying to work out their plots and scripts.

Intelligence - I think what we call intelligence resulted from the our mental equipment trying to work out the plots and scripts of the physical world in the same way as it did social performances. Intelligence and brain size in the natural world are associated with social performance. Intelligence developed as social creatures developed increasingly sophisticated deceptive performances to make their own character appear more interesting or impressive. Counter intelligence evolved in parallel to enable social creatures to see through the tricks and deceptive performances of others. Smart creatures try to make sense of the physical world by ascribing human attributes and intentions to inanimate objects and natural forces, as if they are characters in a social drama. The stories that scientists redraft and improve are hypotheses which become theories.

Creative Intelligence - The mental equipment that evolved for deceptive performances enabled smart creatures to imagine stories to explain behaviour, some of which turned out to be not real. They had to edit their story to shape it to match the physical world more closely.

It was a short jump from that to using the same mental equipment to imagine stories of the physical world that were not real, but instead of adapting their mental version to match the real world more closely, they adapted the physical world to match their imagination. It might have been a small jump but it was a profound one.

This is where creative invention came from. The mind thinks in analogies, taking a component of one concept and applying it to another concept to create something new.

Anthropocene - The name that has been given to what happened to the planet once humans started adapting it. This is a very new epoch in the history of planet earth. Instead of being shaped by astronomical and geographical forces, it is now being shaped by an infectious life form called human beings. Creative invention set off the anthropocene. Who knows where it will end?

Anthropomorphism - A tendency humans have to attribute human characteristics to the physical world, the weather, inanimate objects and other creatures. They make sense of the universe by creating stories in which all the characters have intentions and cause things to happen. This default form of thinking was explicit in ancient stories, for example those of Greek mythology, but it continues to this day. When two things happen in close proximity, humans cannot prevent themselves from linking them into a story. They cannot understand coincidences. This is one of the bugs in our mental software.

Maladjusted - Our physical bodies, brains, and minds have not been able to keep up with the rate of change brought about by our own creative invention. Our bodybrain finds itself in a world for which it is not adequately prepared. We are all maladjusted to some extent. As our ways of living continue to change at an exponential rate, we risk becoming even more maladjusted because our natural behaviour keep reverting to natural reactions that are less and less relevant to modern life.

We need to understand ourselves better, and take more care of the way we are shaping and organising our world, so that it accommodates our nature, instead of expecting human nature to change dramatically any time soon.

Sympathetic Nervous System

This is the system that fires up the bodybrain for action and shuts down general housekeeping activities, such as digestion and maintenance. It wakes us up, it enables us to relax and daydream, it makes us pay attention when we become curious, it helps us to learn new tricks and remember events in our life story, and it helps us to perform the tricks we have learned at an optimal level. To do all of those things it needs to be at different levels of stimulation. When the stimulation level is wrong, things go wrong.

When it is under-stimulated we get bored, daydream and fall asleep. With mild stimulation we enter a learning state, in which both bodybrain and heart & mindbrain work together in harmony to store new memories. At moderate levels of stimulation we perform well learned skills and remember better. Unfortunately, at even higher levels of stimulation the performance of the heart & mindbrain begins to tail off. We quite enjoy being excited but can be a bit silly as the bodybrain system starts to take over. Extreme levels of stimulation are associated with fear and can shut down the heart & mindbrain completely, leaving the bodybrain in charge.

Parasympathetic Nervous System - This works in opposition to the sympathetic nervous system to calm things down. Stimulating the parasympathetic nervous system slows the heart, reduces blood pressure, calms activity in the amygdala (the fight and flight centre) and allows digestion and body maintenance to start up again.

Mood Management - People do things because they feel like it. They do not always understand why they feel like behaving the way they do. If people were completely satisfied, comfortable and entertained they would not feel like doing anything.

Mood management is at the heart of behaviour management. They are really the same thing. It is also at the heart of wellbeing and happiness. Humans spend most of their time trying to manage their own moods. They are torn between a bodybrain that wants to enjoy the present and a heart & mindbrain that wants to create a life story and central character that it feels good about. They would be more successful and ultimately more contented if they understood what they were doing a bit better. This book is intended to help them do that. It is also intended to provide a comprehensive framework of understanding for all professionals who have to manage the moods, emotions, and behaviours of others, so that they can provide more coherent and effective support.

About The Author

Bernard Allen led a series of schools over a period of twenty years before becoming a full-time writer, consultant and expert witness. He writes books and provides training on the psychology of behaviour, working across the UK and abroad, advising courts, insurers and governments on liability issues relating to behaviour. He is on the register of expert witnesses, a member of the Society of Expert Witnesses and a graduate member of the British Psychological Society. Bernard has taken an interest in reducing the use of restraint for the past 25 years and trained in various models. In 1996 he produced the first UK video training package for children's services, "Holding Back", and later trained as a Team- Teach instructor at principal tutor level. He is co-author of the Team-Teach workbooks and training manuals.

Made in the USA
Charleston, SC
21 February 2017